What the'

(Reflections of a Black Country)

By
Dr E.T.M. Cooke

Paperback ISBN – 978-1-910667-84-2
.epub ISBN – 978-1-910667-86-6
.mobi ISBN – 978-1-910667-85-9

To Dad…

William Edward (Bill) Cooke
Without whose wisdom and guidance I would never have contemplated the career that I followed, thus enabling this book to be written, and to my mother, Olive May Cooke without whose procreation…

I would never have been here in the first place!

Introduction

Many books start with a quotation or a clever poem.

This quotation is usually from a person of some repute, made to impress the reader with the intellect and the humility of the author.

You are then expected to believe that the author is really someone very well read, despite the somewhat undistinguished book the reader may be about to explore.

No such introduction is made to this book.

Benjamin Franklin was our coalman. He came from Tipton.

An acknowledgment

I am indebted in the design, editing, format and production of this book to all the team at Spiffing Covers of Colchester for their guidance and excellent professional advice, for all the aforementioned, including "on line presence", IT information etc.

Their front cover design alludes to the purity of Black Country folk despite their bleak surroundings, expressing hope and showing the purity of the miner's canary, with the colour and improvement of times to come. The medical coat is meant to give the reader some idea of the content and contrast of the book enclosed.

All of which expresses the content and atmosphere of the book entirely as intended by the Author.

Dr ETM Cooke M.B.Ch.B D.L.O.

Prologue

This is a book about the "Black Country", that area of the Midlands north-west of the Birmingham conurbation, the descriptive name of which was first used about the time of the birth of the Industrial Revolution. No one knows who first used the term, but in modern times the region has been fully described by Carl Chinn[1] of Birmingham University, though it was first chronicled in about 1803 by Robert Southey who was later to become Poet Laureate, and the historian Thomas Carlyle when he visited the region in 1824, and it was mentioned in the diaries of the then

13-year-old Princess Victoria, later to become queen.

By this time the Industrial Revolution was in full swing resulting in severe pollution of the countryside by coal mining and the manufacture of iron and other heavy metal industries. The earth was black. The sky was black. Iron and later steel production provided the engine for the development and expansion of the Victorian era and the British Empire which went on for over 100 years. These heavy industries continued well until the middle of the 20th century, as did the widespread environmental pollution.

With the demise of coal production, in the last 50 years or so of the 20th century, the economy of the region had to change from its reliance on heavy industry, to that of a light manufacturing base. With all this change, and because of the resultant pollution, some areas became very socially deprived with high levels of unemployment and a high incidence of industrial illness within the population. Despite all this, the people in this region have always had a fierce sense of identity in their Black Country. They have a very specific language and dialect, and they have a sense of independence and an unusual and very strong sense of humour, different than the rest of the country.

An attempt to analyse this language was made in 2007 by Ed Conduit[2], a clinical psychologist, who purported and explained how the grammar may have had an Anglo-Saxon derivation. This and the folk, however, have changed little with the times.

The modern Black Country occupies that area of the country formerly known as (West) Mercia. This was the home of the Anglo-Saxons, who resisted many later changes and retained their own language, "Old English", a remnant of that of post-Roman Germanic invaders. Much of modern-day Black Country language and place names contain eponymous remnants of this ancient Celtic Anglo-Saxon language with Germanic origins and perhaps this is seen also in the stoical attitude to life in general of the people here. Following the Norman Conquest, both French and Latin became the languages of the official administration of the country, eventually developing into Middle then modern English as we know it. With all these Germanic names and expressions still, does this mean then that Black Country people are the "True Brits" of folklore?

In this book, the author, a Black Country man himself, looks at the last 50 years of the 20th century as seen through his eyes, as reflections on his life. These reflections are expressions of one of the "war babies", not a post-war baby boomer. His origins are from an earthy working class, when after primary and grammar school education he left his home in the 1960s to follow a university and then a postgraduate education in medicine, eventually to return to his roots and live with "my people". The author attempts to enlighten the reader with his reflections on how Black Country people look at life and how they see the world outside with a stoical and matter-of-fact attitude, and how with their odd sense of humour they can raise a smile or see a joke in the most obscure or abstract of life's situations.

There is some poetic licence taken, but the stories are not fiction. All the escapades and incidents, the births and sadly the deaths in this book are true. They all actually occurred. Only some of the names are pseudonyms, altered both for anonymity and confidentiality. The references with comment from the author are meant to be both informative and interesting to the reader, possibly amusing, maybe controversial (see "Cot Deaths"), not just statements of facts, and they are situated at the end of each chapter, nearby for pertinence of reading. Whilst the expression is simple there is some strong language at times, and there is particular dialectal expression, all as it was spoken at the time.

Any resemblance to anyone living or dead is at times quite intentional.

Any offence given is accidental.

Any offence taken is regrettable.

References and Author's comment:

1. *Black Country Memories*. Carl Chinn. 2004. Brewin Books:

Carl Stephen Alfred Chinn M.B.E. (06/09/1956 – is a true Brummie, i.e. one born and bred within the geographical area of Birmingham, and Professor of Community History at the University of Birmingham. In his book and his many other publications he describes the development of the area in excellent detail. He himself is renowned not only for his knowledge of local history, but his love of the retention all British dialects and the preservation of regional identities. He has a markedly broad Birmingham accent that disguises a sharp intellect. He has been involved in many local industrial issues such as the preservation of the Longbridge car factory and others, such as the preservation of local buildings and practices, and he is known for his criticism of replacement developments such as the new Bullring Centre in Birmingham, that ignored long-standing street trades and traders.

A deceptive man. Until I actually attended one of his lectures,

I did not realize that he had such a very deep and comprehensive knowledge of all British history and colloquial expression.

2. *The Black Country Dialect.* Ed Conduit. 2004. Laghamon Publishing:

In his book, Ed Conduit, a practising clinical psychologist who actually works with the people he that he describes, includes a complete and complex analysis of the folk, the language and the grammar, and the derivation of the dialect of the Black Country.

"Growin' up"

1. The forties and fifties

We were posh. We had an inside loo. We had a detached house, one of only five in our village. We had a garden with a brook alongside. We had no garage, we didn't need one. We didn't have a car! We didn't have a fridge. Had they been invented? We lived with Granny and Grandad and my Little Auntie Ida. Mother kept ducks in the old air-raid shelter at the bottom of the garden. Grandad, Ted, bred bull terriers. He was a coal miner, a deputy at Baggeridge Colliery. My father was a foundry foreman. Big blokes both. We were deliriously content. Five adults, and me. We didn't recognize then that we were overcrowded. My niece, her husband and their young family now live in the same extended house. Two adults and two children; they think it is too small. The men in the village either worked in the local collieries which were closing in the 1940s and 50s, or worked in the iron and steel foundries and other factories nearby.

Preschool reflections from this time are vague. I remember the war. I was scared of the blackout. Black curtains covered the windows every night, and you got a telling off for peeping out. The noise of the anti-aircraft guns didn't scare me; they were just guns. The blackout was scary though. At this time I remember I had a three-wheeler bicycle. Even at that age I liked speed. I once tried to do a two-wheel turn at a million miles per hour down the drive with cousin Pauline standing on the back axle. It was great. It was also a disaster... We went right over the rockery. I've had a scar on my lip all my life since, and I think, very unfairly, I got a terrible chastising from my mother. Scratched my bike as well it did, and buckled a wheel.

Our Pauline? Oh, she was OK. She just broke her arm or something! She was all right. She went to hospital, I think, but got better.

The war years are now faded memories, but some are retained. At one time while playing in the garden with my Granny feeding the ducks, I saw a low-flying aircraft emerge from over the Wren's Nest hill[3], now a nature reserve, at the rear of our house. At even an early age I had seen our aircraft and knew that they had red, white and blue rings on the wings and fuselage. They looked very nice.

This one was different. It was grey and had black crosses!

"Look Gran," I called out. "A new airplane."

"Our Edward, gerr in the house," she cried as she, Granny, grabbed me and dashed me inside.

Then after a few minutes all the guns on the Wren's Nest anti-aircraft gun battery opened fire, crash, bang, wallop, at the aircraft, which by then was 10 miles away over towards Birmingham!

On another occasion late one night my mother, father and myself were returning late from a trip to Dudley along the Birmingham Wolverhampton New Road, when two Home Guard sentries jumped out from behind a tree. It was a foggy night.

"Halt! Who goes there?" exclaimed the smaller man, "Little Leonard" Halford, at least 4 foot 6 inches tall, who thrust his rifle forward, with a large bayonet attached, towards my father.

"What the '. Bloody hell, Leonard it's me, Bill," my father exclaimed, using an expletive that I later used myself, with modifications.

Now my father, a moulder, you should be aware was about 15 stones in weight at this time with the physique of a hypertrophic weightlifter.

Little Leonard weighed in at about 7 stones wringing wet.

"Friend or foe?" said Leonard, again thrusting his gun forward.

My father knew Leonard quite well having gone to school with him all his young life, and having lived but a few doors away in the same street for over 20 years! He also knew that both guards had but one gun and one bullet between them, and it was Leonard's turn to have the gun but not the bullet tonight. My father was thus undeterred.

"Leonard, if yo stick that sword towards me again, I'll bost y' one in the gob fust and then wrap it round your bloody neck," he stated very firmly.

Leonard backed down. He did not wish to be hit in the mouth or anything similar. We were allowed on our way. Typical reflections of the war years.

We were a strong family unit at this time. We visited all our relatives on a regular basis. Big Auntie Gladys kept pigs, in her garden. Note, I had "Big" and a "Little" Auntie Gladys and "Big" and a "Little" Auntie Ida at this time. Great-aunt, and aunt. We had "Big" and "Little" uncles as well. Big Auntie Gladys' husband, Uncle Jim, used to let me feed the pigs on occasions. He showed me how they would eat anything. Once he boiled up an old boot and I saw them gobble it down, hobnails and all which they spat out. Oddly though now, on reflection of my early childhood, my particular main role models were my grandfathers, not my father at this time. I simply accepted my father as father. My grandfathers, however, they ruled the world.

Grandad Edward (Ted) who we lived with was a hard man. A coal miner, as I said. He had had for many years his own pit where he was buried alive, but then rescued, on at least three occasions. When the National Coal Board was introduced he was snapped up and worked on "the deep coal" at Baggeridge Colliery[4] as a "deputy", a charge man at the coalface, the most dangerous place, with his own team of miners. They were all hard men. They had little time to eat at work. He often had shin of beef stew for his breakfast and woe betide her if Granny had not got it ready on time.

He said he was a religious man, but I never recollect him going to church, not even on one occasion, but I do remember him telling me once when I had been singing in the choir at St. Peter's church in the centre of Wolverhampton,

"Yo'm alright gooin' thea our Edward. We've bin digging under thea at the pit, but I've left a column of coal under that church. It wo fall down 'ow ever loud yo sing."

By this time the coalface was 6 to 8 miles from the pithead and starting to make production uneconomical, but when I later enquired about the market hall nearby, now the site of the town civic centre and Wolverhampton council offices, a huge new building, he replied,

"Well, if yo goo in thea, be careful. I tell ya, doe jump up un down!"

Current Wolverhampton Council employees please note. Don't jump up and down. This is a true story.

I remember visiting my other grandparents. They were posh as well. Mind you they didn't have an inside loo like us. Instead they had a two-seater. Yes, a two-seater, a two-seater loo. One day as I sat down, about to do a "big job" the door opened. What the ' I thought at this, when to my surprise, Grandad Thomas (Tom) came in and sat down beside me.

"Our Edward, ello. Gerr ova," and plonk he sat down, and plonk, he did one too! A big job so to speak.

Well, even at that age, barely 5 years old, I recollect being a little taken aback, but then I sort of accepted that it was normality to have a side by side lavatory seat, only with male members of the family, of course. We had some decorum. Whilst I have learned in later life that other societies also go in for this unisex type of system, I have still not discovered the correct terminology for such "side by side" toileting. The precise Oxford Dictionary definition of the term "side by side" is that of "Standing close together, especially for mutual encouragement". There must be something wrong with me. I never did it standing, nor close together, and I never felt mutually encouraged either.

We were not posh enough, however, to have proper loo paper at this time though. My only childhood recollection of posh loo paper was that made by Izal[5], the sort found in hotels and other public places. Slippery it was. A sort of greaseproof paper. Your bum cheeks just slid off it. I was brought up on sterner stuff. Proper newspaper. You had a better grip, a bit like the modern nonabrasive paper that all the world has now. I remember one night getting undressed to go to bed to see that I had used a wet bit at the loo. I had a tattoo on the cheek of my behind. Not a very good tattoo though, as in the mirror it just read "Dudley Herald-late edition" i.e. the local now defunct newspaper. It looked great though, I thought. I carefully avoided wetting "my tattoo" for over a week until Fatty Smith at school saw it when we were doing PT and he spat on it and it rubbed off. Git!

Grandad Tom, was different to Grandad Ted. He was a *grand seigneur* of the old school. A Victorian leftover character. Tall he was. Sat up straight at all times. Polished shoes, you dare not touch; he had bunions. He had his own haulage business. Even with the introduction of motorization he still used heavy horses and carts. He was resistant to change. He was a brilliant horseman who could turn a heavy waggon around in the street. Try and get a horse to go backwards pushing a heavy cart. It is not easy. He had his own tea and sugar bowls and ate alone. He never mixed. He never talked. He merely gave edicts. He was vile. Universally disliked by all, especially his wife, Grandma, and my mother and her sisters, my aunts. He ruled the house with a rod of iron as if it was still Victorian times. He would cut out and burn any unused coupons from his food ration book[6] rather than share. He disliked all his grandchildren with a venom. I was accepted by him though. Just accepted, that is, he didn't actually like me. But we had a secret scam going. I would cut out my meat coupons, and he would cut out and swap his sweet coupons for me. What do you need meat for when you are 7 years old? It was our secret.

When he died he was accidentally put into an unmarked

grave. Grandma said it served him right, and she never bothered to mark and erect a gravestone, so we didn't have to visit him thereafter. Saved her some money it did.

"I can remember 'im in me yed, that's bad enough," she said. "Now 'e's jed I doe want t' look at his grave an' orl, do I? Any road, it's cheaper as I ay gorra buy a gravestone now, an I?" she questioningly explained.

Overall though, although the family itself was close, society in general struggled in these early post-war years. They were grim times. Shortages still abounded. The empire was going. Grey days, grey clothing, grey times were all my childhood memories. The weather always seemed cold and miserable. We only had coal fires but we were never short of heating, unlike neighbours in the village, because Grandad Ted had his allowance from the pit. Central heating had not been invented. Had it? We had a coal fire even in the bedroom. I do not remember sunshine in my childhood, but we must have had some. In 1947 when I started school the cold weather lasted for weeks, and neighbours were digging in the snow in the fields for surface coal of very poor quality. The men all wore grey coats and jackets. We wore grey pullovers, grey trousers and grey socks. We only ever had black coloured shoes. Cars were all black or of sombre colour. The Black Country was indeed black and grey, as was life in general.

References and Author's comment:

3. *Geological Handbook for the Wren's Nest National Nature Reserve*. R.J.O. Hamblin. 1978. The National Conservancy Council:

This book explains the geology and origin, and how today the preserved park stands as an isolated remnant of wooded countryside in an urban and industrial landscape.

In my boyhood times the Wren's Nest, including Mons Hill at the rear of our house, was an open hill park of geological limestone that had been worked on from before the Industrial Revolution. It had been used for agriculture, building and iron smelting. An oasis in the detritus desert of the post-Industrial Revolution Black Country, it was an incredibly exciting yet dangerous place to grow up in with many open workings and caves still. The most famous of these was the conjoined Seven Sisters cave, with a domed roof, hundreds of feet high with giant pieces of loose rocks abounding and many caverns to explore. In addition the area also contained a huge collection of easily obtainable and well-preserved fossils. The most well known of these is the "Dudley Locust", a trilobite (a Calymene arthropod) which is represented on the Dudley town coat of arms.

The whole area today represents a remnant of the edge of the ancient prehistoric Midland seabed.

4. *The Sinking of Baggeridge Colliery*. Mick Pearson. 2003. Black Country Society: Baggeridge Colliery, near Sedgley, was the last operative Black Country coal mine. This book tells of the sinking of the first shaft in February 1899 until the mine closure in March 1968. It tells of "the deep coal", the 24-foot rich seam that had been mined in total for over 300 years in this area.

There were many small superficial coal seams that allowed opencast mining, and in my boyhood I recollect poor, almost desperate women digging in the fields for "slack" i.e. surface dust-like coal, especially in the very cold winters that we had in those days. All this coal was the reason why the soil in the area was and still is black in colour. The deep coal, the thick stuff, extended from an outcrop near Stourbridge in the south, right across to a fault line near Bentley, outside Wolverhampton in the north. There is plenty still there.

5. Minor British Institutions. Izal toilet paper. The Independent. 14/11/2013 www.independant.co.uk:

Izal is a medicated toilet paper, first made in Sheffield in 1890 utilizing disinfectant produced as a by-product of coke manufacture!

It is still manufactured and available in modern form, but genuine original rolls can be obtained as "collector's items" for sale on the Internet and on eBay, if you are into that sort of thing.

6. Rationing in the United Kingdom – Wikipedia, the free encyclopedia:

Food ration books were issued to all UK residents in 1940 to ensure equal distribution of food in the Second World War.

They were buff coloured for adults, green for pregnant women and infants, and blue for children 5-16 years of age.

Intended for wartime usage, they continued to be used until July 1954, no less than 9 years after the war had ended! I hated them.

2. Food. Language, good and bad. School

In my childhood we ate grey food, and I developed my first hatred; SPAM.[7] This Specially Prepared Artificial Meat, or luncheon meat, was a meat substitute. It could be used in many combinations, in stews, casseroles or alone, when it could be fried, grilled, boiled, battered and cooked in any other way you could think of. It is still produced today. I developed "Spamaphobia" at quite an early age and it has not deceased today. Yes, deceased. It's not a spelling mistake. Telling my children of this brings smirks and sniggers. They think SPAM is electronic junk mail, but they should beware. With global warming and thus the expected food shortages, it has been whispered that the production of SPAM may be expanded again to help solve some of the world's future dire food problems. It may be stuffed down their throats again, like it was mine. It will serve them right. They still sell it at some of the big stores.

Things began to improve though as time went on. In the late 1940s I had my first banana, and I saw, just saw mind you, a pineapple. I never got to taste or eat it. I thought it was a funny coconut that I had already seen at the fairground. I was also taken out by Mother's sister, Aunt Amy, on one occasion for my first delicious restaurant meal. Baked beans on toast, the main course. Wow! I'd never had anything so delicious. This was in Birmingham. Auntie Amy lived there. She was Black Country who had become a "sort of Brummie".

The language and expression of the Black Country was, and still is, different from that elsewhere in the UK. In the 1940s and 50s we visited relatives, "Brummies", in Birmingham regularly, cousin Pauline especially, she still liked me, and I first became exposed to outsider language and behaviour. I had no idea of my insularity and I found it no different than when I went abroad and visited the Rhineland on my first school trip in the early 1950s. They, the Germans, were just the same, foreigners. From just as foreign a land. Indeed, I found to my surprise the German language somewhat easier to comprehend than that of the Brummies, and examples of this Black Country language similarity can be seen in phrases still today.

"Ar bin" means "I am" in Black Country, which is "Ich bin" in German.

"Yo bist" means "You are" in Black Country, which is "Du bist" in German, and there are many other similarities.

Furthermore about this time I discovered I had a very strong sense of regional identity to the Black Country, almost greater than that of being British. When my accent was confused by outsiders in later adult life to be that of a Brummie, then, as now, I felt a sense of upset that has persisted even into my (pre) senility. Despite knowing that nothing derogatory is intended I still feel a sense of dire insult when this mistake is made.

My mother thought school was where you went just to learn to read and write, as she had in her time. She didn't see the need to expand knowledge beyond a local horizon. In 1947 at the age of 4 ½ years she took me to my first day of infant school. We didn't have a four-by-four, we walked. It was only 3 miles away! I came home at lunchtime and returned to afternoon school alone, by myself.

All this at 4 ½ years of age, and on my first school day. There was no school run in those days.

She never took me again, first morning was enough she said, "Doe want t' be saft, an' spile 'im."

I looked nice. I was a pretty child. I became "teacher's pet". I had blue eyes and short very curly hair.

"Just like Googie Withers[8] the film star," said Mother, and her sister, Auntie Edna, agreed. I totally detested curly hair. I used to pinch my father's Brylcreem to flatten it out. Brylcreem is a hair dressing, somewhat similar to petroleum jelly, which is mixed with goose fat and made into a sort of cream with mainly beeswax. On your hair? It is still available and used by some of my friends. Wow! Despite this I was such a pretty favourite that the teacher used to send me to fetch children who had not turned up for school. Yes, but by then I was getting older. I was 5 years of age! "Sooty" Harper, guess why he got his name, was one of them. He was always late. When you went to his house the Harper's kitchen table had three legs and a pile of bricks. They were a big family. They were really poor, couldn't afford a proper table, the Harpers.

We moved twice in my first 3 years at school which meant that I attended three different infant (primary) schools, something unheard of today. Accordingly my academic progress was poor. It didn't matter to Mom. I was at school. Despite my blue-eyed, curly-haired exterior, I had itchy infantile eczema on all my covered up bits. I was also a wimp at anything physical. I was useless at all games as well as academic studies, the latter probably because I kept changing schools.

Towards the end of junior school, however, I discovered something had changed. Firstly I started to grow and get bigger. Then I became good at exams. All this was noted by my father who for a working-class man had an enlightened attitude to education.

For my tenth birthday he proclaimed, "Our Edward, I'm gonna buy you a book t' 'elp your education."

So what did he buy? Incredibly he bought me the whole *Encyclopaedia Britannica*, all 11 volumes it was at that time. A huge collection. I was enthralled. I was engulfed. It took me 6 months to read all the volumes, and then what did I do? I read them all again. It took another 6 months. As well as a huge volume of knowledge, some of which has been useful all my life, all this reading taught me how to educate myself. It taught me how to store facts in that cupboard, the human brain that has attributes superior to any modern computer. It taught me how to evaluate theory and philosophy, how to stand alone and think independently.

Eleven-plus exams were a doddle after all this. Grammar school beckoned.

Post Second World War higher level state education was via the grammar school system. Places were obtained by successful candidates in the eleven-plus examination. Unusually though, there were also a number of "more select" grammar schools where the top 5% of eleven-plus successful pupils were creamed off into higher level academies with more or better facilities. With the demise of this system sadly many such wonderful centres of education have been lost to the nation. The school that I attended, Dudley Grammar School, founded in 1562[9] was one of these, now absorbed into the homogeneous mass of like-for-all state education. Some centres of excellence remain. The Grammar School Wolverhampton, and King Edward School in Birmingham are fine examples. Go anywhere in the Black Country now at 8 a.m. and you can see the bright children being bussed to these few remaining centres.

I was taught at a high level. On arrival it took most of us years to ascertain the standards required. We were taught elitism. "You are the cleverest. The brightest". This included the entire curriculum, even sports. At the town sports day we were expected to win almost everything every year. Many of our graduates became not only university students but high level athletes also. It was expected to obtain six O-level grade GCEs as a baseline. Eight passes was normality. Sixth form graduates were expected to obtain at least two or three A-level GCE passes at high level. State scholarships were regularly obtained, with entry to Oxford or Cambridge or other universities as normality. Furthermore, in addition to all this academia, we were also taught to respect our fellow man. To be kind and generous to others. We were taught of honesty and reliability. An all-round education of high standard.

My very first day at grammar school I had my first French language lesson.

What a load of "Jimmy Rollocks" I thought. Even in those days I had learned to swear, but never, never openly. Why French, I didn't know any Frenchmen? Were there any Frenchmen or French persons in Dudley in the 1950s? No. I didn't know anyone who spoke French or had even been to France, and I never intended to visit the place at that time. What a stupid language, masculine and feminine nouns. Anyway, the *Encyclopaedia Britannica* had taught me how they lived on snails and frogs legs! No wonder they spoke so peculiar. How horrible. I treated the subject with revolt for 5 years. I just got the pass mark in French, 40% at GCE O-level, my foreign language pass to get into university.

Mother said that I have been "revolting" ever since. My wife agrees.

There's a mix up with terminology here somewhere.

This system of schooling, however, had its faults. Think what you may about the teaching of elitism. The majority of pupils in the 2 years prior to GCEs were streamed out into "arts" and "science" classes. These classes were for the boys (it was an all-boys school) with an academic bent who were expected to go on to higher education, university etc. For them this was an excellent system. For the pupils streamed into the "practical" stream, however, it was another matter. Whilst they did some practical subjects, only in a very poor way were they equipped to leave school at the age of 16 years to go into the workplace. They received little or no career guidance and much of their specialist teaching was somewhat wasted, and as they were about one third of the total number of pupils, it was a sizable deficit.

My attitude to education at the time showed the incomprehension, immaturity and lack of understanding of youth. Now having owned a second home abroad for a number of years, when my wife and I are given the courtesy of being addressed as "Cher voisin", (Dear neighbour) by our friends, my basic French grammar learned at this time has been of immeasurable value in later life.

Only in later life does one realize the importance of a broad-based education. History, geography and art appreciation were subjects similarly misunderstood. My scientific studies, mathematics, botany and zoology, chemistry, the physics of light, heat, and electricity (I detested physics) were all crucial to my final career, and have never been forgotten.

I loved my school. Leaving was the first loss of a love in my life. Whilst I still contact a few names, many of my classmates I have never seen again since the day I left. Their names are but reflections in my memory. They are never forgotten.

References and Author's comment:

7. *The Book of Spam.* D. Armstrong and D. Black. 2008. Simon and Schuster:

SPAM is Specially Prepared Artificial (or American) Meat, a type of luncheon meat, an American invention first marketed by the firm Hormel in 1937. The name was created following a competition and is supposed to be a combination of the words "spiced" and "ham". It was widely exported during the Second World War for the troops and for consumption by the general populace. It contains chopped pork, shoulder meat of indeterminate origin, and ham, salt, sugar and water and modified potato starch and preservatives.

It is still manufactured today with multiple even coloured variations available, mainly as a foodstuff, but also for other purposes. It is marketed widely for schools and some variants are purportedly sold for supposedly art sculpture purposes!

8. Georgette Lizette "Googie" Withers CBE (12/03/1917- 15/07/2011), www.britmovie.co.uk:

Googie Withers was a well-known actress of the war and post-war period. She retired to live in Australia for many years. It was mentioned in an episode of the Coronation Street television show in 2004 that "Googie Withers would turn in her grave", which was unfortunate, in that she was still alive, and lived until 2011!

9. *Dudley Grammar School 1562-1975*. Trevor Raybould. 2010. Bassett Press:

The book tells "A History of the School in its Times" and is written by an Old Dudleian. As well as a history of the school and its pupils, it outlines the closure of the grammar school and its conversion into a modern comprehensive.

The conversion of this grammar school was a process that was much against the wishes and views of many local people, a process that occurred in the education system on a nationwide scale at this time. The demise of the grammar school system nationally is still debatable, but is thought by many authorities to be a lamentable step backwards.

3. Family life. The Pub

In 1950 we moved to "The Pub". My father by this time had graduated from his wartime protected occupation of foundry foreman. He became a foundry manager and then owner, and eventually, literally built his own foundry. Grandad had put him into this occupation as it was "not s' dangerous as goin' down the pit" and he only learned to lift half a hundredweight of molten metal by the time he was 16 years of age. But now we were going up the social scale, beginning to enjoy the "you've never had it so good" life as expressed around this time by the prime minister, Mr Harold Macmillan[10]. The family was expanding. Unlike many women at the time, however, my mother had to work as we were still financially insecure and we had additions, two brothers, and then later yet another brother to support and finance. Mother, in her odd bit of free time between pregnancies applied successfully to become the first female public house licensee in Dudley, which was unheard of in those days. She had to attend the magistrates' court with the local brewery owner, Mr Holden to obtain this. We spent the next 10 years in The Pub, when in time with all this reproduction father's XY chromosomes[11] became quite exhausted and the female i.e. XX chromosomes began to get the upper hand. Two sisters arrived. All delightful additions. Happiness ruled, OK.

I became the big brother, and thank goodness my brothers and sisters were all better looking than me. Everybody forgot about my curly hair. I had to help out at home as my father was so busy with the foundry and mother was caring for my siblings. I had to open the pub bar at 6 o'clock, evening opening time and I served behind the bar until the barmaid arrived an hour later. I commenced this at 8 years of age and continued until I left home some 10 years later, when my brothers took over. Would this be allowed in this day and age? I doubt it very much. As a family we had little money, and we did not realize the wonderful times we had. Only by thinking back can I see that we lived in delightful domestic bliss.

My brothers were enchanting, and became charming rascals. On one occasion Norman, aged but 3 ½ years came to me.

"Our Edrud (he always had difficulty with "Edward"), there's a very big budgie on the roof," he exclaimed.

He was and still is a very bright fellow, but not this time it appeared, and he looked a little alarmed.

"Why, y' dope," I retorted. "Everybody knows budgies live in trees or cages, not on roofs."

I went outside to have a look. What the '!

I came back inside pretty quick, looking even more alarmed than he was.

"Daaaad," I shouted upstairs. "There's a big parrot sitting on the roof."

"Why, y dope," he cried back. "Everybody knows parrots live in trees or cages, not on roofs."

Nevertheless, despite this reply he came down from upstairs where we lived, and he went outside to have a look. He came back even quicker. There was a ferocious looking 4-foot tall vulture sitting on the roof that had escaped from Dudley Zoo!

All was sorted out when keepers from the zoo came and fired ropes over the roof and recaptured the "budgie-parrot-vulture" thing.

We took more notice of our Norman after this.

Then another time, elder brother Allan, disappeared with his younger brother, and only after some time were they discovered 4 miles away on the other side of town! He had taken little Norman, still in his pushchair, to the circus ground to see the human cannonball. They were missing for hours. He was 4 ½ years of age at this time, and was, and still is, fascinated by guns. Mother almost had apoplexy until the police search discovered them both safe and sound. It was my fault. I got a telling off again and a smack round the earhole for showing them the circus brochure. Nothing I could do about the situation, just had to accept it. Black Country attitude.

Eventually, however, the arrival of the other youngsters caused us to outgrow the pub accommodation that we had lived in for over 10 years, all of my teenage life. We did not need the income from the pub into the 1960s as my father's foundry was doing well, so we moved out into normal housing. If it had been nowadays we would have been summoned to court for overcrowding. All eight of us lived in a three-bedroom detached house. We were very typical of Black Country large families of those days. It was normal to share a bed as well as a bedroom. When relatives came to stay, as they did regularly, we were even more overcrowded. At Christmas time or other holidays we would sleep four or even six to a double bed. Two up. Two down. I hated waking up in the morning next to Uncle Harry's feet. They smelt OK, they just looked grotty and awful. He had terrible corns and toenails in all directions.

It was normality for those days, these arrangements. I did not have my own bedroom until my second year at university. I was by then 20 years of age.

References and Author's comment:

10. Harold Macmillan. Biography. John Simpkin. 2013 Spartacus Educational:

Harold Macmillan. Wikipedia. The free encyclopedia:

One of the most misquoted and misunderstood speeches ever made by a prime minister was made by Mr Maurice Harold Macmillan (10/02/1894-29/12/1986) at a Tory rally in Bedford, in July 1957. He actually said that "most of our people have never had it so good" implying that not all were included in having it so good, and he went on to further qualify the phrase, urging wage restraint and common sense and warning of the dangers of inflation and such.

The phrase continues to be misused. A continuing example of this was made in as recently as November 2010 by Lord David (Ivor) Young (27/02/1932-) the government "Enterprise Advisor." He caused great offence, using Macmillan's phrase, stating that most Britons had "never had it so good, despite this recession, this so-called recession". This was described both as insensitive and inaccurate and he later apologized, and actually resigned his post, only later somewhat quietly to be reappointed!

11. Sex Determination of Chromosomes. Stevens and Wilson. 1905. Carnegie College report:

Every cell in the human body contains in the nucleus of that cell the genetic material conferring the characteristics of that particular person, everything, their sex, their eye colour, tallness, shortness, intellect etc. etc. Every single cell has the full genetic material of that person. These characteristics are arranged in long chemical chains for which only recently has the full order i.e. the genetic code, been identified for that particular person, carried in a spiral helix formation called chromosomes. Human cells have 46 of these chromosomes arranged in 23 numbered pairs, one pair of which are known as the sex chromosomes, and every single cell in the body is either male or female in type.

In females the sex chromosomes are known as the XX chromosomes and in males the XY chromosomes, the Y chromosome being thought to be somewhat inert in action.

The sex chromosomes were remarkably first described by the American biogeneticists Edmund Beecher Wilson and Nettie Maria Stevens as far back as 1905, long before the discovery of the full chemical helix containing our genetic codes.

The Y chromosome is actually shrinking in size and losing some of its genetic material (genes), and it is estimated that it may stop functioning totally in about another 10 million years or so!

Look out chaps!

31

4. Holidays. Hunting, shooting, fishing

In his book in 2007 Andrew Marr[12] described how the sharp sense of class distinction in post Second World War Britain came much from where you lived, and this in turn defined what entertainments you might enjoy. The post-war changing face of working-class Britain i.e. approximately 60% of the population, can be studied in many ways. One of these many changes was the increased freedom of recreational activity, and in particular how the people took their holidays. In the immediate post-war years there was little money, not many had their own transport and other than the old holiday resorts such as Blackpool or Brighton there was little development of any holiday industry for the general populace. This is reflected in the story of our family holidays.

In 1947 Mother, Father and I took our first holiday together. We stayed in a wooden hut, a supposed "bungalow", in a field near the village of Claverley in Shropshire, a mere 15 miles from home. Water had to be fetched by hand, and toilet facilities were a "bucket and chuck it" into the field. Other than "bracing walks, chaps," and visits to the pubs in the village there was nothing to do other than "get away from it all". My father went fishing and drinking at the pub. Mother and I did absolutely nothing except look at sheep. This was typical of the holiday of working-class Black Country folk at this time.

We were not perturbed. We were relaxed. It was normality.

In the early 1950s, however, things began to change. "Billy" Butlin, i.e. William Heygate Edmund Colborne Butlin (what a mouthful, poor fellow), 29/09/1889-12/06/1980, who was later knighted, and who not unnaturally tended not to use his full name, was one of the first post-war entrepreneurs to envisage cheap holidays for the masses. In 1947 he opened a holiday camp on the converted army camp at Pwllheli, with road and rail access to the Midlands. It dawned on others, mainly the English, that there was a whole coastline of easily accessible disused army facilities that could be expanded in a similar but somewhat cheaper way as caravan parks. Accordingly over the next few years a whole series of holiday parks were opened on this the so-called "Welsh Riviera", from Pwllheli in the north to Aberystwyth in Mid Wales and to all these the Midlanders arrived. These camps and caravan parks were expanded over the next 20 years with a vibrant tourist industry developing by the mid 1970s and 1980s. Today's tourists, who are much more discerning, however, would be surprised by what these first visitors found.

At Butlin's camp the visitors were housed in tarted up army huts surrounded by nothing but farmland, with a huge fairground, with bumping cars (Black Country speak for "dodgems") and merry-go-rounds to keep them happy. The nearby beach was at times a boring mudflat. The town of Pwllheli was actually some distance away, and was a real dump in the 1950s. Indeed, visitors were always not welcomed by the locals. It may be somewhat unpalatable to disclose, but even up to the 1990s such attitudes continued. The staff at the market café at the end of the central car park always served Welsh speakers before they served outsiders.

Pleasingly, this sort of behaviour has now (2014) been resolved.

The caravan parks originally had little or no amenities and were often ill-sited, away from the towns. Other than visit pubs and clubs there was little to do, other than take "bracing walks, chaps" said the brochures. Yes, walks again. You had to like walking in those days. Welsh licensing laws were restrictive, with early closing times and no opening at all on Sundays in many counties, the day of exodus over the respective county boundary, for an alcoholic drink. The weather didn't help with many resorts situated close to the mountains of Snowdonia, precipitation was heavy. Not just the amount of rain though. For some peculiar climatic reason, rain in Wales always seemed wetter than elsewhere. Everybody agreed on this. Why it is, I do not know. Nevertheless, because of cheapness and easy accessibility, in the 1950s and 1960s thousands of Midlanders and Black Country working-class folk started to invade this coastline throughout the summer months. There was not much sun but the grey times had started to brighten up a little.

In the 1950s we went *en famille* on holiday to Dyffryn Ardudwy near Barmouth in Wales. We had a car, a Hillman Minx, bog-standard black colour as all cars still were then, and at home we now had a fridge and a telephone. We holidayed all together as a family with Auntie Edna, Uncle Harry and cousin Pauline. We booked a "De Lux Caravan and Bungalow" at Dyffryn. "Beautiful and quiet, nearby to the sea" said the advertisement.

The bungalow was a Nissen hut just like the air-raid shelter at home that Mother had kept her ducks in during the war. She flatly refused to even let us across the threshold it was so dirty. Mother had a thing about clean, her own definition.

"We are not stoppin' in 'ere. It's bloody dirtier than where I kept me ducks, Bill," she announced to my father on arrival.

In the "De Lux" caravan the floor had come away from the walls and grass was growing through the floor. The earwigs and other bugs were leaving, it was so smelly. If this was the De Lux accommodation, the mind boggled as to what a non- De Lux caravan was like. The main road was half a mile away down a dirt track, and the beach a similar distance, supposedly nearby. We had to share the field with a flock of turdy sheep where we, the children, were to play, and was the place quiet? The first morning we were all awoken with an incredible start by the loudest noise

I still have ever heard to this day. Bang, crash, b-boom! Father was getting his fishing tackle sorted out to go fishing when he spilt his box of maggots all over his bacon sandwich. Took him several minutes to clean them all off, before he still ate it! Mother sloshed her early morning cup of tea all over the bed and knocked the jug over containing Dad's false teeth which also fell amongst the maggots. He wiped his teeth before he put them in. Just once though, that was enough.

The noise was so loud that Uncle Harry was woken up and exclaimed,

"Bleedin' 'ell, Ed," to Auntie Edna. "That bang nearly woke me up."

He was an amusing man, Uncle Harry, a true Brummie with, to us, a terrible accent, and how one could be nearly woken up I knew not, but we understood his logic that day. I suppose to be "nearly woken up" is a little bit like being "nearly pregnant" both of which are a sort of *fait accompli* to me. Only in Wales would one be allowed to develop a caravan site at the end of the runway of an active Royal Air Force base, RAF Llandbedr, with flying Meteor and Canberra jets and target planes including de Havilland Venom fighters and such. You could wave to the pilots, the planes were so low. We had 4 days of boiling hot sun. We had 10 days of miserable rain. As a result we came home sunburnt and very damp. We were all very bug bitten and all our shoes were covered with sheep turds. My little brother Royston, who could just walk, had all his clothes covered with it as well. Caravan sites in those days did not offer clothes washing facilities. Dad, furthermore, was convinced many years later that his noise-induced hearing loss commenced at this time.

"Due to all those bloody airplanes and the nuclear bombs they was carrying I say, our Edward," he insisted, i.e. after only 2 weeks of intermittent noise exposure, and no radiation, it was nothing to do with 40 years of foundry noise that he had been exposed to in his employment. Oh no, no!

We returned home totally cream-crackered, and happy. We had been on a proper holiday. Away from home, at the seaside.

The emancipation of the post-war working class was taking place about this time, and the increased wealth of the populace meant that people were starting to purchase their own homes. Family car ownership also became common. Everyone now had a television and this lead to increased public awareness and expanding interests. The post-war working-class younger generation were beginning to enjoy grammar school and university education, although both of these were still expensive for families, despite state grants, and the working class began to expand into the middle class, which was to become the dominant class within the country. Increased prosperity in the Black Country led to the onset of an annual summer migration to the north and central Welsh coast (Costa del Cymru?) which began to resemble a giant caravan park. Some northern coastal resorts, such as Abersoch and Porthmadog became the Mecca for the "sharp set", the yachting fraternity, such as e.g. The South Caernarvonshire Yacht Club at Abersoch, with mainly English membership. Butlin's camp and Pwllheli town centre itself had a facelift, and some caravan sites such as "Sunny Sands" near to Barmouth started to enlarge to become almost towns in their own right with expansion and a multiplicity of improved facilities. You could still watch the young men at the Outward Bound School at Aberdovey attempt to "improve your moral fibre chaps" by half drowning themselves in the river estuary, but local old trades and activities were declining. The fishing boats at Barmouth and other old ports began to disappear. Inland places also began to wake up to the fact that this influx of Midlander visitors was to their benefit and halfway towns such as Llangollen, Welshpool and Newtown all began to cater for, and welcome, these new visitors.

The colour of life in general was changing and society began to enjoy more pleasant times. Even the weather seemed to improve. As well as brighter coloured family clothes and cars, sports cars began to be available and affordable to the masses, although these latter still had specific colouring. British sports cars were often green in colour, French were blue, posh German ones were usually silver, and Italian ones were any colour you liked, as long as it was red!

By the late 1950s and into the 1960s our family had begun to fit into all these common criteria. Father now had his own foundry business and we joined the annual holiday summer migration by car, a blue one now. A Ford Zodiac, a huge vehicle, which was an increased status symbol and able to cope with the great volume of luggage that Mother always took on holiday. Interestingly this "must-take-bloomin'-everything-itis" is an incurable disease, commonly found in ladies still, but not mentioned in medical text books or articles. My wife has it. We found that as well as clothes, Mother would often take all sorts of totally useless things on holiday that were never needed. On one occasion we couldn't sleep. We all awoke in the night thinking there was a fault in the plumbing of the caravan. Eventually we discovered that Mother had brought my brother's pet gerbil that we didn't know about, and he, in the cupboard, was taking his midnight wheel-turning exercise, causing the noise! The dog yes, but who takes the family gerbil on holiday? Well we did. My father was driven to despair at times.

By now we had our own caravan which was sited at Neptune Hall Caravan Park, at Towyn, in Merionethshire, where we were welcomed by the enterprising owner and his family, and we began to enjoy the sunnier summer times, and happy family occasions.

None of the occasions were so unusual, however, as the time when Auntie Edna was sexually assaulted! Yes, sexually assaulted she was.

It was late one night after a hot day on the beach and after an evening of playing cards, when the whole family group were all about to go to bed. At this time we did not have flushing toilets in the caravan, and "taken short" Auntie Edna had surreptitiously gone outside into the night. Preparing for bed, our intended repose was suddenly disturbed by a great shout of alarm and a scream, and she reappeared at the door pulling up her somewhat voluminous drawers.

"Help, help," she cried out. "Somebody grabbed me from behind and pinched me bum. I could be scarred for life," she exclaimed, not really bothering to fully clarify whether she claimed to be emotionally or physically scarred.

My brother Allan, now grown up, was always ready for a fight (ask his wife), jumped up at this and took hold of the fire iron from the stove.

"Come on. Come on our Edward. We'll sort him out," he cried out, jumping up and volunteering me at the same time. He was very good at volunteering me. Nevertheless in bravado I joined him and grabbed the nearest weapon, Mother's frying pan from the stove, and a torch, and we rushed outside. It was very dark but a bright moon lit the night. All was quiet and no one was seen in sight. Then I heard a rustling sound.

"He's under the van, Allan," I called out.

I shone my torch and bent down. Yes, yes, there he was, the brute. Two bright eyes and a dark nose. A sharp looking chap. I grabbed hold of him and dragged him out and back into the van.

Well I didn't actually grab him. I sort of picked him up, and put him on to the frying pan. Everybody, except Auntie Edna, totally fell about semi-collapsed with laughter, at her assailant, a hedgehog! A very spiky chap that she had sat on. He, not understanding all this, looked extremely scared and, pardon my expression, somewhat "pissed off" (author's apologies), actually "pissed upon" it should be, I suppose, at the predicament that he now found himself in.

The laughter went on for some time. Eventually though the mirth died down and Auntie Edna managed to control her embarrassment, and Mother, always a kindly soul, decided to take pity on her assailant and stuck him in the oven which was warm, to dry him out. This terrified the little fellow even more, as he thought he was about to be had for breakfast as well as being "rained upon".

Next morning when he was nicely dried out, Mother kicked him out, bang! Her kindness had resolved, back into the field again he went, never to return. I wonder why? All our jaws ached for weeks. Auntie Edna never showed us her scars.

Black Country folk were becoming integrated into Welsh society by the late 1960s and 1970s. Father became the first English member of the Towyn Working Men's Club because of his friendly and generous personality. Close friendships were formed with names such as "Kitch" and "Gwillam" and as my father's son, still in my teens I was supplied with a twelve-bore shotgun and gun dog. I went rabbiting in the fields and dunes nearby. The first time I used the gun it I nearly dislocated my shoulder and I had a ringing noise in my ears for 10 minutes. My brothers, even younger than I, were given the same privileges, which would never be allowed these days. They all hunted rabbits, birds and the wildlife, and grew to know the topography and fauna and flora of the area intimately. Then on special occasions, weather permitting, with my father and friends we would go on the "Big Hunt".

One very dark moonlit night, myself in my early teens and a close family friend, Tony, were given the job of going across the moor on the Towyn army camp grounds. We had two dogs which were trained to zigzag across the moor. This would drive any rabbits or other wildlife out and across the road where our fathers and Kitch had set up a long line of nets alongside the road to entrap them. As we were coming across the moor half a mile or so away we saw an army jeep arrive, fitted with a searchlight. The officers inside had seen the nets. They swung their searchlight across the moor. Tony and I dropped to the ground on to the dogs that were brilliant and didn't move a muscle. Then to our absolute alarm they started firing over our heads. They were armed and we were trespassing on army ground!

Tony said to me, "Shit, Edward, was they bloody bullets goin' over our 'eads?"

Pause. And I replied, "Tone [his nickname], yes, I think they bloody was!"

This was the only time in my life I have heard the sound of bullets whistling over my head. It made me swear. Scared, we became very flat.

39

Eventually though, after a while they ceased firing, and sped off into the night, back to the camp. They were off for reinforcements. We crept back up to the road. Kitch grabbed the nets and any rabbits and sped away over the nearby railway line. We saw lights approaching. The army was returning in strength with the police. We all sat in the car with the dogs. Figures approached.

"Wat yu doin 'ere then boyos?" said Police Sergeant Bryn Evans. He was Welsh you know. You could tell by his accent. We knew him well anyway, drank in the Working Men's Club with my father.

"Just takin' the dogs f' a walk Sergeant," said my father.

"What the ',' cried Sergeant Evans. "But it's 2 o'clock in the morning it is," he said.

The police and soldiers were all mad with rage. There was nothing they could do. Kitch had hopped it with all the evidence. They let us go home. The dogs slept soundly under the caravan all night. Kitch collected them next morning, bringing Mother a brace of rabbits all gutted and nicely dressed.

Then there was the "Big Fish" which was similar to the "Big Hunt", but an even more dangerous escapade, a method of sea poaching, off the beach with our Welsh friends again. This required a clear dark night, after a warm day when the tide was coming in bringing in the feeding fish to the beach. A large net fixed to a 10 to 12-foot pole would be taken out some 30 to 50 yards by three large tall and strong men and then others would dig the pole at the opposite end of the net, into the beach sand. The pole men who were fully clothed and smoking cigarettes so that they could be seen, would then walk in an arc back to the beach thus scooping up any fish entrapped that way. This was tiring and cold work and wetsuits were not available in those days. It could be dangerous. One night as we pulled in, the net was very heavy and we heard the sound of snapping. I shone the torch on to the catch. All one could see was a huge mouth with huge teeth coming towards us.

"Jesus, we've catched a shark!" cried somebody as we all ran off.

Kitch fetched a lump hammer he just happened to have. Thump, smack! The snapping stopped. He was always well equipped for all emergencies. Only next morning did we discover what we had caught. A monkfish[13] with huge "reproductive organs" that fascinated all the ladies on the campsite, a heavy fish and over 3-foot long. No wonder we had all been scared; it was all mouth and teeth. I later discovered that these fish are usually all genetic females, and the large appendage seen hanging from the undersurface is the atrophied and shrivelled up remnant of the male fish that they require to reproduce! The ladies on the site would have been quite disappointed had I explained all this, as they all thought it was a male "showing his tackle" so to speak. Father even got his photograph taken and published in the local newspaper with the fish. "Caught with a rod off the beach at Towyn" was the caption. Lying toad. What softies they were for believing him. He made but one derogatory comment on the magazine article.

"Well, if they 'm saft enough to believe that story, they deserve to be took to the cleaner's."

Father was ever innovative as regards his sport. He would try all sorts of methods. Impatient with simple river fishing when good sites required an expensive fishing licence, he decided to improvise with the "Little Fish".

"Our Edward yo'm doin' chemistry at school. What 'appens when you put sodium into water?" he asked.

I explained that in our chemistry labs at school "when utilizing small amounts of refined organic sodium mixed with water there was a profound yet simple exothermic chemical reaction that produced latent energy and sometimes profuse amounts of radiant heat"! Wow, that took him aback. Straight from my chemistry book verbatim. He didn't understand a word. Exothermic meant little to him. He thought it was some sort of itchy skin rash. Well, he had used sodium in the foundry and he professed to be familiar with sodium, so he thought. It was used to put in the furnace to mix up various alloys. He took me then late one afternoon up to the mouth of the Dysynni river by the quarry, and showed me a large jam jar that he had prepared, containing an oily liquid and what looked like Oxo cubes, actually metallic sodium in a protective foil, and he had a tin can full of holes tied to a long piece of string. The idea was to throw the can into the river with an amount of sodium, after putting a net across the flow, to catch any fish that might be temporarily stunned by the reaction, and salmon trout was what he was after, his favourite fish. He wasn't quite sure how much sodium to put in the tin, so the first time he put in half a cube and we lay down on the bank as the can was thrown into the river. There was a loud hissing noise and some bubbles in the water. Nothing much else happened. Pause. Father believed in overkill. Again we lay down on the bank but this time he had put six cubes in the tin, and he threw it in.

I wish I hadn't lain down. I was hit full in the chest as the bank came up and hit me. Kaboom! What the'. An incredible bang, and a huge fountain of water and sparks shot 50 foot up in the air.

"Jesus, our Edward. Yo day tell me it was goin' t' be like that," father cried out.

"I didn't know that you were intending to emulate the sinking of the bloomin' *Graf Spee*, Dad," I cried back in response.

He didn't know what "emulate" meant so he wasn't upset. What I hadn't told him was that when sodium in large quantity was mixed with water, the violent chemical reaction induced produced not only sodium hydroxide, but large quantities of exothermic energy and very inflammable hydrogen gas.

We looked aghast at the river. Stun the salmon? We had killed everything in the river for 100 yards on either side of us, fish of all types, millions, large and small, crabs, frogs, everything floated past. It was like the Americans when they later defoliated Vietnam. We defoliated a river in Wales long before they started in the game. We quickly grabbed up our gear and left, never to try this again.

Later that evening in the Working Men's Club my father was asked if he had any luck fishing that day.

"No nothing was biting," was his fisherman's reply.

"I'm not surprised," said his friend. "You could hear the bangs even in the town here 3 miles away, blasting away at the quarry up by the river, at teatime today, louder than ever. The noise they make would stop any fish biting."

Father agreed. Quick thinking. I looked away and just admired the barmaid's legs and her "big lungs" and said nothing, grinning inside my head.

On looking back I recollect many such idyllic summers and the years passed quickly by as all the family grew up. By the 1980s and 1990s like other Black Country folk we had become very closely integrated into North Welsh society. The local Welsh folk had become firm friends now though still staunchly maintaining their own particular regional identity. Years later, but an example of such established friendships, was the appreciated attendance of a large group of Towyn folk at my father's funeral, a round-trip journey for them in excess of 200 miles. Lovely folk.

With reflection I see a change. In the new millennium, for one thing holiday property prices have markedly escalated. At Abersoch, still the home of the "smart set", prices just for a beach hut run into many thousands of pounds and house prices generally equate to those of southern resorts such as Poole and Dartmouth, and purchase of just a static caravan can cost in excess of £25,000. Furthermore, taxes for UK properties or caravan sites often exceed those paid for abroad in such areas as inland France or on the "Costas Geriatrica" in southern Spain. Although I have holidayed abroad for some years it was never easy, by road or rail, air travel being far too expensive, but my children and those of the baby boomers are much more emancipated. They want cheap and easy travel abroad.

With the deregulation of European aviation in 1997 this was eventually enabled, when the "Irish Luftwaffe", Ryanair[14] appeared and started cheap European flights abroad, and then the Greek Cypriot "Flying Corpse" (correct spelling), easyJet[15], added to this.

In the first few years cheap oversea holiday access was

openly welcomed, but with the increasing restrictions later being imposed such as travel with no luggage, standing up with just the clothes that you are wearing and being unable to use a toilet without paying a forfeit, Black Country folk like the rest of the country have become less enamoured by such flights. Disillusionment of late has been further compounded by suspicions aroused by the statements of "smooth-talking, smarmy, slimy, obnoxious-know-it-all, obviously lying through his teeth Irish Mick" type (you might gather not one of my favourite persons) airline chief executive officer who always purports to be supplying the ideal service that his customers require, when such customers blatantly don't believe him. Well, "Lyin-Air" realizing this disillusionment, have introduced a new "spokesperson" (spin doctor?), but unfortunately he has the identical "smooth-talking, smarmy, slimy, obnoxious-know-it-all, obviously lying through his teeth Irish Mick"-type accent and attitude (I don't like him either) to their chief executive officer, so still nobody believes them! One suspects that with the recession that began in about 2008 all this disservice and dissatisfaction could lead to an exodus back to holidays at home. Time will but tell.

References and Author's comment:

12. *A History of Modern Britain*. Andrew Marr. 2007. Pan Books:
Andrew William Stevenson Marr (31/07/1959-) is a Scottish-born journalist and political commentator, who was editor of *The Independent* newspaper from 1996-1998 and political editor of BBC News from 2000-2005. His book takes a very comprehensive look at post-war Britain up to the present day, with some sharp analysis and particular comment. Despite suffering a stroke in 2013 with residual paresis, he commendably returned to presenting the weekly BBC television Sunday morning "Andrew Marr Show" discussing political and current affairs.
The Marr family appear to have an ability to cope very well with physical disability. He is married to Jackie Marr née

Ashley, and his father-in-law, the peer, Lord Ashley of Stoke (06/12/1922-20/04/2012) had a long history of public service despite a profound and total hearing loss. Mr Marr, together with his wife has many other interests including support for the Deafblind and Rubella Associations.

13. Monkfish of the family Lophiidae, order Lophiiformes (class Actinopterygii, ray formed fishes). *The Columbia Encyclopedia, 6th Edition.* 2000. Columbia University Press:

The monkfish, or anglerfish, a voracious predator, is so called because the head of the fish is supposed to resemble that of a cowled monk, and is so large that it is often mistaken for a shark. The body is an edible delicacy sometimes sold in the UK labelled as "scampi" which is actually illegal, as this contravenes the Fish Labelling Regulations 1996 et al. Scampi is the term given to the fleshy tail of the langoustine or Norway lobster (Nephrops norvegicus) itself often incorrectly labelled as a "Dublin Bay prawn".

14. *Michael O'Leary: A Life in Full Flight.* A. Ruddock. 2008. Penguin UK:

UK Ryanair. Wikipedia. The free encyclopedia:

Ryanair low cost airline was established in 1984 by the unrelated Christopher Ryan, a former Aer Lingus ground handling agent, and Thomas Anthony "Tony" Ryan (02/02/1936-03/10/2007) a pioneer in the business of aircraft leasing, and Liam Lonergan, owner of an Irish travel club. The company made an operating loss until 1991, since when it has undergone massive and profitable expansion, under the current Chief Executive Officer Mr Michael Kevin O'Leary (20/03/1961-). The company is now listed on the Irish and London stock exchanges, and the American NASDAQ.

Appointed in 1994, Mr O'Leary is a controversial character, a known cost-cutting fanatic who in the interests of cost and efficiency at one time registered his own private motor vehicle, albeit a Mercedes S-class saloon, as a registered taxi, to enable him to get around more efficiently using taxi lanes in heavy Dublin traffic!

15. *easyJet: The Story of Britain's Biggest Low-cost Airline.* L. Jones. 2005. Aurum Press Ltd:

easyJet. Wikipedia. The free encyclopedia:

easyJet low-cost airline was established 1995 by the Greek-born businessman (Sir) Stelios Haji-Ioannou (14/02/1967-) whose family originate from Cyprus.

Although he describes himself as... "Lucky because my angel was familiar with the industry" (self-quote 09/04/2003), luckily at the age of 25 years he was given just £30 million by his father that initially he used to set up a shipping company when first entering the business world! A self-described workaholic who dislikes holidays, nevertheless, luckily the airline company that he built up has expanded profitably from its onset and luckily was floated on the London Stock Exchange in 2000.

He still retains a large percentage, some 37%, of the company shares at the time of writing (2014).

5. Puberty, respect, sex education and swearing, logic, career

At the age of 12 years I found that I was changing into a gorilla. My voice got very gruff and I started to grow everywhere and become big. I started to become hairy under my arms, and on my face and around my vital bits, which also started to enlarge. I was not very happy about the hair but the enlargement of the vital bits was encouraging. The curls on my head started to straighten and I became ugly. Well, not actually ugly, let us not get carried away with self-denigration, but not as pretty as I was when I was a child, and my teachers appeared to begin to dislike me as well. Great.

I didn't realize it, but I was also changing psychologically. I became aware that not all females were a total pain, and indeed some were actually quite nice, and I was changing from being a wimp, as one of my semi-bully friends was to discover.

What is a semi-bully you ask? Well, a 100% full-blown bully is an obviously obnoxious person, totally and is always picking on the underdog, and is often a coward when confronted by an equal. A semi-bully is similar, but different, often a "friend", often a long-term friend, who from time to time has to reinforce his or her authority over you. Their bullying is variable.

Now at the age of 14 years I was following the family trend.

Father was built like one side of a house at that time, working in the foundry all his life. I likewise became 5 foot 10 inches tall like him, and began to grow sideways. A metamorphosis that I did not realize was puberty. So when one day I was pushed by a semi-bully friend, he was surprised when I did not buckle as in the past, so he did it again, for the last time. As well as a big push back he also received a sort of "smack in the gob" that flattened him. I was never semi-bullied or even fully bullied again.

It was about this time that I began to comprehend not only the physical stature of my father but his ability to use this largess of personality to communicate. He became my role model, in spades. Sadly my sisters born later in his life never remember all this as his huge presence and personality started to regress as he aged, a common deficit of children borne to parents in their forties and later life. On one occasion when at the age of 16 years I had the temerity to answer him back sharply, I don't recollect what it was about but I recollect the response, he quickly turned, a grimace of disdain on his face. Smack, I got one. With a flick of the arm and wrist he struck out. We had a settee in the middle of the room and I was flung back against it, went backwards in a complete somersault reverse Fosbury flop[16] and landed on my feet again! I was astounded by the power of the blow, given so quickly and adroitly as not to really hurt me. Just to establish an authority. My esteem and respect for my father was established thus and never lost from that time. With that blow we communicated fully forever.

I now know that this time was the age of puberty, the onset of maturation. The time of growth, of learning and of assimilation, an insidious process that we all go through and that like myself many don't realize what is going on until educated by their peers. We only had self sex education in those days. It was mostly learned in the school playground. It wasn't easy. There were no "girly magazines" or such available, no blue movies, no DVD or Internet porn. Everybody became nudists and read *Health and Efficiency* magazine[17]. Actually nobody ever read it, but we all just looked at the pictures, old fat guys with flabby

WHAT THE ' - REFLECTIONS OF A BLACK COUNTRY

goolies and with some quite attractive women playing tennis and the like. Peculiarly though, pictures of the suprapubic area of the women, who clearly had no clothes on, were blanked out, so you either had to imagine what was there, or to fill it in yourself, as some oddballs did, or go and peep at women elsewhere which was much more normal. According to this magazine women appeared to have no genitalia, but we all knew that they did, and so we were intrigued further thus. This magazine greatly helped to breed a generation of post-war young men and their attitudes, budding anatomists perhaps?

Father was not very helpful on the subject of sex though, he was quite a prude, and at the age of 16 years he announced,

"Our Edward yo'm doin' biology now at school. I think we need to discuss sex and the facts of life."

A little bemused and confused by this sudden outburst, I misunderstood him, already having had some "close encounters of the second kind" on several occasions, and being very well acquainted with the biology of sex by now, I replied…

"Well Dad, what would you like t'know about it?"

Result, a smart smack round the ear, and a snort… "Bloody kids of t'day."

We never had another deep and meaningful conversation on this subject again, neither as far as I am aware, did any of my five siblings.

Sex was never mentioned in our house and swearing was not allowed. Oddly, swearing outside and away from female company was quite acceptable, but not in the home. This pertains in most Black Country households and this rule continued into adult life.

When I remarked once that,

"It's bloody cold out today," one icy winter's day on arrival at my parents' house.

My Father retorted,

"Our Edward there's no need for such bad language like that, not in our 'ouse please."

I was 58 years of age!

49

This is an example of the Black Country parental attitude that the age gap between children and parents never closes and that decorum has always to be observed, especially in the home. This is also why modern forms of the media, with open attitudes to both sex and profanity are still frowned upon in many West Midlands households.

Out of the family house though it is different. If you think television chefs swear a great deal, you should hear a gang of Black Country workmen getting upset over something. Black Countrymen swear properly, with reason, and gusto, not for effect. One day when laying slabs with brother-in-law Carl, he was 6 foot 2 inches, no fat, he dropped a 2 foot by 3 foot concrete slab on his toe.

What the ', and then you should have heard him swear!

If the house hadn't had hardwood window frames the paint would have blistered. I will not repeat it, but I didn't know a slab could be "haemorrhaging" or "crudely engaging in sexual intercourse" and be "illegitimate at birth" ...(work it out), all at one time. Following this he picked up a sledgehammer and proceeded to smash the offending slab to smithereens, to bits, to pieces.

When I enquired as to why he had done this he replied,

"So it wo drop on me toe again, wull it?" was the simple (to him), explanation.

Now to an outsider this might seem odd behaviour. I found it completely acceptable, another example of Black Country logic and an abstract view of a life situation. After this we had to lay the other 25 slabs, not one of which offended or assaulted him!

The 1950s was a time of great transition. To be a teenager was wonderful. More social pursuits were available. Sports halls and youth clubs were opening up. There was a revolution in popular music from the post-war ballad era to the more appealing skiffle and folk music period. In the late 1950s rock and roll artists from the USA began to appear; Jerry Lee Lewis, Little Richard, Elvis Presley etc. The UK had no home-grown big stars, yet. But as ever with growing up, life had to change. The colour of life was changing. "Fast food" started to arrive, although we did not yet have the full takeaway meal, one could visit a Wimpy Bar to have a burger, or a Chinese restaurant with its strange food and tastes. Clothes were brighter. As well as sports cars appearing, car colours lightened, silver, blues and greens began to appear, and one could even buy a car with a roof in a second colour. Like the rest of the country, the Black Country and life in general was brightening up and becoming less drab. Content with life and soaking up all this though, I was in for a big shock. Career. The big world, all alone, on my own two feet, had to be faced.

I had been in the local church choir for many years and appeared in school operatic society concerts. Like many of my generation in the 1960s I had a guitar and after skiffle had been in a local early rock/pop band. I aspired then perchance for a musical career. I hadn't thought too deeply about it, when in my 17th year my father one afternoon made an announcement.

"Our Edward we need to talk about your future."

This statement preceded another deep and meaningful conversation, this time regarding my future career. We met with his close friend and confidant,

Mr Edwin Holden, who owned both "The Pub" and the local brewery at the rear, my mother's boss, and who was at that time a governor of my school. The brewery was the biggest industry in the village. Mr Holden was an important man. His ales were sold all over the Black Country, as they still are (in 2014). I do not recollect the exact conversation but it was not like that of today. Your father decided on your career in those days. It was expected of him. The conversation went something like…

"Me and Teddy, Mr Holden to you, have looked at your school record and we 'ave decided that you are goin' t' university, t' study medicine!"

Wham, just like that, in an instant. No discussion. No opinion taken. I was flabbergasted. Me, a "Jack the Lad" type. Big now, good at sports. Playing in a new thing, a pop group, a band. All would have to be given up to do this. Medicine!

The so-called discussion that day took approximately 5

minutes in the empty bar of the pub where we lived. Sometime later my brothers and sisters were to have similar "lengthy" and meaningful career discussion although Father had mellowed somewhat and modernized and did ask them for some opinion. To me, however, the order was made in short sharp fashion and it led to a life-changing experience. I didn't discover until years later that my father had made this decision only after lengthy discussion with Mr Holden and several others including various school masters. At this time it was quite normal for your parents alone to decide without consultation on your future career. I had to put away my guitar and begin to concentrate on my A-level work. Things were getting serious. Intensive study was only made possible by moving to living quietly with my grandparents for a while, before taking my A-level examinations, to find a quiet oasis away from the pub, to absorb the knowledge for the grades required.

Three advanced level GCEs of high grades were obtained. I obtained "provisional" places at Birmingham, London and Cambridge universities so I accepted a "definite emplacement" at the Medical School of Leeds. I had only a vague idea where Leeds was. Up north somewhere. All I knew was that at 18 years of age I was going to have to leave home and leave the Black Country.

Somewhat in a daze still, nevertheless, I left home full of expectations not knowing what was to come. I thought I was well prepared for university and higher education because of my strict schooling, but nothing was to prepare me for the almost cataclysmic realization after the first month or so of the immense volume of knowledge and level of expertise a medical student was, and still is, expected to assimilate and learn. With my A-level grades I managed to skip the first university year so I estimated that I would be away from home for about 5 years. How wrong I was. As I left home in September 1961 all those years ago I recollect seeing my mother with a tear in her eye.

I attempted to reassure her with a now commonplace phrase, "I'll remember every one of you. I'll be back. Don't you forget that. I'll be back."[18]

References and Author's comment:

16. The Fosbury Flop. The U.S. Hall of Fame. 2013. www.usaf. org:

The Fosbury flop is a reverse head-first high jump technique that was first introduced in 1968 at the Olympics by the American, Dick Fosbury (06/03/1947). Devised by himself whilst still at high school, the jump was only made possible by the introduction of better athletic ground landing facilities, when he explained the safety of the jump involved landing on one's shoulders, not on one's neck. Despite winning the gold medal at the 1968 Mexico Olympics, he later found that reputation alone meant nothing, when he failed to make the grade for the 1972 American Olympic team!

17. *H&E* (formerly *Health and Efficiency*) magazine. Editor S. Hawcroft, 2008. Hawk Editorial Ltd:

The naturist magazine *H&E* (*Health and Efficiency*) has been produced monthly for over 100 years since 1900 i.e. before the death of Queen Victoria in January 1901. The magazine is now also available electronically online. Because of public attitudes towards naturism, authors were anonymous until the 1950s, but now all is much more open, and although still discreet, pictures involving "private parts" are at a distance or otherwise obscured and are no longer blanked out in the magazine.

18. *On the Waterfront* (1954). Film site Movie Review. www. filmsite.org/:

The Oscar-winning film (Best Motion Picture) *On the Waterfront*, was produced by Sam Speigel, directed by Elia Kazan (Best Director), and starred Marlon Brando (Best Actor), in 1954.

The phrase "I'll be back" first became a notorious punchline when spoken by the crooked union boss "Johnny Friendly" played by Lee J. Cobb (08/12/1911-11/02/1976) at the climax of the film, many years before it was adopted by others such as The

Beatles and the actor/politician Arnold Schwarzenegger.

The film won many accolades and although Cobb was nominated for an Oscar himself for his role as Best Supporting Actor, this eventually went to Edmond O'Brien for his part in the film *The Barefoot Contessa*.

The Author aged 3 years. ?
A Googie Withers lookalike. See Chapter 2.

WHAT THE ' - REFLECTIONS OF A BLACK COUNTRY

Father and mother behind the bar at "the pub" (Chapter 5 The Park Inn, Woodsetton) in 1958 after she, the licensee, had been awarded the upgraded licence to sell "beers and wines and spirits". The caption behind the bar reflects Black Country Humour and states...

How to live on 30/- (£1.50) a week

	£	s	p
Beer		18	0
Wife's Beer		1	6
Meat, fish, groceries	CREDIT		
Rent	CALL NEXT WEEK		
Mid-week beer		3	3
Coal	BORROW NEIGHBOURS		
Burial Club (for wife)		1	0
Dog's food		3	0
Holiday Club		1	0
3 o'clock certainty		1	0
More beer		1	9
Pinch of snuff		1	0

This means going into debt, so cut the wife's beer!!

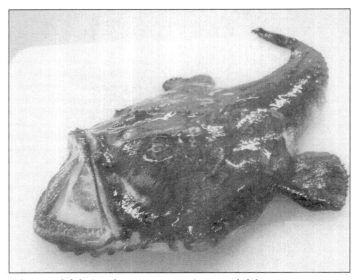

The Monkfish (Lophius Piscatorius), an oral delicacy, sometimes confused as a shark, as caught by the Author's father "off the beach" at Towyn in the 1950's. See Chapter 4.

Mr Dennis Turner MP, seen here in 1990 who advised the author on many matters including the terrible conditions that steel workers were exposed to.

Mr Edwin Holden senior, who "advised" the Author on taking
up a career in Medicine, seen here with his son Edwin
junior, on holiday in Blackpool in the 1940's.

"Interlude"

6. University. Medical School

I left the Black Country in my 18th year. The blanket of academic study descended over my head. The swinging sixties has been written of as the time of "sex, drugs and rock and roll". Like the majority of my student colleagues I saw little of the drugs that were supposedly available, perhaps only to the wealthy few, though sex and rock and roll were another matter. Other than sport and alcohol at weekends I just remember a time of grinding study, night after night, as well as day after day.

In retrospect, all too soon, after 5 years university came to an end. The great day of graduation and attainment of a doctorate arrived and my class quickly dispersed all over the world. After the sheltered cocoon of university life it took some time to realize that once qualified to practice, other than the statutory year of compulsory preregistration hospital house jobs required to obtain full registration with the General Medical Council, there was little or no career help or structured postgraduate education available for medical graduates at that time. This included advice into both the specialities, and into general practice. Medical students at this time felt a sensation of years of their life lost from the normal world in order to obtain their qualifications and early experience, and of then being pushed out alone into the wide world. Because of this experience shared, those in my class retained an incredibly close bond that is difficult to express to others, and we still meet for reunions, many years later.

Then, like many, little did I realize at the time of leaving the Black Country that I would be away from my roots for almost 14 years, as once qualified, my postgraduate education had yet to begin.

After graduation and 2 years of junior hospital posts in Leeds and Birmingham I spent the next 5 years working and studying and practising in the subject of otorhinolaryngology i.e. ear, nose and throat (ENT) surgery. As well as clinical work mainly in hospitals in and around Birmingham, this meant residing in London, at Lincoln's Inn Fields at the Institute of Basic Medical Sciences, adjacent to the Royal College of Surgeons of England. Whilst I adored the folk of Leeds and Birmingham, and overall I liked my time in London, I was astonished to discover that in the daytime, in the week, the place was enjoyable, but then at the weekends all the so-called "Londoners" went home somewhere and the place then became occupied with what seemed to be a variety of foreigners. It caused a discomfort. I began to feel the pull of my roots, the Black Country. More and more I missed the folk, the humour, and the dialect. Then when I returned back to "Brummie-land" hospitals to further my ENT experience, my heart was not in it. Inside my chest I had a deep sense of longing, to return. In 1974 I renounced my specialist subject and I came back to the Black Country as a general practitioner.

"Grow'd Up"

7. The National Health Service. General Practice

Black Country definition:

A "general practitioner" is a doctor, who knows a little bit about a hell of a lot. In time he or she gets to know less and less, about more and more, till eventually, a general practitioner becomes a doctor who knows nothing about everything!

A "consultant" is a doctor, who knows a hell of a lot about a little bit. In time he or she gets to know more and more, about less and less, till eventually a consultant becomes a doctor who knows everything, about nothing!

The swinging sixties had come and gone. Life was now full of colour, seen in music, and the arts, clothing, and even names (see postscript at the end of the book).

The grey days had gone. Cars were of any colour and mixture, with chequered flag roofs and stripes. Fast food appeared, Chinese takeaways and kebabs. The changes extended to all walks of life. I recollect all this, and what now follows is the story of my life and the general practice of medicine that I entered into, in the 1970s…

Tommy Jones took it out and smacked it on my desk.

"Theer yo bin Doctor. Tek a look at that."

I certainly did. What a whopper!

My return to the Black Country was not an auspicious occasion, on a cold wet Monday morning in October. There was no clap of thunder, or reception committee. Only Tommy Jones and my first GP surgery. After nearly 5 years at medical school and more than 7 years of hospital experience, foolhardily I thought I knew it all. I'd seen everything. I'd done everything, or so I thought. Tommy Jones quickly revealed to me my inadequacies.

"Morning Doctor. I think I've gorra verruca," he stated in a questioning voice.

"Well, let's have a look Mr Jones," I replied, expecting him to take off his shoes and show me his plantar wart[19]. He started to take off his trousers.

"Whoa, where is this verruca, Mr Jones?" I said. "There's no need to take your trousers off."

"It's down below, you know Doc," he replied with a manly, machismo-like nod, nod, wink, wink. I must have looked perturbed, so he added. "Y'know, it's on me thing Doctor. Me gun, me chopper."

That's what he smacked on my desk. There it was, in *flagrante delicto.* Well, I had been taught all the ramifications of venereology and I had been as a student, for teaching purposes only of course, to the "Clap Clinic"[20]. I had seen genital warts galore but never anything as insignificant as the tiny dot on the end of his foreskin that he pointed out that day. I was completely underwhelmed. Well, what to do about Mr Jones I thought?

I had seen such conditions in hospital with lesions as big as a piece of cauliflower, (called condylomata) and I knew how to treat them… Excision, "chop it off", or diathermy, "burn it off", yes, burn it off, cautery therapy with an electric needle, treatments were the norm at that time. Cryotherapy, "freeze it off", or laser therapy, "light it up and off" were years away still. I couldn't send the poor man off to be circumcised by a surgeon or to be spot-welded, so to speak, for such an insignificant lesion. I consulted my medical reference bible, the BNF[21]...

Found it, Podophyllin Compound Paint, composed of Podophyllum resin and Compound Benzoin Tincture i.e. "friar's balsam", on your private parts. Wow!

The book said "Advise patient: This paint is very irritant to the eyes. Just dab it on daily with a cotton wool bud"!

I carefully prescribed this to Mr Jones then and gave him the advice.

"Keep it away from your eyes Mr Jones," I instructed.

He blinked at this, thinking I'm not that cack-handed and off he went.

I saw Tommy a week later.

"Gun as clear a whistle Doc, and firing on all cylinders," he assured me with a pleasurable grin. It must have worked.

I learned that day that obtaining my medical degree and having all my postgraduate education, was a little like passing one's driving test. It merely gave me a licence to practice. Like my grandfather used to say, it was at the coalface where you obtained your experience and expertise i.e. in real life with the patients. I still had a lot to learn about this general practice lark, and 40 years ago it was very different than today.

The National Health Service[22] came into being on the 5th of July 1948 when Mr Aneurin Bevan was the first National Health Service Minister of Health.

It was founded on three core principles:

1. To provide a universal and equal care for all throughout the United Kingdom.
2. It was to be comprehensive covering all health needs.
3. It was to be free at the point of entry to all citizens on the basis of need, not ability to pay.

Within one month of inception 90% of the population had registered with a GP who took on the responsibility of all their medical care with the controlling access to specialist hospital care. Fourteen Regional Hospital Boards were created to administer the majority of hospital services, and GPs retained their independent contractor status under The Executive Council and local authority control.

The grandiose ideals of the NHS set-up were quickly forgotten. Prescription charges of one shilling (5p) were introduced in 1952, then abolished in 1965 and reintroduced in 1968. Whilst it quickly became apparent that there were problems with the quality standards of the service e.g. highlighted by The Collings Report of the 1950s little had changed by the late 1960s and 1970s. Indeed, 50 years later are there still the same problems? Although at the onset of the NHS it was envisaged that GPs would all be rehoused in health centres, by the 1970s many GP practices continued to be small or single-handed, often practising from premises within or adapted on to their own homes. GPs themselves were poorly trained for their specific role having the vast majority of training within the specialist hospital situation and never setting eye on a GP surgery! Despite The Royal College of General Practitioners giving evidence in 1966 to an NHS Commission, only in 1976 was a 3-year mandatory postgraduate training programme instituted for GPs under the programme Modernising Medical Careers. This period was increased to 5 years in 2005 and onwards.

I thought then that I was lucky in 1974 when after doing investigative locums all over the West Midlands I joined my new senior partner in Wolverhampton and Dudley, practising from custom-built surgery premises and a local authority Health Centre. My very enlightened senior partner also allowed me 1 day off per week to continue my hospital speciality post in ENT surgery that I held, although this meant me giving up my weekly half day off that GPs had at that time. This hospital job involved a drive, after a night on call, over the busiest motorway in Western Europe, to Spaghetti Junction on the M6 motorway, for the next 33 years! Folk at the hospital never realized that on many occasions I had been up half of the night before, and after an outpatient clinic I had a full operating session to perform, sometimes on less than 2 hours sleep the previous night!

The main surgery from where we practised in Wolverhampton was huge and modern by standards of the day. We had only a 20-foot square waiting room for a list size in excess of 4,500 patients. We had two dual-purpose consulting/examination rooms, one so small that old grannies couldn't unlace their corsets, but we did have separate staff and patient toilets, albeit no male or female segregation. There were just us two doctors, and we had to share all this with another single-handed practitioner and his practice as well (in total approximately 7,000 patients were treated within the building). There were but few group practices in those days to encourage medical discussion between partners. There was no sharing of knowledge. No audit. No clinical governance. General practice quality of service to the patient was virtually unsupervised and was totally at the individual practitioner's discretion, in those days.

Within the surgery where I practised we were well equipped. We had a sterilizer, a stainless steel water container that was electrically heated just like a large electric kettle, that no one knew how long to keep dirty instruments in for them to be sterilized, and the same instruments were all used over and over and over again. There were no "disposables" in those days. We had five glass syringes that we resterilized and repeatedly reused and reused for all injections and vaccinations!

Oddly we had very little cross infection.

We performed no investigative procedures, blood tests, X-rays etc. We had no access to hospital laboratory or other facilities. If you needed an investigation you were referred to a hospital, although because of the high incidence of respiratory disease, peculiarly for some reason we could get chest X-rays arranged without appointment, at the local Chest Clinic. We performed little or no proactive investigation or treatment. It was all virtual crisis management.

As elsewhere at this time there was no such thing as the now much maligned "appointment system", to see the doctor. Patients just turned up *ad hoc* at surgery times, often some 50 patients per day, per doctor. Large queues resulted, with waiting times in the surgery of several hours. Febrile patients would often collapse with the wait.

I found it was normality to perform some five or six home visits per day between surgeries, getting home regularly at 8 or 9 o'clock in the evening. Dinner was after a 12-hour non-stop day. Then I was on call on alternate nights and weekends for "emergencies". Everything to the patient, I quickly discovered, was an urgency. His or her problem was, and still today now is, invariably but understandably, unique to them so it is "urgent", and out of hours, "it's an emergency". There were no mobile phones. Many patients did not even have a telephone. Once the doctor had left the surgery or home, the receptionist of the day (or wife or husband with an out of surgery hours problem call) had to try and contact the doctor already on a visit, or dial 999 for an ambulance. There was an out of hours district nurse but invariably she could not be contacted as they were not "practice attached". There were no such speciality nurses as Macmillan nurses[23], there were no hospices. There were no paramedics. There were no locum services or triage telephone services to speak to the patient.

The system was rough on the staff and the doctor's family, and the system was especially tough for the poor patient in distress.

References and Author's comment:

19. Verruca(e).Viral infections. *Davidson's Essentials of Medicine.* 2009. Churchill Livingstone:

A verruca(e) is the term used to describe a skin lesion(s) that occurs on the thick skin of the soles of the feet and palms of the hands. They are no different than warts found elsewhere, other than they contain a more thickened outer epidermal layer of skin. Warts are caused by the human papillomavirus (HPV) and they are spread by direct contact from shed skin particles. There are numerous types of the virus, and subtypes 16 and 18 spread by sexual contact are associated with the development of cervical carcinoma in women. A vaccine has now been developed for these that is available to all schoolgirls from the age of 12 years onwards in the UK.

Warts can occur anywhere on the body and those that occur on the genital areas of both sexes can become raised and thickened into large growths that are called condylomata acuminata. These require medical advice for both confirmatory diagnosis and treatment.

20. The Clap Clinic. www.medical-dictionary.thefreedictionary. com:

The venereal disease gonorrhoea is commonly referred to as "the clap". Hence the term "Clap Clinic" used by many hospital staff in both a derogatory, yet in a somewhat affectionate fashion to describe the "Special Clinic" the term introduced to avoid patient embarrassment when attending venereology departments.

The venereology clinic name itself has been further modernized (Disguised?) by renaming the clinics nowadays as within the "Department of Genito-urinary Medicine".

21. The *British National Formulary* (BNF). Published jointly by the British Medical Association and the Royal Pharmaceutical Society. Print upgrades are made in March and September. G.G.P. Media GmbH. www.bnf.org/:

The British National Formulary was first established in 1946 to compile a comprehensive prescriber's formulary for both doctors and pharmacists.

Up to 1966, following my year of graduation, there had been only seven editions of this book produced in 20 years! It was a small hardbound book of only 360 pages giving little or no clinical information or explanation.

Despite repetitive government prescribing restrictions it is now a much larger soft covered book, with over 60 editions, all of A5 size with over 900 pages giving in-depth advice on drugs and their various preparations. The doses of medicaments required are clearly specified and for what clinical conditions drugs should or should not be given. It now includes a vast wealth of prescribing knowledge.

It is the rapid reference drug book that should be available at all times to all medical practitioners both in general practice, and the specialities, for modern good medical practice to be performed.

It is supplied by health authorities to all registered GPs approximately twice yearly, and it is their reference bible used constantly by all and every day, but oddly whilst supplied to hospitals, quite incredibly it is not specifically delivered to individual doctors, neither junior hospital doctors, trainee specialist registrars, nor consultant surgeons or physicians etc.!

In actual clinical practice (author's hospital experience) specialists such as anaesthetists, particularly in the operating theatre scenario and elsewhere, constantly despair at ever finding an up-to-date departmental copy!

22. *From Cradle to Grave: 50 years of the N.H.S.* G.C. Rivett. 1998. The Kings Fund. www.nhshistory.net:

This superb book has a foreword by the then prime minister (Tony Blair), published on the 50th anniversary of the birth of the NHS, and it gives a vast, comprehensive and extensive history of all of the NHS, including comment and opinion.

A wonderful book, it is huge and interesting. It is described quite correctly as the most substantial and complete account of the NHS since its inception.

Dr Rivett, a Fellow of the Royal College of General Practitioners, has written and lectured extensively on the subject, which is regularly updated and can very interestingly be enlarged upon, on the associated website.

23. The Macmillan Cancer Support. www.macmillan.org.uk:

The Macmillan Cancer Support is a registered charity founded by Douglas Macmillan in 1911, providing highly trained specialized nursing care, "Macmillan Nurses", for patients with cancer. They also provide specialized palliative care and pain control management and provide much-needed psychological support for both patients and their families. The nursing posts are all initially funded by Macmillan for a set period, usually 3 years, before becoming fully NHS funded.

In 1970 there were only 10 Macmillan nurses in the whole of the UK. This number had increased to over 3,700 by December 2011.

Macmillan nurses supposedly do not provide an emergency or out of hours service.

This does not match their work ethic. They are quite a superb lot.

In all my career, I never had a refusal to visit from them, both day and night in over 40 years of both my hospital and GP medical practice!

8. Signs and symptoms

In the 1970s the number of patients seen by the doctor in a day in general practice was very tiring, with many simple self-limiting viral infections, and other regular complaints not seen today, such as the infective diseases of childhood, measles, German measles, mumps etc.

Furthermore, many consultations were frustrating to both the doctor and patient as the attendance was for the dreaded sick note. You needed sick notes from your doctor to obtain your wages if you were ill, and in those days if you didn't return to work after a bank holiday due to illness, you forfeited your holiday pay as well. As a consequence the clinics on a day after a bank holiday were especially crowded.

The incidence of disease was very different to that seen in the new millennium. Whilst the major psychiatric disorders, schizophrenia and so on were still seen as today, one saw few complaints of depression or anxiety disorder, and if you had psychological symptoms it was expected that you just had to accept them. There were but few psychiatric drugs, and no NHS counsellors or psychologists. There was also a high incidence of industrial-related disease in the menfolk, with musculoskeletal problems related to heavy manual work, and many cases of respiratory disease due to the pollution of coal mining, and foundry industries, and worst of all in our practice, the steel works nearby. The loss of the British heavy industrial base has been bemoaned in some quarters. Not by me. I had to deal with the health consequences. Good riddance I say. In my first 10 years as a GP I lost about one patient killed per year in the local steel works[24]. I saw numerous men injured in various ways, almost daily. To see a 40-year-old man out of breath at the slightest effort as he had been exposed to what he called "pickling fumes Doctor", hydrochloric acid bath fumes, was distressing. As a result many men were physically worn out by the time they reached their 60s often caused by the development of chronic disabling disorder and malignancy. To be called in the night by a teenage lad, who would not allow his mother to see his father collapsed in the bathroom, blood everywhere, dead from a massive pulmonary haemorrhage from his lung cancer, caused great sadness and unbelievable empathy with the families affected (see Chapter 22).

All this distress started from birth… whilst we had had a community attached midwife and a specific antenatal clinic, most deliveries were still at home and consultant obstetricians had to be called to the house when difficult deliveries arose. Worse of all the suffering though was seen in the children, in paediatric disorders. The infectious diseases of childhood were prevalent and seen every day and whilst population vaccination had started there were no computerized recording and recall systems in place. They just hadn't been invented at that time.

Life was not all doom and gloom though. The vast majority of consultations were convivial and light-hearted. I quickly learned that Black Country folk were very easy-going and stoical, and accepted whatever their lot, and in those early days service complaints were almost unheard of occurrences.

The expression of Black Country signs and symptoms was unusual though and could be difficult to interpret and sort out even for a local-born doctor such as me.

Fanny White (First World War name) was a septuagenarian, with a stick insect figure, a widow who did not have much to occupy her life. She lived in a council bungalow and she enjoyed ill health. Because of easy access to her doctor, her notes were voluminous, and it was a cold February morning when she crept into the consultation room at the health centre. She "liked it better", the health centre, as it was warmer and she could chat to all her friends. She was in dire straits.

She limped in and so I looked at her legs assuming a lower limb problem, but oddly she stated,

"It's me shoulder Doctor. It's killing me."

"Which one Mrs White?" I asked, while questioning myself as to why she was limping then.

"Me left. Me left one. Look, last wik are could lift it all the way up 'ere," she said, elevating her left arm to the vertical, up to the sky.

"Now it'll only go to 'ere. Haaaaah!" she cried in a loud voice as she now limited her arm raise just about to the horizontal!

I was dumbfounded. Did I actually see what I had just seen?

After a short pause I thus responded, "Really, Mrs White, show me again please," and she repeated the performance…

Vertical, no pain. Horizontal, agony!

As a clinician you can't laugh at such a patient, it is improper, but to paraphrase modern terminology, one develops so-called "coping strategies". Turn away and write in the notes, slowly, do anything to distract oneself. Scratch your head as if thinking. Switch to the computer nowadays. A pause… helps the reply. I don't recollect my diagnosis or my advice or treatment on this day, but it worked. With my sympathy she never returned with this problem, but I do recollect however, that she walked out of the room quite briskly and normal, forgetting the limp that she came with on arrival!

Such odd, almost attention-seeking symptomatology, was and still is, not just confined to the elderly, however. Olive Green (Second World War name) was only 48 years old, I could see the date of birth on her voluminous notes, and she was a different shape than Mrs White, being wider than she was tall. She had the (in)famous Monday morning disorder, "Tired All the Time" or "TATT" syndrome.

"What's the problem then Mrs Green?" I asked.

"Well y' see Doctor I'm fagged out, tired all the time, even in the mornings after I've been t' bed," she said, adding, "and it's always worse on Mondays, and me bowels don't work very well at the same time," she disclosed. "It all gives me the yed erk at times it does," she went on with, holding her head.

Mmm I thought, I've got some of that, but not on Mondays though, but some folk give me a headache, so I've got that as well.

"Then in the evening after me tea, again on Mondays I'm so tired I g' t' sleep, and me bowels don't work again, twice daily that is," she continued.

Well I've got that as well, I thought, without the bowel thing though, but I never did manage to differentiate how her bowels didn't work, twice daily, that is. (Author's comment... Think about it.)

"I'm out a breath when I do anything 'eavy, I don't want to do anything at wikends and I feel low and run-down all the time, with no energy. Me bowels are sometimes very slow at wikends as well," she further disclosed.

I was getting fed up now, as she just sounded bored and fed up, except for the bowel thing, just like me and many others. However, always give the patient the benefit of the doubt. Remember my older partner's adage...

"Ed, all neurotics eventually have a physical illness, a complaint that is often missed. Never 'pooh-pooh' them", he advised.

Well, I examined her carefully thus. She was not anaemic. Her abdomen showed none of the "rocks" of chronic constipation. Her blood pressure and heart sounds were normal, as was her chest and respiratory examination. She had no signs of e.g. underactive thyroid, or of diabetic or metabolic disorder. She had no lumps or particular bumps of note. The only real abnormality to find was that she looked much older than her chronological age, and she was very overweight, and she had the facial skin of a window leather, as many women then did due to overwork and/or worry, (when nowadays it's due to overwork and/or worry, and the suntan lamp). She looked worried but otherwise well. Really I could find nothing substantial amiss here. Was she possibly menopausal? A delicate roundabout approach was required then. Many ladies did, and still do not like, the suggestion. I posed thus a guarded question.

"Tell me Mrs Green, how is your cycle these days?" I asked, a modest request perhaps regarding her menses, or so I thought.

Her answer took me aback. Flabbergasted. How to keep a straight face?

When in loud indignant voice she exclaimed,

"Doctor, yo orta know, I don't ride a bike now at my age any more!"

Turn away, don't grin, and write in the notes again. Do something. Anything. Solve her problems. Pause.

After my internal mirth subsided, a therapeutic trial perhaps? Yes. Mist Rhei Co. i.e. Compound Rhubarb Mixture BPC[25], a medicinal mixture containing rhubarb extract, that's what I should try…

A foul mixture recommended by my senior partner of the time, an absolute gem of a man who taught me many of my life communication skills. Certainly he knew how to deal with the oddballs.

"Try them on this, Ed. It's a vile taste, and a mild laxative to boot. Just taking the cork out of the bottle makes the room stink so badly that the neighbours complain! If ever they come back for a second bottle they are "nutters", they don't have a physical illness. They have a personality problem," was his advice.

Nowadays the diagnosis of such a patient would be described as "challenging".

In those days they were just "difficult".

Mrs Green herself gave me the answer to her diagnosis… She came back for three more bottles!

Difficult cases to interpret were not always women though. Don was one of these.

Quite a character, indeed a Black Country legend, famous for his fleet of coaches and his (Ford) car dealership, he had an enviable reputation especially amongst Wolverhampton Wanderers Football Club supporters when he painted his coaches taking them to away matches, in the club's colours! He was one of the post-war entrepreneurs who built the infrastructure of modern Wolverhampton, a fascinating man. He was not my full patient, but I saw him occasionally both as a neighbour living in the same road as myself and as a locum when his GP was on holiday. Being a neighbour and such a pillar of the community, one time I readily went to his home when requested…

"Gut ache Doctor, feeling off colour and bowels terrible. I've not been for nearly a week now, and I'm off my food and drink," he explained at my arrival. Not much else to complain of though. He looked well.

On examination there appeared little amiss. No raised temperature and he was well hydrated and a good colour. Abdomen was a little distended but difficult to palpate as he was a little pot-bellied. Bowel sounds few, but some present, and normal. Some "rocks" but no significant masses. Simple diagnosis here… acute on chronic constipation, maybe due to his active lifestyle and incorrect eating habit. Not enough fluid and/or roughage intake I suspected.

I gave simple dietary advice then, and to push fluids, and I prescribed glycerol suppositories, "large size", there being two smaller sizes sometimes used for children. These contain mainly glycerine, a mild bowel irritant and a lubricant, thus kick-starting anyone with constipation, and off I went thus leaving him to the care of his good wife.

Two days later I got a recall…

"He's quite poorly now," said his worried sounding wife. "Still not had his bowels open, and he's started to vomit as well doctor," she explained. She was not a panicker.

Heck! I thought. Could this be a misdiagnosis? Intestinal obstruction, all the symptoms. A neighbour as well. I'll never live this down. I rushed to the house.

He looked dreadful now. Dehydrated from vomiting and pale. Colicky pains coming and going every few minutes causing him to writhe in the bed. Oddly though his abdomen was but a little distended, and still no loud bowel sounds that I could hear with my stethoscope that one would expect from an intestinal obstruction. Nevertheless, "send him in urgently for a surgical opinion" was indicated. I spoke to the hospital doctor on call for surgery and arranged an ambulance.

As I was writing his admissions letter, I enquired as to his details... full name, postal address, date of birth, on any dugs, and so on. All was normal until I mentioned his drugs...

"Well I take tablets religiously for my blood pressure," he said. (I've never been quite sure about the term "religiously" regarding the taking of drugs. I assume they mean "rigorously"), "and they are going down OK," he said. "But oh, those depositories," (another word Black Country folk have problems with). "They are bigger than me thumb doctor. Terrible. What a job I have getting them down," he complained, indicating that he had been taking them by mouth all the time!

Glycerol suppositories, twice daily for 2 days by mouth! Wow. How on earth he got them down I know not. Huge things. He was suffering from an overdose of glycerine now, no wonder he looked sick and ill.

I cancelled the ambulance and his admission. I telephoned my district nurse who came around and gave him an enema (or two), and he was better and "operating regularly" within 48 hours. His life, my reputation were both saved.

Now Don was a bright man. It was my fault this arose, not his. I had not fully explained to him how, with what, and why I was treating him, and I learned a welcome lesson that day...

Whatever the intellect of the patient, with any treatment, explain fully why, wherefore and which orifice that treatment is meant to be put into!

I had other problems with orifices i.e. "a hole or opening to the body".

Errol McNish's case was much more difficult. He was a first generation Afro-Caribbean arrival from the 1960s, a lovely, huge 6 foot 4 inches Jamaican man. He had a Scottish surname, like many of his countrymen. Like many West Indian patients he also came with a common problem that was often attributed to the somewhat vague diagnosis of "the Gas, Doc."

Sounds obvious I know, but that's not so. "The Gas" in Afro-Caribbean patients was usually a gastrointestinal problem that could range from anything simple, such as carbohydrate indigestion, to something more severe such as an intestinal obstruction. I have even seen patients with unusual and somewhat exotic complaints such as pernicious anaemia[26] present with "the Gas".

After a short consultation thus with Errol as he looked completely well I gave him a simple mixture of the day Mist Mag. Carb. Aromat. BPC. This mixture contained magnesium carbonate and sodium bicarbonate in an aromatic cardamom mixture. It smelt and tasted quite nice, and it settled indigestion very well. It was a little like gripe water for grown-ups. Off he went. A week later he was back.

"Hit ain't no better Doc," was his complaint still.

Examination of his abdomen etc. still no abnormalities to find. Was this the dreaded peptic ulcer then? Nowadays he would have a full blood count and biochemical assay, his Helicobacter pylori[27] status checked, blood tests, and even be referred for an outpatient endoscopy. In 1979 open access endoscopy was not available to GPs and thus in this case a trial course of the first so-called peptic ulcer "wonder" drug, cimetidine[28], was indicated. I wrote the script and off he went.

A week later he was back. No better. I must admit he did look unwell now, although illness is often difficult to observe in very dark-skinned patients such as he.

"Hi can't sleep Doc with this gas, and Hi's feelin' very sick now," he exclaimed.

He was a genuine chap. Not a weakling this fellow. This needed further investigation.

"Tell me more Mr McNish about this gas. Where does it start and does it spread anywhere?" I asked. Was this a referred pathology like cardiac pain down the arm or such?

"Well Doc, hit starts in my stomach and hit goes into my chest, even at night in bed," he replied.

Yes, perhaps a hiatus hernia, symptoms worse on lying down, I thought.

Then he added, "Hit goes up my chest and then into my troat Doc."

Got it, gastro-oesophageal reflux, can bring symptoms right up into your mouth especially lying in bed. Problem solved.

No it wasn't.

"Hit then goes up my neck Doc. Hinto my 'ead, and hit comes out my left hear hole. Hi can't sleep with hit." He dumbfounded me while still adding all his H's in odd places to his conversation.

It was time to examine him comprehensively. Abdomen, normal, his chest and respiratory tract normal. Everything again, no abnormality to find. His mouth, his nose, his ears. Getting to the small print stuff now, all normal. Well not completely normal. His eardrums, his tympanic membranes, were intact, but the left one, the side of his symptoms, showed a healed central perforation. It was clean and dry, not infected. The dawn hof realization 'it me. (Wow, I'm doing the "H" thing now).

"What's your job, Mr McNish?" I questioned.

"You know Doc, Hi'm in the rolling mills now for 22 years since hi been 'ere. An 'eavy and noisy job, man, but hi likes hit you know," he replied.

Solved my problem. Feeling a total fool, yet delighted to help him, I sent him off to an "ear, nose and troat" colleague who very kindly fitted him with a hearing aid that masked his tinnitus, yes it was tinnitus, and helped him to sleep! Whether or not his tinnitus was due to industrial noise trauma or his perforation I never did discover. Probably both. Cured his gas though, it did!

Since then, for many years I have regretted never writing this case up for medical publication as…

"An Interesting Case (possibly the only ever) of Intractable Gas, Relieved by Hearing Aid Amplification"!

There are nice addenda to all these aforementioned stories…

Fanny White lived well into her nineties and died of "nothing serious".

Mrs Green lost her tiredness, left her husband, and ran off

with a rich scrap man (scrap metal dealer) and became "happy ever after", at last.

Don totally recovered from his "moving experience".

And, the following Christmas after his summer holiday in Jamaica, I received a bottle of illicit home-made Jamaican white rum from the cured Mr McNish that nearly burnt my troat away. It was great, maaaan!

References and Author's comment:

24. *South Staffordshire Ironmasters.* Ray Shill. 2008. The History Press.

Steel at Brierley Hill. Ollie Knox. 1957. Newman Neame:

Wolverhampton History and Heritage. www.historywebsite. co.uk:

By the time of my arrival in 1974 into general practice the main remaining large steel works of the Black Country were…

(a) Round Oak Steel Works, Brierley Hill, Dudley. Founded originally by the Earl of Dudley in 1857 to produce pig iron the works expanded in the 20th century to eventually employ at its peak more than 3,000 employees. Like the Bilston works below, there was so much industrial physical injury caused on a daily basis that the works had its own medical centre for treatment with on-site nurses and physiotherapists. I attended here as a locum medical officer for a short while in my early career. It was like attending a battlefield casualty station at times.

Closed in December 1982 many employees became involved with the on-site development of the new Merry Hill shopping complex and malls built on the site.

(b) Bilston Steel Works (Hickman's Ltd/Stewart and Lloyds) Wolverhampton. Work commenced early in 1770, and the blast furnace works were expanded over two centuries to eventually build in 1954 "Big Lizzy", the massive blast furnace that in its lifetime produced 55 million tons of pig iron. Open-hearth furnaces were included on the site as were rolling mills. In 1944 the works made 83 miles of Pipe Line Under the Ocean (PLUTO) to supply fuel to the allied armed forces after the D-Day landings.

Closed in April 1979, more than 1,900 employees lost their jobs.

When I was taken round the site by a responsible employee friend, Mr Dennis Turner, a local councillor, (later an MP and eventually the first Lord Bilston), at my request in an attempt to explain all the injuries to my patients, I had to take out an insurance policy, it was considered to be so dangerous for visitors. I found out why... When the open-hearth furnaces opened I did not think that human beings could tolerate such a heat, the blast was so great, and I was approximately 100 yards away at the time. Men were nearer than me, most stripped to the waist in trousers, otherwise wearing only gloves and goggles. No hard hats in those days. No foot or other protectors. In the rolling mills section the noise was like bedlam. I saw everyone was lip-reading, you had no alternative. No one wore any ear protection or any ear defenders.

No, I don't miss the demise of the steel works at all.

25. Mist Rhei Co. Compound Rhubarb Mixture BPC. *British National Formulary.* 1966 edition. Watson and Viney Ltd:

Mist Rhei Co. was a compound mixture, now discontinued, containing rhubarb extract, with sodium or ammonium bicarbonate mixed with 25% glycerine, all in peppermint or sometimes chloroform water.

Prescribable for humans it was sometimes used also as an animal medication, and as a cleaner for pots and pans! In those days when pharmacists made up the preparation what the patient got could vary. The US National Formulary preparation, as well as the above, also contained ipecacuanha, a drug originally derived from a Brazilian plant, Carapichea ipecacuanha, which has been used medically to induce vomiting, and has been prescribed as both a laxative and a carminative i.e. a drug "facilitating the expulsion of bowel gases thence aiding flatulence". The side effects of all the constituents do not bear thinking about, but as well as these, and the smell, with 25% glycerine it must have been a pretty slimy mixture to administer by mouth anyway.

26. Pernicious anaemia. *Davidson's Essentials of Medicine*. 2009. Churchill Livingstone:

Pernicious anaemia is a disorder characterized by atrophy (wasting) of the gastric mucosal stomach lining. This means that the so-called "Intrinsic Factor" required for the absorption of vitamin B_{12} (cobalamin), from the diet, is deficient, and it leads to an anaemia characterized by abnormally large red blood cells (macrocytes). It leads to complex neurological disorders including damage to all the peripheral nerves, blindness, due to wasting of the optic nerves, and dementia, and if untreated eventual death.

Because vitamin B_{12} is not absorbed when taken by mouth in such a condition, patients with this disorder have to receive vitamin B_{12} supplements by injection, for life!

Dietary vitamin B_{12} deficiency alone will also cause a macrocytic anaemia, but it is not "pernicious" (definition = "causing malicious harm") in type, in this case.

It is not easy to develop this "simple" type of anaemia, because the daily requirements of 1ug/day of this vitamin are so small, yet it does rarely occur in some patients with odd dietary regimes, and it is found in certain groups such as vegans, on a totally plant-based diet.

The resultant anaemia of this type is simply treated by dietary vitamin B_{12} supplements, by mouth, until the deficiency is corrected.

27. Helicobacter pylori. *Davidson's Essentials of Medicine*. 2009. Churchill Livingstone:

Helicobacter pylori is a bacteria that inhabits the stomach lining causing a marked inflammation, and it is found in 70% of patients with gastric ulcers and 90% of patients with duodenal ulcers. It is diagnosed by various methods including serology i.e. blood tests, or more simply by breath analysis tests. Treatment is complex but involves taking an antiulcer drug, a proton pump inhibitor (PPI) and an intensive course of antibiotics, all by mouth, the latter administration of which patients often have great difficulty tolerating in my experience.

28. Cimetidine. (British trade name: Tagamet). *British National Formulary*. No. 64 edition. 2012. GGP. Media GmbH:

Cimetidine is a so-called H2-receptor antagonist drug that inhibits stomach acid production and is used thus against both oesophageal (gullet), stomach and duodenal ulceration. It first became prescribable in 1979 under the trade name "Tagamet."

On arrival it was advertised publically as the "wonder drug" of the day. Doctors at that time were advised to prescribe it with caution as it could mask the symptoms of gastric cancer, but how we were supposed to ascertain this I never did discover. Its use for ulcer disease has largely now been overtaken by the newer and more potent proton pump inhibitor (PPI) family of drugs, although it still has many other uses, such as for the treatment of the intractable pain of post-herpetic (shingles) neuralgia, and for allergic problems etc.

It has even been used to treat verrucae i.e. plantar warts, for which it is totally useless and ineffective

9. Breaking and entering

To most people "breaking and entering" is a phrase associated with the criminal fraternity. In my practice I found that this could be a doing of the police themselves.

My first experience of "breaking and entering" with the police occurred when I was called by concerned neighbours to the home of Isaiah ("Ike") Hughes. He was a widower and a "cantankerous old person", a retired steel worker made very deaf by his army service as a gunner and 30 years or more of rolling mill industrial noise exposure[29]. He was a tough chap though, having married his wife in May 1944, just before he landed on D-Day and they lived happily for many years on his return from the war, with their daughter, until his wife's death from ovarian disease. We didn't have hospices or specialized care in those days. He nursed her alone at home with just the occasional visit from the district nurse, until her death. He never asked for any specialized equipment. He never sent for help. He coped with her alone, himself. It was what he and she wanted, and he now lived alone in their terraced two-up two-down Victorian house. His worried neighbour, Mrs Cherry, who had not seen him for some weeks, had called in the police.

After loudly knocking both his front door and the door in the back entry, to no avail, the constable in attendance asked if I agreed for him to "affect an entry Doctor" and he got me sign some sort of official form that gave him encouragement. I thought that he would attempt to force the lock. No... Crash, bang, wallop,

WHAT THE ' - REFLECTIONS OF A BLACK COUNTRY

he kicked the door in with his size 12 boots! We all entered the house through the entry door that was. The downstairs, the back toilet, the front room, the living room and kitchen were all quiet and empty. I did notice though that the house was quite warm. The officer approached the door at the bottom of the stairs, which suddenly flew open and into the room jumped Ike, brandishing a large spanner in his hand, the sort used to take the propeller off the *Titanic* and the sort that you normally keep at the side of the bed, for emergencies, you know, as you do?

"What the ' d' ya think yo'm doin?" he cried to the officer, pointing to his smashed in back entry door and shaking his spanner.

"It's alright Ike," I replied in his defence. "Mrs Cherry, your neighbour next door, hasn't seen you for some time and we were worried about you, and you didn't answer the door to the officer."

"Well that ain't surprising really Doctor, is it, as I've been on 'olidy t' Bridgnorth, t' the daughter's caravan for a couple a wiks, and I've gone and left me hearing aid there, ain't I, dope that I am," was his reply with an air of disgust.

Well, we all apologized, and with some alacrity I quickly left the scene. I left the officer to sort out the repair to the door. Ike was not a happy man.

After the affair with Ike, I was more careful some time later when I was again called by the police and concerned neighbours who hadn't seen elderly Mrs Potts likewise for some time. She was a lovely and interesting character. Born in the Ukraine, we called her Magnolia, not her real name, which was unpronounceable, but Magnolia was the nearest one could make in translation. She tearfully told me one time how she was taken at the age of 17 years to a forced labour camp by the occupying Germans. Here, her forced labour was of the horizontal type in a Wehrmacht rest camp. On arrival she was made to sit in front of a table with a "buzzing machine under it, doctor, Sir" and she went on to describe an acute abdominal wall burn developing, and how her monthly menstruation never returned after this! She came to the UK as a displaced person having been rescued after the war by a

83

soldier, Mr Potts, who she married, and they first saw me some years later making enquiry re conception. Sadly I had to explain to them, after investigation, that pregnancy was impossible after her radiological sterilization, and that they were too old to adopt, but nevertheless despite this trauma they lived for many years in domestic bliss.

Mr Potts had died peacefully just a few years previously and I saw Magnolia regularly in the surgery after this, as she had become a diabetic, and when I received this unusual call then I looked up her medical notes. I discovered that it had been 5 weeks and more since she had attended the surgery for her very necessary monthly supply of antidiabetic drugs. She was in trouble then by now.

When I arrived at her home I found that as well as myself, the neighbours had already called the ambulance service, a local vicar from Magnolia's church, and a nice policewoman, who was in attendance with a tall and well-built young police cadet, flat hat, blue band around, 16 years and very keen. This grade of police officer apprenticeship has now been abolished in England and Wales (in 2014), but not in Scotland where they continue to serve but with no power of arrest. Somewhat presumptuously, also the local undertaker was there, possibly touting for business?

After introduction, again I was asked to sign a form, to allow them to "affect an entry" and again they did so.

"Don't kick the door in," I cried out in anticipation. "Take your time."

Too late.

The young cadet just charged at the door and hit it with his shoulder. I think he must have been a prop forward as the whole thing came away from the wall, door frame and all, and fell to the floor with a loud bang. He fell into the back kitchen with his momentum, turned to one side to look into the room, went quite pale, and with his eyes rolling he crashed to the floor in a faint, banging his head soundly on the kitchen table as he fell. He was unconscious when he hit the floor. Crash!

Well, what to do? Attend to the living first, the young

policeman, order an ambulance to take him to hospital after he recovered shortly with no neurological deficit. It was pointless to attend to Mrs Potts who had caused him to faint. The flies all flew out of the room at our entry. On the floor bloated and dark, she was very long gone. Not a nice sight even for the experienced. She was beyond all earthly aid or help. There was nothing further we could do for her, medically that is.

This case, however, nicely highlighted the excellent inter-emergency service co-operation involving all of the specialized emergency services that day and I do mean all of the services i.e. the police to police the action and ensure there had been no foul play, and the NHS doctor to attend to the sick and deal with emergency treatment i.e. in this case the police cadet. The ambulance service was also there to attend to the casualty and convey him to hospital i.e. the police cadet, and the undertaker was able to quickly remove the body and take Magnolia to the public mortuary. Finally the priest, Father "Unpronounceable and Unspellable" from the Wolverhampton Ukrainian Church, was available to give religious blessing to the deceased, before she left the scene, and to counsel anybody else who was thought to be in need, i.e. the police cadet again, but this was unnecessary as he had been taken off to hospital by the ambulance men already!

Post-mortem examination later revealed that elderly Magnolia had died of natural causes, and the police cadet made a full and complete recovery. I felt relieved.

Not all my dealings with the police involved breaking and entering though. Sometimes they called me just for help and advice. This was the scenario involved with my dealings with "Old Joe".

Old Joe Badams was called "old" in typical Black Country fashion, as his son Joe was just "Joe", and his grandson "Young Joe", just like in our family with my grandfather, my father and myself, typical hierarchical name calling, based on age. Well, the old man was a friend of my grandfather, a very similar character, and another "cantankerous old person". I loved him to bits. He lived in a custom-built bungalow at the rear of a local

British Leyland sales garage, run by his son, next to the winter emplacement of the Smith family of gypsies (see chapter 10) with his wife and a herd of corgi dogs that were quite polite and well trained, well they never went for me, that is, and his flock of champion racing pigeons in several sheds alongside his drive.

He once disclosed to me the loves of his life... "Numbers 1. and 2. me corgis and me racing pigeons. Then, Number 3. brewing me dark mild beer, and finally, me wife," in that order I think it was! She didn't get a number, but they were very devoted to each other I recollect. I have completely forgotten what the medical reason was though for my regular visits, but his problems were always eventful.

I arrived one day to find him in the drive with his double barrelled twelve-bore shotgun in his hand.

"What's up Joe?" I enquired, (we had become informal and were on first names terms by then).

"Well yo see Doctor my champion Birmingham Roller [a type of acrobatic racing pigeon] 'as just come back from abroad yo know, To-loose, that place weer the painter comes from," he replied. (I never did enlighten him that he was actually quite correct. Although Toulouse-Lautrec was known for his Parisian paintings etc. he originally did hail from Toulouse and Lautrec).

"Yes," was thus my sole reply.

"Well, 'e wouldn't come down yo know, t' get the ring off 'is leg. I tried everythin'. Whistling 'im, 'as normal. Then I put some food out. No good. Then I even brought his favourite hen bird out, no relief," he answered shaking his head in sadness.

"Sadly I 'ad t' turn t' me last resort. Me gun," he continued. "Blowed 'is bloody brains out I did, you know. 'e come down then!" he stated with finality.

It was only at this point that I noticed bits of blood and feathers and the odd bit of bird leg lying around the drive. He had shot the pigeon, valuable as it was, with his twelve-bore shotgun, just to get the ring off his leg in anticipation of getting a prize time, I realized. Joe was a strong and determined character.

One time when examining him in his bedroom I noticed

the gun propped up against the side of his bed and I enquired again as to why he felt need to keep it there. He pointed out the scratch on the floor lino…

"'ad the burglars the other night. After me silver pigeon cups they was Doctor, but I fooled them. They are all locked away in the garage. Trouble is, at the side of me bed was me safe. It only 'ad the wife's wedding ring in it worth tuppence, and they pinched the bloody safe they did, that 'ad cost me £200 t' buy the thing, and scratched the floor they did. Me gun's loaded now," he disclosed.

I felt unable to deepen my enquiry regarding the wedding ring, he was so upset. I was a little alarmed by the loaded gun disclosure though.

My need for alarm was confirmed a month later, when I was called to the bungalow by the police.

This time on arrival I could easily see the problem… on the drive. A large Alsatian dog, or what was left of it, was splashed all across the drive and nearby grass lawn. Brains and bits of dog all over. It was explained to me that this was the neighbour's dog that had gotten into Joe's corgi dog pen.

"Caught 'im shaggin' me best bitch, again," Joe explained. "I'd warned them next door last time that if I caught 'im at it again there'd be trouble. An' I did. An' there was. Well, 'e wo do it again Doctor you see. I've solved the problem," he completed, flatly.

The police officers were not happy with this explanation. Shooting the dog was an offence, especially where it had occurred. We had to come to "an accommodation in confidentiality". They decided not to prosecute Joe for discharging a firearm in close proximity to residential property (he did have a gun licence), providing that I agreed to fail him at his next application for a gun licence renewal, on the grounds of "Physical Impairment, Age and Imperfect Eyesight". It should have been "Mental Impairment". But, everybody seemed happy at that.

Joe made a donation to the Retired Police Officers fund, and was placated by his non-prosecution. His neighbour was placated with a bottle of Scotch. We all had a nice cup of tea and left amicably, I think. It's been a long time since then. Very understanding officers, I felt. I don't think this would have been so easily resolved nowadays.

My escapade with Amrik Singh and the police was a different scenario. I sent for them this time. Amrik, was a very big chap. A UK-born second generation very pleasant Sikh man i.e. when he was normal. Unfortunately he was also a schizophrenic and had mad phases and was not always normal. I became to know his mad phases were caused by his reluctance to take his antipsychotic medicines long term, when after taking them for 12 months or so when he felt quite well, he rationalized "why take them any longer?" And so he stopped.

In the early 1980s this led to my first home visit when his relatives called me in the night to say...

"He has gone mad again Doctor, and he is threatening his wife in the bedroom. Please come right away. Thank you very much please."

I climbed out of bed and went round to their terraced house where three families lived together. I arrived in the early hours. It was a dark and dingy backstreet, in the All Saints area of Wolverhampton.

"He's upstairs in the bedroom, very mad crazy Doctor, and he's got his wife and the baby in there too," I was told.

I was a little wary of this story so I went inside and upstairs somewhat gingerly to find the whole house awake and several men in pyjama-like clothing and long hair all down to their waists, all milling around, and hanging on to the bedroom door. They released the door at my arrival and I entered the room as they indicated.

At this, Amrik, who I initially didn't recognise with his hair all hanging down as well, and shouting in an unknown language, jumped from the windowsill opposite waving a large Sikh sword. Somehow, he grabbed and swung from the miserly 40 watt light fitting in the middle of the room. Oddly it carried his weight as he swung there, with the light, back and forth. I could see his wife and a small child cowering in the corner. Nobody told me about any blooming sword I thought. I made an urgent clinical decision…

I shut the door and came out.

It was obvious I required help here. I sent for everybody. I sent for the Emergency Mental Health Ambulance Team with specially trained ambulance men. I sent for the police. I sent for the district nurses. I tried to get an on call social worker but none were available. The specialized Mental Health Social Worker, in my opinion a superb appointment, was not available, and in my (considerable) experience in those days it was always difficult to get any other social worker out of hours, or at weekends, or after 4.15 p.m. in the afternoon, and at weekends, (did I mention that already?), and if it was dark or it was raining, and Saturdays. Sundays neither. Never even consider calling on a bank holiday etc. They always seemed to be so far away. I sent for the police again.

Within 5 minutes, it seemed hours, a Sergeant Dafydd Taff arrived and the ambulance men. He was a huge pot-bellied Welsh chap (I seem to have met several Welsh policemen at the crises in my life. Is this coincidence?) And I quickly explained the problem to him.

"I'll have a look for you Doctor, to sort this out," he cried, "and by the way, call me Taff, all the boyos do. I'm Welsh you know," he explained in a broad Valley's accent.

He went upstairs to have a look. He quickly came back.

"We need some 'elp 'ere," he stated.

Well I knew that, that's why I sent for you I thought, quietly, to myself.

"I'll go and get some 'elp," said Sergeant Taff.

Off he went into the night and he shortly returned with help, not with a group of officers, but a small van. Didn't look like you could get many policemen in that, I thought.

Then he opened the back door and everybody retreated. Out it came, an animal. I can only describe it as a "land shark", on a huge thick lead, almost a dog, a supposed Alsatian with fluffy hair as if backcombed, snarling, growling and snapping at everybody despite being muzzled!

"Sorry Doc, he's not very fond of Pakis, but he's well trained otherwise though," said Sergeant Taff reassuringly as he hung on to the leash.

"Looks to me like he's not very fond of anybody," I replied thinking that it was no use trying to explain that all the family were Sikhs and not "Pakis" as he supposed.

"We need a plan of action here Doc. We'll disarm him and disable him, me and the dog, and, then when he's restrained you can give him some sedation like, right away and then we can get him off to hospital, OK?" Sergeant Taff suggested.

"Yes, yes. Just give me a moment to draw up the injection," I replied.

I opened my bag and drew up the drug of choice at that time, paraldehyde[30]... Wow, a so-called "basal narcotic". For injection it had to be given with a glass syringe as the modern plastic syringes just coming into usage at that time were melted by this potent preparation! I drew up 10 ml, a good dose, with another 10 ml in reserve. As I said, Amrik was a big chap.

We set off upstairs. Sergeant Taff opened the door, and took off the dog's muzzle and let him go. "Butch", the dog's name I later discovered, took one look at Amrik and flew across the room. A snarling bloody fight erupted with bits of fluff and stuff, and bits of Amrik and Butch, flying everywhere.

Now we have all seen demonstrations on the TV or at RAF shows, where an assailant with a padded arm, runs across a field chased by a dog that then grabs his arm, and they fall to the ground, and the dog handler arrives and the dog sits and retreats to commands. Yes? OK? Well in real life it is nothing like that.

"Christ, Taff," I cried. "He's bloody eating him. Stop him," I demanded, as the dog didn't just grab Amrik, but repeatedly bit and tore at him, when Amrik punched and yelled at him back. Bang, bang, woof, woof, shouting, and bits of blood and stuff flew everywhere.

Taff used his initiative and as the pair rolled around, with first the dog, then Amrik on top, he drew up to his full height, took a deep breath and flew through the air like a wrestler. He performed a huge bellyflop, splat, on top of them both, all 18+ stone of him.

Smack went the dog's head as he hit the floor on the bottom of the sandwich, and he went all quiet, almost KO'd he was! Psssssst went the air out of Amrik's lungs, and he rolled away gasping for breath!

I needed to seize my window of opportunity at this point, but I think a little medical information is required here to aid the reader.

To inject paraldehyde students were/are taught to…

"Swab the area initially and pick a muscle of some bulk, preferably that of the buttock i.e. gluteus maximus muscle. Choose the upper and outer quadrant and then gently palpate to ensure no vital organ, or nerve is beneath the site of injection. Introduce the needle gently through the skin, withdrawing occasionally to ensure no blood vessel or likewise is involved. Gently push into a deeper plane and introduce the medication slowly, to avoid patient discomfort".

My pharmaceutical lecturer was not present in the middle of the night in bloody, and I mean literally bloody, All Saints with Amrik, Butch and the sergeant all tangled up together, as I was. Besides, Amrik's behind, his arse, was invitingly sticking up in the air in front of me and this was an emergency. The needle went straight in through his pyjamas, skin and all. He got 10 mls quite quickly. No swabbing, no palpation, no needle withdrawing. There was no time.

He felt no discomfort. I felt no discomfort, but I was relieved. Sergeant Taff was relieved as well. He was able to muzzle the still dopey dog and drag him off, and Amrik quickly went off to sleep. I didn't need my backup injection. He was sent on to hospital with the ambulance blokes.

"We are all very grateful please Doctor. Thank you very much please," said his (I think) brother, pulling the wife and child to safety, as we all packed up and were about to leave. Lovely folks.

Then, some months later after all this, Amrik returned to the surgery after being discharged from hospital on his medication. He was back to his normal self and terribly apologetic for causing so much trouble.

"Sorry, sorry, so very much when I was mad please Doctor. I am normal again now," he explained almost in tears. A delightful man. A lovely big softie in his normal phase.

I was later asked to recommend Sergeant Taff to the Chief Constable of West Midlands for an award for "Bravery in The Course of Duty" which I was pleased to do so. His bravery had nothing to do with dealing with Amrik.

Nobody could have handled that dog as well as he did.

Amrik then proceeded to relapse in an identical fashion to all this every 2 years or so, despite his apology, for many years thereafter!

It is not always villains that the police have to deal with.

References and Author's comment:

29. Noise induced Hearing Loss. *ABC of Ear, Nose and Throat.* Ludman and Bradley. 2007. Blackwell Publishing:

Hearing and Deafness. Bowdler and Faulconbridge. ENT UK . www.entuk.org/:

Hearing loss affects 25% of all the population of the UK by the age of 60 years with loss of perception of the higher frequencies, a condition known as presbycusis, a degenerative disorder that increases both in incidence and severity, with age. In addition to this, hearing loss is further influenced by many other factors, especially industrial or other forms of noise exposure and loud music, and it was as far back as World War II when aircraft engine noise-induced hearing loss was first described. All employers are now obliged to take action if noise exposure in the workplace reaches an 80 decibel (dB) level, but in my extensive experience, many workers do not always co-operate with the wearing of ear defenders and other types of protectors supplied.

30. Paraldehyde Injection B.P.C. *British National Formulary.*

1976-78 edition. Watson and Viney Ltd:

Paraldehyde injection was used "to control delirious and disturbed patients", for severe agitation, even mania, and for status epilepticus, a constant and intractable type of serial epileptiform (i.e. epileptic in type) convulsions.

Paraldehyde is no longer a prescribable item in the UK although it is still in the pharmacopoeia of some countries and thus still available. It was so potent, and because it was excreted through the lungs, that after being given it could be smelled on the breath of the patient for days afterwards. Vials had to be stored in the dark to avoid deterioration, and injection could be extremely painful and cause abscesses at the site of the injection. It had the decidedly unpleasant effect of reacting with rubber and melting plastic, so that it could only be given in injection format by utilizing a glass syringe. It really did melt the plastic type, and one can only guess how I, the author, know that!

Interestingly paraldehyde administration and other drug usage was implicated in the trial of the suspected serial killer Dr John Bodkin Adams (21/01/1899-04/07/1983) in 1957. He was a wealthy and well-respected general practitioner in Eastbourne, when it was discovered that more than 160 of his patients had died in suspicious circumstances over a number of years, with 132 of these leaving him as a beneficiary in their wills! However, murder utilizing paraldehyde could not be proven in his case, and when charged he was acquitted, only later to be convicted and fined for the much lesser charges of fraud and of lying when completing cremation forms.

This was all many years before the infamous Dr Harold Frederick Shipman (14/01/1946-13/01/2004), also a well-respected general practitioner was similarly charged with being a serial killer doctor, eventually being convicted in the year 2000.

(I.e. after attending the Medical School of Leeds in the same years as the author!).

10. Germuns, J.W.s and "Gyppos"

After a while I felt that I was getting to know my Black Country patients, their needs, their likes and dislikes, and I started to understand their behaviours and reasoning and their views on life in general. They were quite insular in their attitudes at times, being particularly suspicious of outsiders and they were very resistant to any new or lifestyle change. On looking back I feel that it took me 5 years to realize all this, during which I was mentored and aided by my senior partner who taught me all the ropes at this time. These suspicions to outsiders included my partner himself, a kindly Northern Irishman, who had been in the practice for almost 30 years. Being of local birth, however, I was accepted.

Burly Brian was a big bloke, weighed 15 stone and usually gently bounced into the surgery. A local hotelier, he was gay. This day in January 1980, he minced and barely crept into the room.

"I'll remain standing if you don't mind Doctor. It's me back. It's killing me. Bloody Germuns," he exclaimed.

I must admit he did look unwell and not his normal self.

"Why Brian?" I asked. "What's it got to do with Germans?"

"Well, I was in Germuny when it happened," he said. "I fell off the back of a lorry, I did. It's not been bloody right since, and I couldn't get any decent treatment over there," he bemoaned.

I examined him. No abnormal physical signs other than a

rigid lumbar spine.

Looked very like a long-term degenerative problem to me, not recent.

"When did this happen then Brian? Were you on holiday?" I questioned. Medical care in Germany was usually pretty good I knew.

"No, no, Doctor, it was on the last day of the war, when I was in the army," he exclaimed. "Fell off the back of an army lorry during my national service didn't I. If they hadn't started the bloody war, I'd never a been there, would I, and there was no bloody 'ospitals t' go to, we'd blowed them all up by then, 'adn't we?" he disclosed.

Gosh, that was 1945, I thought. It was now 1980. This was a good example of a Black Country retained grudge, albeit a little distorted. Germans were foreigners though you see, like the Brummies.

Suspicion ruled the waves in the Black Country, not Britannia.

In other ways Brian himself was unusual in the homophobic society of the time. He was quite open about his sexuality. He disgusted my Uncle Jim who was a neighbour and a relative of his. Once when seeing Brian out for walk, 6 foot 2 inches, with his tiny white miniature poodle with a real plastic collar studded with real plastic hearts and diamonds, Uncle Jim exclaimed…

"Not a man's dog, our Edward. Bit like a furry rabbit," was his opinion.

Brian on this day apparently was followed by Aubrey, his partner, 5 foot 4 inches, Cassius-like demeanour, lean and hungry, cachexic-looking physique, leading his dog as well, or rather being dragged along by his dog, a Dobermann with a massive metal-studded leather collar.

"Not natural, not natural, you know them two. Cor you give 'em something for it, our Edward? Injections or something?" Uncle Jim enquired.

In this era homosexuality was greatly frowned on, as it was so little understood. Brian and Aubrey had been partners for years and lived out a long-term happiness. They were a charming and devoted couple. Thank goodness that nowadays things have changed and the public has become broader minded and accepted that persons of all sexual preferences have all the same needs as the rest of society. As human beings whether you accept their choice of sexuality or not, they should have the same basic human rights as all.

Jehovah's Witnesses, J.W.s, likewise, were and still are another group of society equally misunderstood, that I had as patients.

Mick Rose came into the surgery late one evening. Rosy he was not. Thickset, a bricklayer, of not great intellect, he'd been to the Royal Hospital Casualty Department Wolverhampton and had an "urgent" appointment in the surgery arranged. He needed a sick note. His arm was in a below elbow plaster of Paris splint.

"Good evening Mr Rose, what can I do for you?" I started. Never make a direct enquiry with a "trauma" problem.

"Soddin' Jehovah's Witnesses, Doc," he bemoaned.

I had many Witness patients. They were usually a very placid lot. I frowned.

"Knocked on the door Doc. 3 o'clock Sund'y afternoon he did. Right in the middle of me dinner. I was fed up. I knowed he was one of them Witnesses 'cos he was wearin' a suit. They always wear suits and 'ave one a them briefcase things under their arms, so before he could say anything, wollop, I bostid 'im one straight in the gob I did. Right in 'is cake'ole. Well, down he went like a sack of terters. Never said another word he daye," was his somewhat incomplete explanation.

He had apparently hit the chap, just for disturbing his Sunday lunch!

"Ha, but Mr Rose it's Monday evening now, what have you been doing since Sunday lunchtime?" I asked.

"Oh well, f' some reason somebody called the police and they locked me up overnight after that, and since I was let out t'day I've been up the casualty at the Royal ever since," was his reply.

"What happened to the Jehovah's Witness chap?" I asked again.

"Oh, they took him away somewhere. He wasn't badly 'urt, I know, cos they only kept him in 'ospital overnight. Just had a few bostid teeth he did. Any road he weren't a Witness at all as it turned out. Apparently he was the insurance bloke asking if we knew if the old lady next door was away this wik. Still, it serves him right an all Doc. Spoilt me dinner he did, and look 'ere, 'e's bostid me ond now and they tell me at the 'ospital I cor g' t' werk f' the next 3 wiks. I need a note, please," he now fully explained.

He had by mistake hit the insurance man in his mouth, his "gob" or "cakehole", thinking he was a Jehovah's Witness, all because his dinner was disturbed on a Sunday. This caused several of the man's teeth to be dislodged or broken necessitating the unfortunate man's admission to hospital. In the performance of this assault Mr Rose had broken some of the bones in his hand, and required thus a sick note from me for his employer as he was now unable to work. It was all someone else's fault, not his. This self-deceiving logic, and his conclusion to all this typified Black Country folk attitudes to strangers when disturbed, Jehovah's Witnesses in particular. They themselves were right and could do no wrong.

On joining general practice I knew little or nothing of Jehovah's Witness-ism. I had the usual limited knowledge of the religion as does the general public, and I had all the prejudiced ideas. All I knew of their religion was of their refusal to accept blood transfusions, and what I had been taught at medical school to be considered good medical practice in the handling of such supposedly awkward patients. With the senior receptionist at my surgery a Witness, and many Jehovah's Witness patients within the practice I quickly became enlightened, and indeed in time enamoured and an admirer, of this group of folk. My views changed only slowly, but overall quite dramatically as time went by.

I gradually discovered from my patients that Jehovah's Witnesses belong to a denomination distinct from mainstream

Christianity, with their own interpretation of the Bible. They live within a strict fellowship directed by their local elders, and they have a strict moral code encouraging obedience within the family, and marriage within their religion. They shun divorce. They do not observe Christmas, Easter, birthdays or bank holidays all of which they consider to have pagan origins, and as well as refusing blood transfusions they also have objections to organ transfer, skin grafts and other such transfers of any bodily materials. Their beliefs are multiple and complex but as a result of these beliefs they have been criticized and even persecuted in many countries, especially as they also refuse military service and refuse to salute national flags.

To an outsider they seem almost like a dictatorial group living within normal society, but in my experience this is not so. As a doctor I have observed them very closely as an outsider, but I have also seen them from within so to speak, and over many years I have developed a very different view and opinion. What is not commonly known is how they finance many of their activities. Members who are "on the district", can be quite young, spreading their beliefs from door to door, often when they have no source of income, when they are sustained by other members of the community in all respects. They have only to ask for finance or accommodation, clothing even, and it is provided. If a member falls ill and e.g. needs a specialist "private medical opinion" and they do not have the finances, or if they require some costly medical need or just an appliance, others will quite anonymously donate the money. The person receiving the money often is not aware from whom it arises. When a member falls ill at home and requires nursing or night sitting care or other specialized home input, volunteers will appear out of the blue to cope with their need. Their work and care ethic is quite extraordinary. They are extremely kind and caring to all. As a family GP over the years I have shared more and more of their life's crises, and become closely bonded into their family circles. When you are allowed into the family circle one finds an incredible sense of happiness in all their lives and all their activities, not seen in society in general. They still have all the physical and psychological illnesses of modern society but it is quite uncommon to have to treat a Witness for e.g. a depressive illness, I found, they are such a happy lot.

In my early days of practice I found them very maligned not only by the general public but also by the medical profession when they were treated almost with disdain. "Oddballs, nutters" I have heard them described. I have seen cases where Jehovah's Witness children deserving of surgery were refused operation because the surgeon would not accept the parental refusal to sign preoperative agreement for transfusion, even when the operative risk of haemorrhage was/is nowadays very low e.g. for tonsillectomy[31] etc. Consensual acceptance here would be tantamount to denial of their religion or the equivalent of excommunication to them. Their depth of belief was, and still is, so poorly understood. In general practice the commonest problems of Witness management that I found did not arise with operative surgical problems or with children, but in the everyday normal care of the pregnant woman who has antenatal concerns. Pleasingly now, there are in place guidelines and protocols issued by the various Royal Colleges and health authorities that set out how to manage not only Jehovah's Witness patients, but all religions, creeds and beliefs and when problems do arise with treatments there are now specific liaison committees[32] worldwide set up and in place to aid the doctors in the management of cases when needed. These various advisory committees take into consideration the rights and beliefs of all of the specific religions concerned, extremely important now in our modern multicultural society.

In the Black Country, "gyppos", gypsies were similarly not accepted.

"I had to see a gypsy child today," I mentioned over a pre-surgery cup of tea to my doctor partner. "What do you think of them?" I innocently asked.

"Bloody thieving, lying, smooth-talking Irish Micks!"

Note the repetition here. That's where I got my description

of the chief executive officer of Ryanair from, I now recollect…
(see Chapter 4).

"Never buy anything off them and never let them lay any tarmac on your drive," he cried, and he was an Irishman himself. My experiences, however, did not always match his opinions. Most of our Black Country gypsy patients were of the Smith, Davis, Lee, or Price families. As a child I remember the ladies coming around with the gift of the gab selling pegs and baskets to my mother. She always bought a sprig of heather off them "for good luck". My father often signed their letters and documents when we lived in the pub, as they were mostly illiterate, when they visited our mining village in their caravans in the post-war summers, always on an intermittent basis. By the 1970s however, the spare land of the post-war years available to them had become very scarce, and they started to live on local authority designated sites. They even began to register with GPs, albeit on a Temporary Resident basis.

Elderly Bert Smith and his wife and others lived on a small piece of land in Bradley, Bilston, entered only by driving through a garage and forecourt, at the rear of Old Joe Badam's bungalow. A pretty awful location, but better than some. Whenever one visited in the winter the caravan was spotless, as ever, with a huge fire on the stove, and various china collections arranged around, and at the end of my consultation the conversation usually went…

""Now, what would you like your cup of tea with today Doctor?" would ask Mrs Smith, with an enquiring voice.

I knew it was incredibly bad decorum to refuse a drink and thus to view their precious china collections, so I always replied with politeness…

"What did I have it with last time Mrs Smith?"

"Well I think it was the Royal Doulton Doctor," she answered. "Perhaps you'd like to try the Wedgwood today for a change, sir?" was her courteous reply, knowing full well what I had had my last cup of tea in, no less than 9 months previously!

In time, with repeat visits, I went around the whole of the

dinner services meticulously kept in the glass-fronted cupboards on view all around the caravan.

Likewise, the Davis's lived on the Highfields Road, local authority site nearby, also in Bilston. What a dump. Reached by jumping a humpback bridge it was a triangular piece of land with no electricity or water supply, it was bounded by the canal on one side, a foundry wall topped by razor wire on the other, and sealed by a fence from a large water-filled marl hole (Ladymoor Pool) on the other side. The pool was colonized by a flock of noisy Canada Geese.

Despite these poor home circumstances, Magenta, Mrs Davis, had a completely uneventful pregnancy, and after a few days of false alarm Braxton Hicks contractions[33] her subsequent 24-hour hospital delivery at New Cross Hospital Wolverhampton was as she described, "Like shellin' peas, Doctor." The next day I had to do my first antenatal home visit... As I drove into the site, what the '!

I had to do an emergency stop. I was scared and startled as various ferocious-looking large dogs jumped up and obstructed my entrance, snarling at me through the car windows, and barking and running around. I was pretty alarmed.

Then I saw an old granny, sitting knitting at one side, in a rocking chair, "on guard" it seemed, as she cried out...

"Ge' down. Si' down. Let the Doctor in," she commanded to the quite nasty looking animals at her feet, who rolled their eyes and snarled their jaws, white teeth exposed, and then all laid down at her feet.

How she knew who I was, I never discovered, but I didn't get out of the car. I drove right up to the Davis's caravan before alighting. I went into the usual spotless van and I was met with a scene of domestic bliss. Mr Davis in his bare feet, was on the settee feeding the new infant after just changing her nappy. Drinking a cup of tea with his other hand. Stove on. Lovely and warm. Very *Gemütlichkeit*. He welcomed me in. I examined the babe.

Head end first, work your way down, I thought. Anterior fontanelle (the baby's head "soft spot") patent, fluctuant, and not distended. Posterior fontanel closed. Flaccid child. Not anaemic, not jaundiced. No cardiac murmurs. Chest clear. Grasp reflex fine. Tone normal. Spine OK, no clicking of hips. Well-nourished babe and feeding well. Cord clean, not yet detached, and so on. A lovely apyrexial babe.

Something was missing, what? Magenta! I need to examine the mother, to ensure the uterus has retracted, to enquire re breastfeeding etc.

"Could I see Mrs Davis as well please?" I requested.

"Oh no Doc that's not possible," explained Mr D. "She ain't been t' work for a wik, you know, havin' this babi, so 'ere's gone out in the HGV truck just t' ger a bit a scrap in t'day. Nothin' 'eavy I tode her, mind you, when she left at 8 o'clock this mornin'. She promised to tek things easy and be 'ome early by 6 tonight. I made her promise that Doc," he confided.

How considerate of him, I thought. I was alarmed and surprised and sat down sharply. We had the usual cup of tea from a particular service as ever, and we exchanged idle chat. To make idle chit-chat I asked as to the origin of the dogs outside and as to why they were so big.

"The dags? Well we gorra be careful of intruders her Doc, you know. They's for security, you see," he explained, as if anybody in his right mind would ever approach the site unannounced, and he went on to say…

"The big one, well he's gorra bit of Rottie in him, he's a nice dag, and the other a bit of pit bull you know. Nice dags both, but the little un, 'e's different you see. I think 'e is a bit mixed up like. He worries me. I think he might have a bit of cat in him as well." Then, before I could enquire further to this rather odd disclosure, even from a gyppo, he added…

"As well as keeping all the local rats and other vermin away, he's started to catch birds, you know Doc. He even brought us a nice duck f' dinner the other day, you know. D' y' want t' 'ave a look?" he said, as he pointed to the kitchen door of the caravan where a somewhat modified Canada goose from the pool next door was hanging.

"We 'm goin' t' 'ave 'im f' dinner t'night if the wife gets back in time t' cook it," he added, whilst offering me a closer look.

I declined his offer, and left soon after, leaving strict instructions for Magenta to contact me on her return, if she could fit me in for a consultation sometime perhaps, between her looking after the baby, collecting scrap, and doing the cooking for Mr Davis etc. at her convenience of course.

In the 1980s the life of the gypsies began to change. The children started to attend regular school and with the formal education of this generation, many families gradually stopped the nomadic caravan life and began to move into council housing accommodation, although some families still do live in caravans from time to time. The poor standards of health that they enjoyed then, also began to improve.

Despite the bad press they receive many families still live in bungalow-type of accommodation on their old sites, some of which are quite appallingly situated.

It was in the mid 1990s when I had to visit a family of Dudley Davis's (related to the Bilston Davis's), in Wall Heath, a supposedly middle-class residential area of Dudley, when I had moved surgeries then (see later), that was reached down a rutted track that really required a four-by-four to visit. I went to see a very ill patient living in a bungalow on a site that I did not think could still exist in the modern age.

As well as piles of rubbish, scrap metal, old tyres, battered cars and such, a cloud of choking smoke with a pungent smell blotted out the sky, arising from behind a fence just yards away from where the lady was lying in her last bed, spotless, doted on by her husband and daughters. It was a surreal landscape. Incredible.

"What is all the smoke and burning?" I asked of her husband.

"Oh, it's nothing Doctor. They'm just burning the bodies again as they always do this time a day," the old man replied.

It was the height of the BSE[34] problem and the government had just ordered the culling of the pre-1996 total UK cattle herd. They were burning the carcasses but a few feet from where these folk lived. It was so bad you could taste the smell and the smoke. I still can. The lady died shortly afterwards, peacefully in her own bed.

The family still live in the same property today. Not all gyppos are a pain.

Incredibly, it was not until July 2008 I remember, that a full and comprehensive study of The Black Country Gypsy and Traveller Communities was commissioned by the Black Country authorities of Dudley, Sandwell, Walsall and Wolverhampton[35]. This then was only in response to the Housing Act of 2004 that required all local authorities to take their needs and requirements into consideration. The study enclosed and identified English Gypsies, Irish Travellers, New Travellers and Travelling Show people. This large and detailed study looked at the populations concerned, and it did include their needs and requirements, and showed how they still form a greatly deprived group of society, with not only housing issues, poor water supplies and such, but other educational deficiencies and health problems, asthma and other long-term illnesses being identified[40].

References and Author's comment:

31. National Prospective Tonsillectomy Audit. The Royal College of Surgeons of England. 2005. www.rcseng.ac.uk/:

This comprehensive audit of more than 40,000 tonsillectomy cases made by the Royal College of Surgeons of England showed an overall operative haemorrhage rate of 3.8% in NHS hospitals. This audit included all methods of tonsillectomy surgery and included the operative experience of the surgeons concerned.

Of these cases only a very small number i.e. 8 patients, out of the 40,000 studied, and pleasingly required actual blood transfusion, i.e. on the balance of probability therefore, refusal for permission for transfusion does not always indicate that surgery likewise, should be refused.

32. The Watchtower Information Service. www.watchtowerinformationservice.org/:

In 1988 the Jehovah's Witness Watchtower Society set up a Hospital Information Service that can be accessed online, setting out information regarding doctors who would consider treatment without transfusion and other therapies. As of 2006 this service had widely expanded and by then there were 1,535 Hospital Liaison Committees worldwide, co-ordinating communications with clinicians and patients on religious and medical matters.

33. Braxton Hicks contractions. ADC Fetal and Neonatal Journal. 1999. BMJ Group. www.fn.bmj.com/content/:

Predelivery contractions of the uterus were first described by an Englishman, Dr John Braxton Hicks in 1872. These are due to uterine muscle fibres contracting then relaxing (retracting) and they are thought to aid the body in preparation for delivery. Not all women experience these contractions which can arise at any time after 6 weeks gestation, but generally they occur more frequently in the later stages of pregnancy. They are precipitated by many factors and they are differentiated from the full uterine contractions of delivery by their short duration and their irregularity, and unlike full uterine contractions they are not painful in the sense that they do not increase in strength and intensity.

34. Prion Diseases: *Davidson's Essentials of Medicine.* 2009. Churchill Livingstone:

Creutzfeldt-Jakob disease. The National CJD Disease Surveillance Unit, Western General Hospital Edinburgh. www. nhs.uk/Conditions/Creutzfeldt-Jakob:

Bovine spongiform encephalopathy (BSE) or "mad cow disease" is a fatal neurological disorder affecting the brain and spinal cord of cattle with a very long incubation period of 30 months to 8 years. The first case diagnosed in the UK was in 1986. It was then implicated in the development of the similarly fatal human neurological disorder variant Creutzfeldt-Jakob

Disease (vCJD) with the resultant eradication slaughter of 4.4 million cattle over a period of time.

The normal nonvariant and sporadic Creutzfeldt-Jakob Disease (CJD) itself still occurs worldwide, with an incidence of about 1:1 million of population per year.

The highest number of human deaths due to vCJD recorded in the UK was in the year 2000 when there were 28 attributed deaths, but subsequently the numbers of deaths per year has greatly fallen. The exact numbers are still unclear due to the very long incubation period of the disorder, with only 1 death attributed to the disease in the year 2013, i.e. they have fallen dramatically.

Although the development of vCJD has been attributed to the eating of beef containing prions, the infective agent, the exact causation is still a debatable subject, and was the slaughter of all those cattle really a necessity?

Recently blood transfusions have been implicated in the transmission of vCJD and it has been postulated that prions could even be transmitted in humans in the Far East and elsewhere, by the practice of cannibalism!

35. The Black Country Gypsy and Traveller Accommodation Needs Assessment. Fordham Research. 2008. www.fordhamresearch.com:

This large 144-page study shows the gypsy and traveller populations throughout the boroughs concerned and their needs and deprivations. It shows how 1960s legislation closed off much communal land previously available and how up-to-date accommodations are of insufficient number and of poor quality. Even when registered with a local authority for health care with e.g. with a GP or for educational needs, many families were/are reluctant to attend because of cultural differences and perceived continuing discrimination.

11. "Retards"

If your IQ is below 70, by international definition you are
"Mentally Retarded".
You are a "Retard".

One of the subjects I knew little about on arrival into general practice was the medical care of patients with what is now kindly termed "Learning Difficulties", and on looking back, it was only in time did I gradually acquire an expertise in the management of such patients, which eventually became a great pleasure.

My initial introduction was made by a pleasant and kindly middle-aged lady social worker, who asked if I would consider to undertake the medical care of a local authority home for the "Mentally Retarded", as such patients were known as in those days, at Stow Heath near Bilston, a long-term residential home for 25 or so such labelled patients. She had had great difficulty obtaining medical cover for these patients because of their complex problems requiring much medical input, and several practices had already refused her request. She pleaded for my help in almost a desperate fashion, and so I eventually agreed to her request, after first obtaining the agreement of my senior partner. I decided that the best way to manage these cases was that I would do a regular ward round at the home itself, to review all the patients in their own environment when their social as well as medical histories were available.

My partner gently warned me to expect a difficult time. I

quickly discovered his concerns. They were certainly not normal patients.

I was met at the door on my first visit by the warden Mr Wood. A small, balding, very smartly dressed and very polite, almost NCO military-type man. He must have been ex-armed forces.

"Morning Sa, Doctor," he greeted me with a smile. I was almost saluted. Smashing chap he was.

I soon discovered that due to low staff to patient ratios, a poor financial budget, and possibly lack of training for the post, although being an extremely caring man, he had no alternative but to run the home almost like an army barracks. I began to call the patients "inmates" as indeed they were like prisoners, when they had all to get up together at a certain time, they all had a set breakfast, whether they wanted it or not, at a set time, and they were then all washed and dressed and sent off to work together to the sheltered workshop where they worked, down the road together, all at a set time. They all got a comprehensive education together at the workshop, and were employed according to their intellectual capacity such as the making and painting of garden furniture, keeping livestock for profit; chickens and some sheep etc. They were collected and came home together for a set dinner. They went to bed all at the same time and "lights out" was likewise all at a certain time.

It was the only way they could be managed with the facilities available. Despite very caring and hard-working staff, the patients had no freedom, no independence. They were taught little or no social graces or skills.

This was the way "retards" were cared for and managed at that time in the Black Country. This reflected the attitude of society in general to these folk.

Allan had Down's syndrome[36].

"He's an awkward cuss doctor. He's a mongol and retarded. He's almost blind Sa," was my introduction to him by Mr Wood.

He was one of the oldest patients in the home having been originally cared for at home by his well-to-do parents and then into middle age by his very caring sister, a single lady, our local authority housing manageress. Because of her extremely busy job she could only have Allan at home weekends and so he now lived weekdays at the hostel. He himself was generally well, but his main problem was that of visual impairment, he used a white stick, and he had a chronic resentment of authority, especially that of Mr Wood. However, Allan and I established a rapport quite quickly and we got along fine. I gradually got to know and like him very much. He was irreparably totally blind in one eye and in the other he had a severe cataract, yet, still with a large hand lens I discovered him reading and writing complex items one day, quite remarkable for his syndrome and with just one useable eye. His records showed that he had never been considered for an ophthalmological referral and opinion despite his abilities and disabilities, because he had Down's syndrome! His disabilities had just been accepted. He supposedly didn't qualify!

I began to realize the prejudices that were rife against these patients who were "retarded", and even now many years later, I recollect feeling of being quietly enraged by all this. I decided to fully review all "the inmates" with their medical and social notes and histories and to rectify any medical problems that I discovered... starting with Allan. So, after discussion with his sister I referred him to a local surgeon colleague. He had the first intraocular lens implant[37] that I had ever seen, and he discarded his hand lens away. He became much easier to manage at the home, but he would not let go of his white stick that he was almost addicted to. He only occasionally thrust this at other residents who were getting on his nerves. It appeared that we had solved his awkward personality, or so I thought.

I was called out as an emergency. Allan had assaulted Mr Wood with his stick causing him to be admitted to hospital with a head injury, a suspected fractured skull, and I found Allan very agitated on my arrival. The staff were also very wary of him. Chaos ruled, again.

"Why, what's the matter Allan?" I questioned. "Do you feel

poorly? Why did you hit Mr Wood?"

"No, no Doctor. Not poorly. Can't see properly. Mr Wood wouldn't let me have my looking lens again. Shouted at me he did. Said I was naughty. I'm not naughty Doctor. Just want to read my books. He's the naughty man, not me," he poured out a reply in his typical staccato-type speech, shaking his head, rocking and nodding rather oddly for him.

Allan never told lies. I examined him gently in his agitated state. I had another first. His lens implant had come loose and was flopping about in the anterior chamber of his eye, going up and down as he spoke and moved! It was quite bizarre. I had never seen this before. This was what was upsetting him. I calmed him down and gave some mild sedation. I sent him back the next day to my ophthalmologist friend who surgically refixed his implant, pleasingly for good.

Vera was different. She was charmingly co-operative. A big grin, lots of teeth in all directions, and such a smile welcomed me at our first encounter.

"She's mentally retarded and deaf and dumb, doctor Sa," was her given diagnosis.

"She's also very awkward at eating, and can be quite stubborn at times with certain foods. She's not very bright, I'm afraid," completed the explanation.

Her notes detailed how she had been born deaf, of elderly parents, and had always been difficult for them to manage. When in her early teens, not long after the Second World War, she had somehow become pregnant, the father of the child was never discovered and an abortion was procured. The social stigma of this, at the time, was such that her parents could not cope with the embarrassment and she was admitted for institutional care, where she had resided for more than the last 30 years!

"Good morning Vera," I introduced myself, in a normal voice.

"Guh mnin Dcta," was her immediate reply.

What the ' I thought!

She had replied immediately to an unraised voice. There

was more to this. My ENT speciality kicked in. She was supposed to be retarded and completely deaf and dumb, yet clearly she was lip-reading, and whilst she gave a reply, it was not the "deaf speech" of the profoundly deaf, but just distorted normal speech. This required a full ENT examination. I got her up to my surgery where I had the required examination instruments, which showed that she possibly had some hearing, but a full diagnosis was outside that of my capability without more specialized audiological equipment. A long medical referral was then made to a specialist hearing/psychiatric unit in Manchester that I knew about, that dealt with unusual and complex syndromes.

She returned after comprehensive investigation and treatment, which included the fitting of powerful bilateral hearing aids, and surgery to both her temporomandibular jaw joints. She was diagnosed as having an amplifiable hearing loss, and although she had spontaneously taught herself to lip-read, it had been discovered that she could not communicate, or eat hard food properly, because of congenital problems with her jaw joints. Her IQ level assessed was "normal to superior" i.e. 115-120, "Possibly above average for the general population"!

She had been locked away for years because of failure of medical diagnoses!

This was now over 30 years ago. I have rheumy eyes. My heart still weeps at this reflection.

The age range in the home was from teenagers to middle age. David was another Down's syndrome patient, a boisterous teenager, short and stocky, similar to a mini prop forward, a delightful and lively chap. He was a keen footballer who was allowed to play with the local lads in the park. He was also a class 1 insulin-dependent diabetic[38] on twice daily insulin injections, when at the time insulin was either given personally by a suitably trained patient, or by the district nurse at home, utilizing only the glass syringes then available. The prescribing of these syringes for a patient could only be made by the approval of a specialist consultant physician, a diabetologist also at this time. It is quite important that such patients receive their injections in the correct fashion, and on time, but due to nurse time constraints it became quickly obvious to me that it was difficult to do this with David, who went off each day to his training centre at a set time, especially when the nurses were very busy. He was often given his morning dose too early. He was often given his evening dose too late. I thought then that if the staff at the home were prepared to give his injections, this would be beneficial both to David's health and at the same time relieve somewhat, the workload of the very busy district nurses. All concerned were in agreement, and I just had to get consultant approval for the syringes and other equipment required. I telephoned Dr Bramble at The Royal Hospital Wolverhampton with my request. His reply was as sharp as his name…

"We can't afford to divert expensive NHS resources and supplies in this fashion. Anyway he's a mongol, he's a retard. Why should he have such special treatment or equipment that others don't get?"

What "special treatment" was this? Prejudiced attitudes were not just confined to the general public, but also to the medical profession it appeared. I could not be bothered to point out that David had all the human rights as others and this system would be both beneficial to his health as well as actually saving some NHS expense. At my next hospital ENT clinic the following week I just went up to my very understanding ward sister and explained it all to her. She kindly supplied me with all the syringes needed and anything else that I required. I just shifted "expensive NHS resources and supplies" i.e. I pinched (removed, stole) the syringes and other equipment off the ward. David's diabetic control became good and stable. His football improved as well.

Disaster struck. One day when I arrived at the home, the staff were all in tears! David had been caught in the park changing rooms, with a group of lads, masturbating in public! He had been arrested by the police and put in jail. He had then been charged with an offence and compulsorily admitted, by a (lady) magistrate under a court order, for "Corrective Therapy" to St Margaret's Psychiatric Hospital in Birmingham. He was gone, and disappeared for 3 months. He came home like a zombie, he could barely walk unaided, and had large breasts! He was discharged with drug sedation to "calm him down", and he was the only male patient that I have ever seen on the female oral contraceptive pill. The oestrogen content was intended to make him a chemical eunuch! No one seemed to have noticed that he had severe varicosed leg veins and that he had a strong family history of thromboses. Within one week, before I could get him mobile and gradually reduce all his drugs, he was readmitted to hospital in Wolverhampton with a deep-vein thrombosis in one of his legs, and multiple secondary embolic blood clots, pulmonary emboli, in his lungs! He nearly died. They saved his life at New Cross Hospital, they did. They stopped "the pill" and all his sedation. They got him back on his feet and mobile. They treated him as a normal human being.

Now all this sounds a little depressing. It fills one with sadness and a feeling of doom and gloom. However, society attitudes in general over the years have markedly changed and now patients with difficulties with cognitive ability and learning difficulties are no longer locked away to be cared for, but they are included into normal society, and their basic human rights are respected and accepted at all times. Moreover, I am pleased to say that for all the aforementioned stories regarding my "retards" locked away for years, there were happy endings for all.

Mr Wood never returned to work after his head injury. He was replaced as head warden (now called a "manager") by Miss Glenys Brown, a kindly lady born in the UK of West Indian family extraction. She had a huge smile and a booming laugh. She mothered and smothered and took all the patients so her very ample bosom(s). She believed in letting the patients have newfound freedoms and be taught life skills and social interactions. She was ably aided in this by her new assistant manager, Mr Michael Bright, a young Black Country man straight out of college, full of new ideas and new ideals.

Together with the new staff, we took a risk with Allan. After a chat, when he explained his resentment to care was, "Don't like living here Doctor. They are all thick," we realized that he resented being with his supposed peers. His behaviour would now be classified as "challenging", although I never found him a challenge in the true sense of the word. He was just difficult to manage. We transferred him thence to an elderly care residential home, on one condition, that he gave up his stick, which he agreed to do so with reluctance, and I saw him there afterwards taking the afternoon tea out to the old folks and helping out in the kitchen. He was very happy doing his own thing there ever after with,

"Nice normal people here, Doctor, like me!"

Furthermore, the early 1990s Wolverhampton local authority purchased several small houses, "Cluster Homes" just down the road from the home, where residents were rehoused after being taught life skills by Miss Brown and Mr Bright prior to transfer. They were taught how to cook and house clean, and do clothes washing etc. They were taught how to go shopping and buy food, even go into town on trips on the bus. They were taught all life's daily required skills that we "normals" just take for granted. Vera was put in charge of one of these homes, with others, where she kept them all in line, being visited by Miss Brown or Mr Bright or their staff, for daily supervision. She now still lives in happy, but supervised, domesticity.

But poor compensation for all the lost years.

David? Well, he survived his (drug induced?) pulmonary emboli, and we got him off all his sedative and hormonal drugs on discharge from hospital. His diabetes, on an in-house given insulin regime became stable and well controlled. He came back to the home still very young and boisterous, but his hospital experiences had dampened down his previous exhibitionist behaviour, and he showed no more signs ever again of what had been his form of sexual maturity.

He is still being taught life skills in the hope that eventually he might be able to go into community living, despite his years of institutionalized care, and he has had psychosexual counselling.

He goes to watch professional football matches on a regular basis.

References and Author's comment:

36. Down's Syndrome. www.nhs.uk/Conditions/Downs-syndrome:
Down's Syndrome Association. www.downs-syndrome.org.uk/about-us:

Down's syndrome is attributed to having been first described in detail by Dr John Langdon Down in 1866, despite being previously described by various French physicians. Subjects with this syndrome have a complex syndrome involving delay in cognitive abilities, altered physical growth and particular facial characteristics. These facial characteristics include epicanthic skin folds to their eye fissures giving them an Asiatic appearance, hence the term "mongoloid" or "mongol", a term now rarely used. They often have a degree of intellectual disability with an average IQ of around 50, as well as a predisposition for other physical disorders such as congenital heart disease, eye, and hearing disorders, thyroid disease and infertility. Females are, however, not uniformly infertile, although the offspring of Down's syndrome patients have a 50% chance themselves of having the same condition. Male infertility is almost uniform and there have been only three cases recorded of male Down's syndrome patients having fathered children.

The incidence of the condition varies from country to country, and occurs in about 1:650-1,000 live births, increasing with increased maternal age. Maternal age itself has been increasing in the UK for some time now, and despite markedly improved systems of screening, there were still over 700 live births with this syndrome in 2012.

The syndrome is due to a chromosomal abnormality known as "trisomy-21", first described in 1959 by Dr Jerome Lejeune...

Humans have in the nuclei of all their cells, from the tip of their toes to the top of their heads, 23 pairs of intertwined chemical strands called chromosomes (i.e. 46 in all). These pairs of chromosomes are numbered 1 to 23, and at conception half of these is provided by each parent in the paternal sperm and the maternal egg (ovum) cells. The chemicals in sequences carried on these chromosome structures are known as DNA, deoxyribonucleic acid, and each DNA sequence carries the genetic code to their offspring, equally from both parents.

In Down's syndrome something goes wrong with this process and instead of being "deficient" as they are often labelled, they have an extra chromosome attached to pair no. 21, and they have in total 47 chromosomes in their cells. The extra one of these chromosomes, in the vast majority (88%) of cases, originates from the maternal part contribution, and Down's syndrome patients have this extra chromosome, trisomy-21, in all their cells from the tip of their toes to the top of their heads.

Saying all this, however, as always in nature, nothing is ever simple. Further complicating this issue is the discovery that not all Down's syndrome patients, (approximately 2-3%) have trisomy of chromosome no. 21 in all their cells. Some of their cells have the normal number of chromosomes, as well. These patients with a mixture of chromosome numbers are known as "mosaics" and usually they have a greater intellect than expected, and can often read and write etc.

In the aforementioned story I strongly suspect that patient Allan, was so bright that he was indeed a mosaic Down's syndrome patient.

37. Intraocular lenses. Optical Express. 2010. www.opticalexpress. co.uk/:
Biographical Memoirs of Fellows of the Royal Society. D.J. Apple. 2007. Royal Society Publishing:
An intraocular lens is an artificial lens surgically implanted in the eye as a treatment for cataracts and short-sightedness, i.e. myopia. With a cataract the lens is clouded over and removed and replaced. For myopia the new lens is placed over the existing lens. The pioneer of such surgery was Sir Nicholas Harold Lloyd

Ridley (10/07/06- 25/05/01) who during Second World War service noticed that when splinters of acrylic plastic became lodged in the eyes of wounded RAF pilots it did not cause rejection reactions as did similar glass splinters. Although he performed the first lens implant surgery in 1949 using Perspex, there was considerable and prolonged opposition to his techniques from the medical community and it was not until the 1970s did the surgery become widespread and accepted. Procedures have now become so refined that nowadays patients after just a local anaesthetic and surgery can expect excellent vision within 24 hours of operation.

38. Diabetes Mellitus. *Davidson's Essentials of Medicine*. 2009. Churchill Livingstone:

Diabetes UK (formerly Diabetic Association).www.diabetes.org.uk/:

Diabetes mellitus, "sugar diabetes", is a disease characterized by the development of a raised blood sugar i.e. serum glucose level, which leads to a complex multisystem disorder and illness. It was first described in humans by the ancient Egyptians and it is now known to occur in animals.

It is due to a disorder of the pancreas gland found in the abdomen which...

1. Does not produce enough of the hormone insulin, i.e. type 1 diabetes.
2. The insulin produced becomes ineffective even when produced in large amounts, i.e. type 2 diabetes.
3. There is also another type known as gestational diabetes, seen only in pregnant women with high blood sugar levels that return to normality after delivery.

These patients invariably develop the disease later in life, and I, the author, have seen this many times.

Type 1 diabetics require the administration of insulin, which is a protein denatured by digestion, and that can be given only by injection, usually the subcutaneous route just under the skin.

Type 2 diabetics require diet and/or various drug

combinations given by mouth, to lower their blood sugar.

Newer preventative therapies, newer drugs and routes of administration such as insulin being given intranasally, or using embryonic stem cells to replace insulin-producing cells etc. are still being evaluated for all types of diabetes.

Insulin itself is normally produced by cells in the pancreas known as the islets of Langerhans, and it causes peripheral body muscle cells, and other cells such as liver cells, fat stores and other sites to take up glucose, the body energy transmitter, from the blood.

Type 1 diabetics just do not produce enough insulin, thus producing the symptoms of clinical diabetes.

Type 2 diabetics, however, do not develop symptoms of clinical diabetes until they have lost 60-65% of their islet cells which are by then working overtime to produce an insulin that is ineffective, a condition known as "insulin resistance", and about 30% of these patients continue to lose 5% of their islet cells each year till eventually they have virtually none. They then become type 1 diabetics thus requiring insulin administration.

Insulin was first synthesized by the Canadians, Frederick Grant Banting (14/11/1891-21/02/1941) and Charles Herbert Best (27/02/1899-31/03/1978) in 1921 but it did not become widely available to all in the UK until the Diabetic Association charity was set up in 1934 by the famous authors H.G. Wells and D.H. Lawrence, both who had the disease. They wished to ensure that insulin was available to all, whatever their financial situation.

The disease globally now affects an estimated 285 million people and its incidence in all countries is increasing rapidly. It is estimated that this number will double by 2030 and the cost of care to the NHS will be both huge and exponential.

Hopefully more effective preventative measures will ensure a reduction in these figures, as well as more effective treatment.

The disease was supposedly not very common until the 20th century, and although there are many other causative factors now involved in the increasing incidence, presumably then, as it was often undiagnosed and thus untreated, with this disease, you died!

12. Favourites

Doctors should not have favourites, but I did. Children, kids. I could not help it I just liked Black Country (and Brummie) kids.

I suppose they are delightful elsewhere, but I can only reflect on my experiences.

Black Country children are still taught…

Rule Number 1. "Don't talk to, and stay away from, strangers."

Rule Number 2. "Don't let anybody touch you, that you don't know."

This rule applied both in my working-class Wolverhampton practice and my later Kingswinford practice, the latter of which most of the following examples are from.

Then, Grannie, who is caring for the family as Mom (Amber) has gone out to work, brings little Willie, and Coral his baby sister, to the doctor's surgery and says…

"Si' down. Sit still, and tell the nice man what's the matter. Let 'im examine ya, an' I'm just poppin' outside to change Coral's nappy cos it stinks. She's got a bit of the squitters [diarrhoea] Docta," she said.

She leaves him there, alone with the doctor and off she goes to change the baby's nappy. Now to Willie, a little bemused, this contravenes rules number 1. and number 2. and just about everything he has been taught for the last 6 years. Furthermore he vividly remembers the last time he came to the doctor's place. He felt perfectly fit and well on arrival, when somebody, who he is not sure, his memory time clock isn't too great, stuck a needle as big as a poker into his arm, which really hurt, and he didn't feel at all well when he left. Accordingly he becomes completely nonco-operative. He sits still, and he does not and will not say a single word, whatever the current problem. He ain't stupid.

Then, next time Amber herself brings Cerise, aged 8 years, an older sister to the clinic because of suspected wax in her ears and orders…

"Lie on the bed and let the doctor man examine your ears," which raises alarm as she has never seen me before and this is contrary to rule number 2. Then this is followed by the statement guaranteed to raise alarm in anybody's mind…

"It won't hurt!"

Little Cerise likewise, ain't stupid. By her probably unconscious reasoning, if something "won't hurt" it means that hurt or pain has to be contemplated. She wasn't even aware that there might be "a pain" here until her mother mentioned it wouldn't hurt. She will not lie down, and immediately covers her ears with her hands making ear examination impossible. She definitely ain't stupid.

I quickly discovered that much of the volume of paediatric medicine that I had been taught at medical school had to be put aside in the initial approach to children of the Black Country, as everywhere else. A very personal relationship is required. You must establish a rapport. You have to become a "nice friend".

The NC or "name and clothing" approach works well as an introduction I found.

"Is your name Cerise young lady? That means cherry in French, did you know? And that's a nice cardi. Do you go to (so-and-so) Infants School Cerise?" I asked, seeing that she was wearing a name badge on her cardigan and the school emblem was on her school blazer to give me the answers anyway.

"Does it, does it?" …pause…then, "Oh, yes, Doctor," was the somewhat surprised reply, with a smile.

The ice was broken. I went on to examine her ears with impunity.

"Football" or the SC, "sports clothing" approach is even better with boys.

In my Wolverhampton and Dudley practice the boys and girls I discovered showed their allegiance by wearing Wolverhampton Wanderers or West Bromwich Albion Football Club logos and clothing. In my hospital clinics in Birmingham it was Aston Villa or Birmingham City.

"Are you a Wolves or a Villa supporter?" I sometimes asked.

"Oh, yes Wolves (or Villa) Doctor," was the quick reply.

"Oh, well that's bad news. You see I only treat Albion or Blues supporters here," I learned to respond, always with a wry grin and a smile.

There was then a slight pause as this information was assimilated. Pause… Then a big grin. They invariably realized my joking.

The ice was broken. We established a rapport.

Examination with a medical instrument is more daunting, but can be done in a similar way. Children are little adults. They have the same apprehensions and concerns as grown-ups. Show them the tool or instrument. Explain what it does and what it is for. Get them involved. Give it them to hold while you do something else, curiosity is very calming. Explain, an auroscope, a fierce-looking thing to have stuck down one's ear is… "Just a special torch for looking down little boys and girls earholes." Or… "Has your daddy got a torch, well this is just like that only a little different?" Once the doctor-patient relationship has been established then one can go on to real paediatrics and disease mode. Well, that is, in most, but not all cases.

Amber came in one Thursday morning with Charlie, her eldest, who clearly didn't want to be there. 10 years of age. A hard chap. He stood totally disinterested with eyes to one side staring up the wall, hands behind his back and ignoring us both. He had a completely tough guy, scruffy appearance. Shoelaces undone, socks rolled down round his ankles, dirty knees exposed. His woolly jumper had seen better days, it was covered in bits of, I dared not ask. He had a snotty runny nose. Bright red cheeks. No

WHAT THE ' - REFLECTIONS OF A BLACK COUNTRY

fat, but not thin. He looked dirty, very fit and disgustingly well.

"There's something the matter with him, Doctor. He come 'ome passin' blood in 'is water, 'is wee, last night, but he's alright t'day," his mother exclaimed.

Sounded like haematuria[39] I thought. This needs looking into.

A cursory examination of a silent Charlie revealed no physical abnormality other than general unwashedness. Incontinent children often smell of urine. Not him. Query a urinary infection? He was apyrexial, no raised temperature, and was generally very well.

Simple urine examination with a dipstick showed no evidence of albumin (protein), blood or sugar, and when I dared ask if he had any pain when passing urine I did eventually get a reply.

"No."

He was quite definite, pretty brief and to the point. I got the message.

"There is no sign of any problem now, such as infection," I explained to his mother. "Just make sure he has plenty to drink, even at school, Mum, and let me see him again should this occur in the future," I explained.

Off she went, just nudging Charlie out of the room.

Next Thursday she was back again, with Charlie, who look even more fed up this time. Same problem.

"He's bin passin' blood in 'is wee again Doctor, last night, 'e's still well though. Y' doe think 'e's done it wankin' an' playin' with 'imself, do you Doctor? 'e's getting' near that age when boys do it you know?" she asked, raising a diagnosis that had not occurred to me immediately, although I was not quite so sure of the age of onset of masturbation, as she appeared to be.

I examined a silent Charlie, yet again, somewhat more thoroughly. Again, nothing to find other than a very fit looking child. Certainty no signs of self-trauma. I suggested we send off a sample of his urine to hospital for further and more detailed analysis. A bottle and form was supplied to Amber and Charlie.

They seemed to be getting fed up with each other. He went out, but with a shove this time. She was definitely getting fed up of this.

His urine report came back from the lab within a couple of days. No growth of any bacteria on culture. No abnormality on microscopy, no evidence of raised white cell count indicating any infection. No evidence even of a raised red cell count which could have indicated blood in the sample not detectable to the naked eye i.e. microscopic haematuria. A normal analysis.

Third week. Amber and Charlie. Same day. Same symptoms. Same no abnormality on examination.

"Well that's funny," she said. "'e came 'ome from school last night, again with blood all over the pan when he wee'd," she explained, somewhat indignantly now.

At this, I had a thought, and questioned her out loud.

"You know, he hasn't been eating beetroot, has he?" I asked.

"No, no, we never eat the stuff at our 'ouse," she said.

"Yes, yes I 'ave," said Charlie!

"No, no, yo 'avan't," she said, eyebrows raised.

"Yes, yes I 'ave. I 'ave," he said. "We 'ave it for school dinners every Wednesday, an' an' Mrs Smiff, the school dinner lady says I'm, I'm a good boy for eatin' orl mine, an' an' 'er give me another 'elpin's yesterday, like she does every week now," he disclosed in a repetitive pattern, to emphasize to both me and his mother, all in a burst and a single breath!

She turned on him in her embarrassment, her face like thunder. He received a clout round the ear from his mother for... "Tellin' the doctor fibs an wastin' the doctor's time testin' and torkin',"... although I actually never said a word, and he was dragged out of the room, by his hair this time, and with a very big push.

Bang went the surgery door. Off they went down the corridor.

Beeturia[(40)] was the answer.

Sometimes it is not the doctor but the parents who lack the rapport.

124

References and Author's comment:

39. Haematuria. *Davidson's Essentials of Medicine.* 2009. Churchill Livingstone:
Haematuria is the condition where blood is found in the urine. It can be visible to the naked eye i.e. macroscopic haematuria, or invisible to the naked eye i.e. microscopic haematuria. It can be painful or painless, and bleeding can arise from anywhere in the urinary tract, from the kidney itself, or from the ureter, the tube from the kidney to the bladder, from the bladder where urine is stored, and from the urethra, the tube out to the exterior.

Causes are multiple. Congenital malformations from birth in the tract can cause bleeding, and bleeding can be due to trauma and accident. Tumours, commonly in later life also can often cause bleeding, and oddly 10% of such tumours of the urinary tract that arise in the bladder are of the so-called "Transitional Cell" type, very similar to a transitional cell tumour found in the nose, a condition that also presents with (nose) bleeding, known as epistaxis.

However, by far the commonest cause seen both in general and hospital practice is urinary tract infection, usually of the ascending type, originating from the exterior.

40. Beeturia. Food Idiosyncrasies. S.C. Mitchell. Drug Metabolism and Disposition. Vol. 29. April 2001:
Beeturia. Wikipedia. The free encyclopedia:
Beeturia is the condition caused by the eating of beetroot containing the pigment betanin, or foods with a similar pigment, when pink or red urine, and sometimes even discoloured faeces, are passed by some folk. Such individuals are unable to break down the pigment in the gut or the colon, and this condition affects approximately 14% of all humans.

It also depends on the type of beetroot eaten as some varieties contain twice as much pigment as others.

Other edible foodstuffs can be similarly excreted in the

urine with abnormal effect. Asparagus excretion in some folk supposedly causes a very malodorous urine that smells like rotten cabbage!

13. Sex 'n…

The swinging sixties were supposedly all "sex and drugs and rock and roll"[41].

I don't know where I was. I never saw any of the drugs. I saw plenty of the others.

Sex and sexual dysfunction was supposedly never a problem in grey post-war Britain, as were other conditions now, such as depression or obesity. Well, it appeared that way in the Black Country. If you did have a problem with any of these, you just put up with it and dealt with it yourself. One didn't go to the doctor. In the 1970s these attitudes began to change.

I was brought up in the backstreets of Dudley. Everybody had a gasworks at the bottom of their garden. I was "streetwise" by the age of 10 years. I knew of "sex" by the time I finished junior school at the age of 11 years, the practical side that is. The theory came later. (Yes, I got those in the correct order!) I spent much of my teens and student days "expanding" on them both. After qualification, at "Jimmy's", St James' Hospital in Leeds, then the biggest general hospital in Europe, we were 24 preregistration junior male doctors. There were 1,500 nurses, as well as lady doctors! At mess parties we were overwhelmed, annihilated. The girls had to dance with female partners, the men were so outnumbered. I then spent another 8 years in postgraduate hospital training, furthering my education of the subject. I attended various hospital Nurses Homes or Halls of Residence where I was physically aided in my quest by very obliging young ladies.

This was normality for a young male doctor at that time, when unlike today, only few graduates were married.

When I arrived in general practice the subject of psychosexual medicine had barely been mentioned in my medical school curriculum, and with my self-education I didn't need it. There was nothing I did not know or had not heard about, sex.

Or so I thought. I quickly discovered the inadequacy of my "training".

Mrs Woodcock opened my eyes. She was a dark-haired petite Scotswoman who came to my clinic one morning shortly after my arrival in the practice. She was married, I knew, to an ex-school colleague of mine. His unthinking parents had incredibly managed to give him the name Norbert! Well, I say! Guess his school nickname? A real wimp he was, 2 years below me at school. He only enjoyed art drawing and chess, the so-called strategy board game, all non-touch, non-violent recreations. Never anything very physical. How he ever managed to marry such a delightful woman I could not understand, and they had four children already when I caught up with them, both still their 20s.

She was complaining of abdominal pain, bellyache. She had been to see my partner already some fortnight previously and on taking a history alone he had prescribed a simple antacid remedy. She was no better.

How to approach this? In a woman of her age enquire first as to her bowel habit.

"Are your bowels normal, for you, Mrs Woodcock?" I thus enquired.

Now this is not a leading question. "Normal" bowel habit is what is "normal" for you, you personally. Everybody is different. For some, normality is once a week. I have had a patient respond to this question with… "Regular as clockwork Doctor, every month!"

Mrs Woodcock, however, said that she had had no problems from this point of view. I followed on further then questioning her "waterworks", i.e. any problems with passing urine, micturition, then her monthly periods, her menses, etc.

All was normal, to her. A physical examination was required.

"Please, jump on the couch Mrs Woodcock," I said, and she quickly complied.

There was no abnormality to find on abdominal examination but as she got off from the couch she looked sad and worried. She sat down slowly, with a tear in her eye.

Approach her carefully I thought, there's more than just a simple physical problem here.

"Why, what's the real problem then Mrs Woodcock?" I quietly requested, hopefully in a sympathetic voice.

"Well, you see it's my husband Doctor. He doesn't love me any more," was her somewhat languorous reply.

A pause then before the next question.

"What makes you think that?" I said.

"Well, you see Doctor it's like this. He doesn't make love to me as much as he used to," was her sad reply, continuing openly with, "We don't do it, you know, make love, as often as we used to," she disclosed.

"Ooooh?" I replied, as a sort of query while thinking. Fairly obvious what my next question was to be to this, but she gave the answer herself before I could ask.

"We only do it, 4 or 5 times a day now," she completed, quite unabashed.

A bigger pause here, before the next even more obvious question then.

"Why, errr, how many times a day did you used to do it before?" I questioned with some apprehension.

"Oh, perhaps 8 or 10 times a day in the past you know, Doctor," she explained, with an air of normality, normality to her that was!

"8 or 10 times per day?" I queried again, a little bemused. "Errr... 8 or 10 times per day? How did you find the time?"

"Oh, you know Doctor, well normally in the evening and at night, like all folks, but then he used to come home to his dinner, as well," she replied, as if that answered my question.

I was astounded. My old mate. (He'd suddenly become one.) What a bloke. What a performer. He kept alive our school ideal of elitism in a funny way. He rose in my estimation. I had been so wrong. Lunch time conjugal relationships.

It was difficult to maintain a professional face. Indeed, I had difficulty speaking. She was so deadpan, flat, and open, to reveal this to me. Could she enlarge?

"Tell me, Mrs Woodcock, did you do this, every day? Every day of the week?" I asked, thinking that they couldn't keep such performance up long term, so to speak, or so I thought.

"Oh no, not every day you know Doctor," she replied with respect.

Yes. Of course. No one could do it that often, and long term, I thought.

But then she added… "No. No. Not every day. Naturally we did it more when we had the time, like weekends and 'olidays you know," was her final somewhat incredulous response!

I was taken aback, speechless. I had to retain an air of acceptance, normality to her, but it was difficult. Was it me, or was it them who were normal? But then doubts began to arise in my mind. Poor chap, was he well? With all this exertion and ejaculation he was probably exhausted, maybe dehydrated from loss of bodily fluids and such. He could have electrolyte disturbance in his blood, protein deficiency or other problems. I had to offer her a reply, reassure her, whilst somehow get to see him. I pondered what to do.

OK, I promised I would speak to him. We would have a "man-to-man chat, all in confidence, of course," and I would come back to her and speak again.

At this, she nodded in agreement, and smiled, and went off looking a little brighter. I was still perturbed though. It was becoming obvious to me that my sexual education was inadequate for my current practice. However, at this time there was little I could do to expand on my knowledge before the next problem arose.

Mrs Dipper was a big woman, in every sense of the word. Her voluminous bosoms were matched by her very blond-blue hair, and her full voice, and her often somewhat nebulous illnesses. I soon became a little wary whenever she presented. Mr Dipper on the other hand was a little chap, dark-haired, and somewhat inappropriately named by his parents. Now if you think that naming your offspring after the site of their conception is a thing of modern times viz. "The Beckham's" in 1999[42] then you are incorrect. This was a Black Country concept first initiated by Mr and Mrs Dipper senior, after their honeymoon at Blackpool in the late 1940s when they thought giving their son the Christian names "Barrington, Ivor, George" was very appropriate as they had had such a good time on their honeymoon at the Pleasure Beach, Blackpool[43] where they had many pleasurable rides of various sorts. Anyway, the resultant B.I.G. Dipper was not a large fellow in any way when he grew up, although his presentation in the 1980s in my surgery was very big and dramatic indeed.

What the ' was going on?

"Gerrin, gerrin," I heard a shout in the corridor outside during one evening surgery. Then crash, and a bang, and the consultation room door burst open, followed by Mr Dipper who flew into the room. The source of his flight quickly became apparent as it appeared to have been precipitated by a kick from his wife's foot up his backside!

"Si' down, si' down," she snarled at him, and pushed him into the examination chair at the side of my desk.

I needed to intercede here, she appeared to be about to assault him.

He cowered in the chair, looking even smaller than normal.

"Why what's the problem Mrs Dipper?" I commenced. I thought it diplomatic to address the question to her.

"It's 'im. It's 'im Doctor. You need to give 'im something. He needs treatment, the dirty little sod," she cried, smacking him round the earhole as she did so. Smack!

"Why, what's the problem Mrs Dipper?" I asked again, repeating my question. She was going to injure him soon it appeared if I didn't stop this.

"Well you know I work at school meals Doctor?" she answered.

"No, I didn't," I said.

"Well I do," she said.

"And you know it was one of those new teachers' training days today Doctor?" she said.

"No, I didn't," I said.

"Well it was. It was," she said, repeating herself, as if to emphasize the point.

"I came home early, you know, and 'is car was in the drive. Now, that's unusual I thought, so I let myself in at the back door, not the front as normal. I went in the 'ouse and I quietly took my shoes off. They were wet. It's been raining all, afternoon you know?"

"Has it? I didn't know." I said.

"Yes it has. It has. Well, I took me shoes off and went upstairs. I could hear 'im, a noise in the back bedroom, and guess what I found?" she demanded.

"I don't know. I don't know," I replied frustratingly. I had started to repeat myself, like she did.

"Well there 'e was, on the bed, on the bed you know. We have one of those new video cassette players, and there 'e was, 'e was, watching one a them blue movies, it was, and he was y' know, y' know?" her voice faded away and she nodded to me questioningly, nod, nod, wink, wink. I was supposed to respond.

"What?" I queried.

"He was. He was errr, errr…" she couldn't get the words out. She paused, unusual for her. Suddenly it came out with a gush…

"Masticating[44] he was Doctor. Masticating!" she cried out.

I didn't dare tell her of the confusion of words here, but I fully grasped the gist of what she meant. She then went on to further enlarge her story, becoming quite red in the face and by now the amplitude of her story was such that the whole thing was becoming very noisy.

"Well I wouldn't have minded that, I suppose Doctor, but

what really upset me, what really upset me," she said emphasizing the word "really", "was 'is get-up Doctor," she followed with.

"Why what do you mean Mrs Dipper?" I followed with another query. I was a little lost with all this. I hadn't got the full story yet, it appeared, "get-up" was the Black Country expression for clothing, attire, or dress, I far as I understood.

"Well, well 'e was naked, naked 'e was Doctor, except for wearing my black stockings and suspenders, and my best new black bra! My best bra! He never takes any bloody notice of them normally when I wear 'em," she added, swearing with disgust in her voice.

"You dirty, dirty little sod," she concluded with, as Mr Dipper got another clout round the ear. Smack!

I was thus immediately reminded further of my inexperience in such matters by this scenario. It was all so very odd. Now 30 years ago the terms "cross-dresser" or "transsexual" had not been heard of or invented, had they, at this time?

All I could do was to perform my first duty of service as the doctor, to pour oil on troubled waters, calm the situation, and offer explanation later.

My training had taught me to first deal with the "offended", who needed calming, offer sympathy and reassurance. The "offender" I didn't know what to do with, but I could deal with later.

I told her to sit down and him to stand up. I took her, Mrs Dipper's blood pressure, which diverted her attention, and it was quite naturally elevated as expected. I gave her a simple prescription for some night sedation to help her sleep, and possibly avoid further trauma to Mr Dipper. I gave him a prescription for an "active treatment", for both of them really, as they both needed something to be seen to be done. I wrote him a script for "Valium[(45)] 5 milligram tablets, take 2 three times daily, when required". These I instructed were "to act as a relaxant should he get unusual sexual urges again".

I realized that it would have little or no effect on his future behaviour, but it did give me time to think what to do further, and I arranged a follow-up appointment. She calmed down somewhat, and just grimaced at him. They both crept out. I felt almost worn out as they exited the room.

Such cases as these caused me to realize that when patients presented with sexual problems, be they acute or chronic, with or without an emotional content, the first and best thing that I could do was to calm the situation. A solution often arrived at a later date. With reflection one learns by experience.

All this stood me in good stead when later in the 1990s I first met Christeen and Sid. They lived at a local Cheshire Home[46] where I had recently become the responsible medical officer. Problems here tended to be more complex. Christeen and Sid's problem was a good example of such complexity.

Miss Christeen Taupe (very appropriate description) was a miserable little person, and understandably so. She was born with congenital dislocation of her hip which was never corrected in childhood and as a result she could only stand for a short while unaided, before her hip came "out again". She was short in stature, some 4-foot-nothing tall, and because of lack of exercise she became considerably overweight. She was emotionally difficult to manage at home in her one parent family and as one of the "Young Chronic Disabled" she became a resident in St Anthony's Cheshire Home in her early 20s. She was dissatisfied with her lot and her life. She was surly and unruly to her carers and nurses. She could be short-tempered and even abusive at times.

Sid, was different. He was from a working-class family background. He left school aged 16 years and became a bricklayer. He married at a young age and by the time he was 25 years of age he had four children. He smoked 60 cigarettes and drank 8 pints of local Wolverhampton "Bank's Brewery" bitter beer every day. By the time he was 35 years of age and now with six children, he regularly beat his wife when he came home from work late, under the influence of "the booze". He paid little attention to, or was not involved with, any of his children's upbringing. He never saw them grow up. By the time he was 45 years of age he was hypertensive, and he had his first major stroke. He had a permanent hemiparesis i.e. became paralysed down one side of his body, and he had also a resultant expressive dysphasia, an extremely frustrating condition whereby he understood and comprehended conversation but could not initiate a reply. He knew what he wanted to say but could not get the words out. He could not be managed at home after hospital discharge, even though he learned to walk short distances, and his wife, totally disillusioned with him, eventually divorced him and she moved away. In the mid 1990s St Anthony's Cheshire Home was starting to take on general nursing care of such patients and Sid arrived. He was one of the younger male patients. Christeen, who knew all the ropes of the home, quickly took him under her wing.

On my Monday morning round I was surprised one day when Nurse Heather, the superb charge nurse, let me know that Christeen and Sid had decided to get married. The whole place was excited. They had not had an inpatient wedding for years. However, there was a problem and they, the nursing staff, had laid on "a display" in Sid's bedroom after my ward round to ask for my advice and opinion. No further information was forthcoming, I was intrigued. So after I had seen all the other patients then that day I was led by Nurses Heather and her assistant Diane, to Sid's room where all had been made ready and Christeen and Sid were in place. She was seated leaning forwards in her wheelchair with the sling from the ceiling-mounted monorail under her behind. Sid was lying exposed on two beds pushed together, clothed just in his pyjama bottoms.

"Go on Christeen, show the doctor what you want his advice about," urged the nurses together… So then, off she went…

Buzz, then clunk, went the motor of the monorail with the controller in Christeen's hand as she was hoisted into the air leaning forward on her stomach with arms outstretched, the sling now around her abdomen, a bit like a flying fairy elephant, she herself operating all the electronic machinery.

Buzz, she slowly went across the room over the bed.

Buzz, then clunk, she slowly lowered herself, still arms and legs spreadeagle-like, down over Sid, and came to a halt.

Buzz, clunk, she slowly lifted herself up.

Buzz, clunk, down again she went. Buzz, clunk. Buzz, clunk.

I got the meaning of the demonstration. I turned to the nurses behind me, who were standing, hands over their mouths, silencing their convulsions of laughter.

I looked at Sid. He wasn't laughing. He was taking the demo very seriously. His face was red, going blue. The veins in his neck began to stick out and that wasn't all. An elephant's trunk was coming up under his pyjamas. He was getting very excited.

"Whoa, whoa. Slow down, slow down a bit," I called out to Christeen.

"But we want to know if we can make babies this way Doctor, me and 'im, and anyway, it's only got one speed," she called back as she zoomed up and down through the air. She was liking this I could see.

Buzz, clunk. Buzz, clunk, she carried on.

Babies, I thought. It'll take him a fortnight to ejaculate doing it this way.

"Christeen, nurses, stop and check his blood pressure. Quick. He's going to have another stroke doing this," I ordered as Sid began to look exhausted. It all looked very dangerous to me.

The whole process came to a sudden halt at this and Christeen, who I suspect had gotten a little aroused herself, despite the audience, sulked off in her wheelchair, and the nurses rescued (resuscitated?) Sid.

The nurses were catatonic with subdued laughter, but they assured me that they had been pressurized into staging the demonstration. I left having no immediate answer to the problem.

Pleasingly though, like the adventures of my "retards", I recollect now that all the aforementioned cases came to unusual and happy conclusions.

I met up with "Nobby" Woodcock who explained his dilemma. He loved his wife but he had difficulty coping with her sexual appetite, and he didn't want any more children. His new job in Nottingham meant that he did not come home for "lunch time recreation" now, which helped, and by a method of subterfuge between us both, I prescribed a placebo tablet to take for his supposed "borderline hypertension", his raised blood pressure, that he hadn't got but was in danger of developing, and we explained to his wife that because of this, he had to avoid heavy physical exercise and reduce his sexual activity. It seemed to work.

They lived very happily ever after, for many years, and they didn't have any more children.

The Dipper's found their own solution to their problems, not me.

They went off to a new clinic in Birmingham run by a Dr Martin Cole[47], a "sexologist", a new speciality word to me, at The Institute for Sex Education and Research, who obviously did them both a world of good. I never knew what he advised or counselled but I later saw them happily shopping together in Sainsbury's, actually arm in arm. (The reader will have to consider the reference and use one's own discretion to infer the solution here.)

Christeen and Sid did get married and prior to this I was able to obtain help with their problem.

By the 1990s the NHS, had invented a new speciality, "Psychosexual Medicine" available to all, by NHS referral, to see specialist advisors and councillors. These services also became available for the physically disabled, such as Christeen and Sid, who I duly referred for opinion and advice.

Their wedding went ahead as planned and all the patients and staff in the home attended the church. Sometime later they left the Cheshire Home to live (hopefully) in happy marital bliss together ever after.

I don't think they used the monorail system again.

References and Author's comment:

41. *Sex and Drugs and Rock 'n' Roll. The Life of Ian Dury.* Richard Balls. 2000. Omnibus Press:

Sex, drugs and rock and roll is often mentioned or quoted by contemporary figures such as the Rolling Stone guitarist Keith Richards in his autobiography in 2010, and others, but the phrase itself originated in 1977 as a "Punk Anthem" written by singer-songwriter, Ian Dury (12/05/1942-27/03/2000). The song was written in his London flat nicknamed "Catshit Mansions" where he squatted, that overlooked The Oval cricket ground, and it was misinterpreted as a song about excess, when he intended it to suggest that there was more to life than simple existence.

It was banned initially by the BBC.

Despite physical disability due to poliomyelitis at the age of 7 years, he was a prolific lyricist. His many other works involved poetry, wordplay, and an acute observation of everyday British daily life. He developed colorectal cancer in 1996 and despite a partial recovery, he died 6 weeks after his last performance at the London Palladium. Knowing of the terminal diagnosis of his disorder, prior to his death, he married his sculptor partner, Sophy Tilson with whom he had two children.

42. *My Side (autobiography)*. David Beckham. 2002. Harper Collins Willow.

www.davidbeckham.com:

www.victoriabeckham.com:

David Robert Joseph Beckham (02/05/1975) footballer, and Victoria Caroline Beckham née Adams (17/04/1974) singer, (note: she is the elder) were married on 04/07/1999. Both are now also known worldwide as fashion designers and style gurus. Their wedding was attended by their elder son, Brooklyn Joseph Beckham (04/03/1999) whose first name it is attributed to his place of conception, although it should be noted that there are a number of "Brooklyns" within the geographical boundaries of the United States of America.

43. Blackpool Pleasure Beach – History Timeline. Roller Coaster Grotto Worldwide database of theme parks and roller coasters. www.coastergrotto.com/:

The Big Dipper (Pleasure Beach Blackpool). Wikipedia, the free encyclopedia:

The Big Dipper is a roller coaster at Blackpool Pleasure Beach originally built out of wood, and opened in 1923 at a cost of £25,000. It was followed by the Little Dipper, built in 1934, and later renamed the Zipper Dipper. The Big Dipper was upgraded in 1936, but the structure remained generally unaltered for many years until closed following an accident in 2009 when trains collided. It was reopened in 2010 after a £500,000 refit, being reconstructed sympathetically to the original design.

The Big Dipper is also a name given from time immemorial to "the Plough", an asterism of seven stars in the night sky constellation of Ursa Major.

44. Mastication. *The Oxford Dictionary*. F.G. and H.W. Fowler. 1988. Oxford University Press:

Mastication is the act of chewing, or biting and/or the grinding of teeth.

I suspect that this was not the act mentioned by Mrs Dipper.

45. Diazepam (British trade name: Valium). *British National Formulary*. No.64 edition. 2012. GGP Media GmbH:

Diazepam is one of the benzodiazepine family of drugs first introduced by the Croatian, Dr Leo Sternbach, employed by Hoffmann-La Roche in 1963 in New Jersey. It was intended as a replacement for barbiturate drugs which were much more sedating and had an addictive effect. It was marketed as a breakthrough drug for the treatment of anxiety states and stress-related illnesses.

It is now used for many other medical conditions such as an anticonvulsant for major seizures (replacing paraldehyde. See chapter 9). It is used widely in minor surgery for pre and post-operative sedation in e.g. endoscopic procedures, and it has many other uses such as a muscle relaxant etc.

Despite it quickly becoming evident after introduction that it had interactions with other drugs and marked dependence inducing properties it became widely overprescribed and it was purportedly the top selling pharmaceutical agent in the world from 1969 to 1982. It was responsible for Hoffmann-La Roche becoming a pharmaceutical giant, e.g. in 1978 selling 2.3 billion tablets of the drug.

(Yes "billion" is correct.) Its use in the UK has now been markedly curtailed and it should at all times be used only for short-term administration.

Like other dependence-inducing drugs this is easy to say, but at "the coalface", the patient-doctor interface, this is not always easy to do. I have been physically threatened on several occasions by various, even well-educated patients, when refusing to dispense repeat prescriptions of this drug.

46. *The Biography of Leonard Cheshire.* Richard Morris. 2000. London Viking. Leonard Cheshire Disability. www.lcdisability. org/:

The Leonard Cheshire Disability charity foundation was set up in 1948 by Geoffrey Leonard Cheshire (07/09/1917-31/071992), later Baron Cheshire of Woodhall.

Her Majesty, Queen Elizabeth II, remains the patron of the charity.

Of the 32 airmen awarded the nation's highest honour, the Victoria Cross, Leonard Cheshire was the only one to obtain the award for a sustained period of outstanding valour rather than a single act, taking part in over 100 airborne missions.

He was the official British observer in the B-29 bomber "Big Stink" at the dropping of the atomic bomb on Nagasaki, and after the war, disillusioned by "the bomb" and the war, he became aware of the nursing problems of care for ex-colleagues, himself learning the nursing duties required to care for such patients.

He dedicated the rest of his life to supporting disabled people and he set up the charitable organization which now includes multiple nursing homes and other care services nationwide.

The foundation was originally created for the young chronic sick and disabled people, providing residential care as well as educational and employment programmes, but in the 1990s, for financial and other reasons, some of the charity homes started to accept a wider spectrum of disorders including the elderly and other patients discharged from hospital requiring care and long-term accommodation.

He obtained a life peerage in 1991 and he and his second wife, Baroness Sue Ryder, were one of the few couples to both hold such titles awarded in their own right.

He died the following year suffering with exemplary and spiritual fortitude from the effects of motor neurone disease.

Indeed, a "Great Briton", in a BBC poll in 2002 Leonard Cheshire was included in the "100 Greatest Britons in History".

47. Martin Cole (sexologist). Wikipedia. The free encyclopedia:
    The British Pregnancy Advisory Service. Stratford on Avon. CV3 9BF. www.bpas.org/:

Martin John Cole (1931) BSc PhD (in botany and plant genetics!) was widely known in the Midlands as "Sex King Cole" in the 1970s having set up the Institute for Sex Education and Research, in Birmingham. His controversial work involved the use of surrogate partners for patients with sexual difficulties, erectile dysfunction etc. He attracted widespread condemnation from MPs and others, and in 1971 after producing an explicit sex education film entitled "Growing Up" for schools, he was all at one time uniquely criticized by both Mrs Mary Whitehouse, Lord Longford and Mrs Margaret Thatcher simultaneously.

He was a pioneer for abortion law reform and he became chairman of the Birmingham Pregnancy Advisory Service on the day when the 1967 Abortion Act came into force. At this time Birmingham and Black Country patients wishing abortion had to travel to London for termination. This service has now been expanded and renamed the British Pregnancy Advisory Service with over 40 branches nationwide, also advising on emergency contraception, vasectomy and sterilization and related conditions.

14. Sex 'n' drugs

Everybody at uni knew everything about "drugs", i.e. narcotics. We were taught quite a bit at medical school of the dangers, of dependence, of addiction, and how this type of drug affected your "psyche" but not your "soma".

Although I had heard of "performance-enhancing drugs", the description had hidden meanings, sexual performance was almost never mentioned, and I discovered that I knew little or nothing about this type of drug or the subject when I first entered general practice.

Up to the 1970s other than hormonal-type drugs, there was nothing available to aid one's sexual activity, but about this time things began to change.

I discovered that as well as athletic performance, drugs could also affect (help?) your sex life.

Leading up to the 2012 London Olympics much publicity was made of athletes using drugs to aid their athletic performance, and for more than 10 years prior to this their use was implicated in other major events such as the scandalous use by cyclists in the Tour de France and other events. However, one should note that the drug Stanozolol[48] was used by Ben Johnson when he was sensationally was stripped of his 100 metre title as far back as the 1988 Olympics, when he tested positive for this drug after the gold medal ceremony.

Well, that's nothing. I first saw such drugs used many years before all this, not well known I realize, but by Mrs Sepia

Small aged 52 years in 1978, a tiny and wiry little woman of Wolverhampton. She had the indrawn skin and lined face of the masochistic exerciser, but she was not an athlete!

Sandy, her husband, came to my surgery one day. He had a bad back and when I examined him I suspected it was "mechanical" in type, secondary to heavy lifting in his manual job. I noticed though, certain bruises on his arms and back at this examination and I enquired as to their causation.

"Oh, it's just me and the wife gamin' about, Doctor," he explained, with a bit of a grin. "Mind yo, her doe arf like it, y' know, a lot these days yo know," he added, sort of implying that I should understand what he meant by "gaming about" and what "it" should be.

Sexual overtones here, I thought?

"How is she doing then?" I questioned with a frown as she had been quite unwell the previous time I had seen her, I remembered.

"Well, 'er's great these days Doctor, since yo gid her them tablets and 'er's put weight on, 'er feels well and 'er 'ands and feet are much better y' know. In fact 'er knocks me about these days 'er's getting' so well, I tell yo 'er's getting' arms bigger than me, and I'm a brickie," he exclaimed.

I pricked my ears up at this, him a bricklayer, it seemed a little odd that she could knock him about. I sent him on his way with the appropriate treatment, and I thought I ought to review Mrs Small as a precaution. I sent her an appointment to see me.

I should explain here, sometime previously Mrs Small, a lovely lady, presented with the worst case of chilblains[49] that I have still ever seen. So bad, they were, that the ends of her fingers were ulcerating and shrivelling up, navy blue, almost gangrenous. Her toes were likewise affected. She was in constant pain and discomfort. I had tried all the usual drugs to no avail, and thus I referred her to a local consultant physician colleague for advice. He saw her, and concurred with my diagnosis and suggested that I put her on to "Stromba", which at that time was in the current "recommended drug bible", the BNF, so I duly did so in accordance with his instructions, arranging precautionary follow-up as I was not familiar with this drug at that time. At Mr Small's later disclosure I then looked up in more detail the pharmacology of this drug, so that I was well informed when she turned up for her review appointment. I was somewhat perturbed as to what I learned.

I was even more perturbed when she came to the surgery... What the'!

A new person walked in. She was not small now. She had put on more than 2 stones in weight since I last saw her, and had a gruff masculine-type voice and a heavy stance and a swagger. She had become big. She had all the side effects of Stromba, which I had discovered contained Stanozolol, a drug that also caused increased virilization, the "gaming about" described by her husband, and she had increased sexual activity and libido, the "it", of Mr Small's conversation. She had increased muscle bulk and more body hair. She had lost her dainty femininity and petiteness. She was becoming male, masculinization!

I was alarmed and sent her back right away to my consultant colleague to review her problem. Pleasingly he started her on an alternative, but complex, vitamin D injection regime that continued to hold her chilblains in check. She gradually recovered her femininity and previous personality. Her chilblains resolved.

But I learned from Mrs Small's case, that drug effects on sexual behaviour, are not always those that are expected or desired.

Over the years following all this I began to notice that due to increased public awareness and more openness, more and more patients of both sexes began to request advice from me, their GP, with sexual problems, something unheard of in my early practice years.

Erectile dysfunction in particular, in men, became a common presenting problem, even in my reserved and somewhat prudish Black Country menfolk.

Gradually becoming aware of the unwanted side effects of drugs used to treat such sexual disorders over years of clinical practice, it was with some trepidation then in 1988 that I received the introduction of Viagra[50], the first widely used nonhormonal drug treatment for such complaints. It was to be taken orally specifically for the enhancement of sexual performance.

With reflection now it is easy to remember the case of Mr Jasper, my first patient given this drug. He was and still is a real brick. A hard-working Black Country man who wouldn't dream of disclosing of a sexual complaint, unless his life was becoming a total misery.

I knew him well. He had a long-term problem, a shaking tremor of his hands, not disabling, but quite a serious complaint in his job as a roofer, and he had been on beta-blocker drugs[51] for this problem for many years. He attended surgery one day and swore blind that his sexual performance had fallen off markedly the day that I started him on these drugs, and that his long-suffering wife was now complaining bitterly because of this, so he purported.

Odd, I thought, he'd been on these drugs for a long time, and only now after several years has he seen fit to disclose this problem. However, this effect on sexual performance is a documented side effect of beta-blocker drugs, so he was to be believed.

"Can you please help me Doctor?" he queried. "My quality in the bedroom is so bad it's affecting the wife," he disclosed. "It all started with them tablets ar tek for me tremors, and it's gerrin much worse lately. My wife's in that menopause thing, y' know, and that doe 'elp," he explained.

He was, as I knew, a very genuine chap who had put up with his tremors for years until they started to disturb and endanger his employment. He must have been pretty upset now to complain of this additional problem.

Just before Millennium Day in 1999 then, I commenced him on Viagra. A new start to the new century, I thought, somewhat guardedly. I explained to him what the new drug was, how that it might help and I explained to him how to use the tablets. He was not to overdose. He was to use them sparingly, only twice or thrice per week, and he was to report to me any upset or side effects.

He agreed, "OK Doctor, I'll gi' 'em a try," and off he went, albeit a little questioningly.

I was surprised when a month later Mr Jasper's wife came in to see me. I was with experience now, wary at her appearance. Did it have any connection to my new prescribing?

"Doctor I've come to have a word about them new tablets you gave my husband last month," she said.

My heart sank. Not another Mrs Small type of thing, I hoped.

"Yes I've come to thank you, very much," she added, to my great relief.

Phew, this could be interesting, I thought, feeling more relaxed.

"Yes Doctor, with them tablets he's a new man in every way. He can perform in the bedroom now, even better than when we was kids," she stated. "But it's not the sex Doctor. The real improvement is in him, mentally," she explained. "He was gettin' to be very difficult, but," she paused, "he's now not so shirty and rat-arsed, sorry for swearing Doctor, but he is a delight to live with. He feels more of a man and he has changed with the children, he's more pleasant, and he's even polite t' the neighbours, and our social life all round is so much better. Please can I have a repeat prescription for him to continue, if that's alright, of course?" she politely added with a broad smile on her face.

Now, "rat-arsed" is not in Ed Conduit's book of Black Country phrases mentioned in the prologue of this book, but I got her meaning. I was delighted to concur with her request.

This was my very first such script given for a nonhormonal drug for sexual dysfunction, and I was uncertain as to whether or not it would be effective in the long term. I had seen so-called "wonder drugs" many times in the past. I hoped for no disastrous side effects, and I hoped that they would not become used in a recreational type of way, in a perhaps frivolous fashion.

On looking back now, after more than 10 years of such

prescribing, I am pleased to disclose that my fears and suspicions have resolved.

Such drugs do work and appear safe with few side effects if taken as prescribed, and although in my opinion lifestyle changes to behaviour still offer most help to those with sexual problems, many of my patients report improvement to their lives, in the broadest sense of meaning, with such simple oral drug therapy.

It would appear that these drugs are safe and are not being abused and overused as I originally thought, I am pleased to recall.

References and Author's comment:

48. Anabolic steroids. *British National Formulary*. No. 64. Edition. 2012 GGP Media GmbH:

Stanozolol (British trade name: Stromba or Winstrol), www.musclefuture.com/:

Stanozolol is a synthetic anabolic steroid drug developed by Winthrop Laboratories in 1962. Like all anabolic steroids, administration improves muscle mass and peripheral blood vessel circulation, without evidence of fat reduction.

It has had several medical uses in the past being used to treat intractable anaemias, angioedema (i.e. severe nettle rash) syndrome and severe chilblains. Its use for osteoporosis in women is no longer advocated and its use as a body builder or tonic is now totally unjustified.

It is known to have many unwanted side effects including affecting liver function and cholesterol metabolism causing a lowering of so called "good cholesterol",

high-density lipoprotien (HDL), and an elevation of "bad cholesterol",

low-density lipoprotein(LDL), within the body.

Nevertheless, anabolic steroids have been used by athletes for performance-enhancing properties for many years now, and for the cosmetic effect of increased tanning to sunlight, and although Stanozolol itself is a banned substance for many sports, it is still easily available for purchase on the Internet and elsewhere.

Anabolic steroids, have also been used in animals, to falsely stimulate dietary intake and growth, and their supposed improvement when they are ill or debilitated!

49. Chilblains. *Andrews' Diseases of the Skin.* W.D. James and T.G. Berger et al. 2011. Elsevier Health Sciences:
Chilblains. www.nhs.uk/Conditions/:
Chilblains, sometimes known as pernio, is a medical condition found in individuals with an undue sensitivity to cold. This causes damage to the small peripheral blood vessels (capillaries) with resultant red painful itchy lesions not only on the hands, but also the feet and other extremities such as the nose or ears. When severe and intractable it can cause extreme pain, blistering and ulceration. It tends to be seasonal, occurring in susceptible individuals on a recurrent basis in wintertime. The condition can also be confused with other medical conditions such as frostbite. It is very similar to a relatively minor, yet exquisitely painful nodular condition of the ear lobes, commonly seen in winter ENT hospital clinics, that is worsened by cold and local pressure such as the wearing of a tight cap or by just lying down on a pillow. This condition has the grandiose medical name of chondrodermatitis nodularis chronica helicis, difficult to spell even for doctors!

50. Sildenafil (British trade name: Viagra). *British National Formulary.* No. 64 edition. 2012. GGP Media GmbH:
Sildenafil was first synthesized in the UK by the drug company Pfizer in the 1990s. It was initially introduced as a treatment for high blood pressure (hypertension) and cardiac pain (angina) when it was noticed that it also induced marked penile erections! It was eventually marketed for this unusual side effect and it is now used worldwide for this property.

As well as improved sexual function in men it has some effect in women, apparently especially if already on antidepressants with which for some reason it has a possible female synergistic effect. It should not be taken lightly, as it has many side effects including drug interactions, and it is very much contraindicated for patients with certain cardiac disorders. It is used for a multiplicity of other problems including pulmonary hypertension, in the lungs, and altitude sickness.

Although postulated, it has not yet been proven to help other conditions such as jet lag, or athletic physical performance, but oddly, when used in water it can have a causative effect on plants. It slows down plant ripening, with effect on some flowers, some fruits, and even some vegetables. It has thus been used to increase the shelf life of flowers in this fashion, when it causes them to stand up straight for up to 1 week!

Its action in humans is not so prolonged, (thank goodness).

51. Beta-adrenoceptor blocking drugs (Beta-blockers). *British National Formulary*. Edition No. 64. 2012. GGP Media Gmbh:

This family of drugs was first synthesized by a Scotsman, Sir James Whyte Black (14/06/1924-22/03/2010) when he developed the drug propranolol, in the 1960s working for ICI Pharmaceuticals. He was also involved in the development of cimetidine (see reference no. 28). The development of beta-blockers revolutionized the treatment of many cardiac diseases, and has been recognized as one of the most important contributions to medicine of the 20th century.

Following his researches, Black, a very private man was horrified to discover in 1988 that he had been awarded the Nobel Prize in Medicine for his works, and he later went on to many other awards including a knighthood and being awarded the Order of Merit by the Queen... (There are only 24 living members of this award at any one time.)

Whilst the phrase "beta-blocker" is commonly used, few of the public know of the derivation of the term...

The human nervous system produces the chemicals adrenaline (epinephrine) and noradrenaline (norepinephrine) which in turn produce all the reactions of "flight or fight" mechanism or response. These complex responses are a remnant of our ancient prehistoric responses with combative and arousal reactions. They have acceleration effects on the heart and lungs, yet slowing effects on the digestive tract, and they cause the urinary tract bladder and bowel sphincters to close. In the central nervous system they cause the pupils to dilate, tunnel vision to develop, and shaking and many other symptoms to occur.

There are widespread receptors in the body to cause all these effects, that respond to these two chemical mediators and these are known as alpha and beta type receptors, depending on their type of action.

There are now drugs developed blocking each particular type of receptor, hence the terms alpha and beta-blockers.

Propranolol was the first synthesized beta-blocker and now there are numerous others developed having a multiplicity of cardiac and other uses. Propranolol was at one time the bestselling drug in the world.

Alpha-blocker drugs are not so commonly prescribed, but in the UK the commonest usage is in the treatment of simple prostatic overgrowth, i.e. benign prostatic hypertrophy, often called BPH.

Reactions to the adrenergic blocker drugs are also seen in other non-human species, when exposure to such drugs has even been known to cause colour changes in some types of fish!

15. Lots of rolls (of fat)

I have to admit that as well as kids, I had other favourites, i.e. "my fatties".

Obesity was not a problem when I entered general practice in 1974, because like many modern words such as "logistics" (i.e. supply and delivery) or "human resources" (i.e. personnel) the word had not been invented, or had it?

Overweight people were described as "fat", particularly in Black Country parlance, just "fat".

In the new millennium there has arisen both an epidemic of fatness, and an epidemic of classifications and measurements of fatness. The commonest measure currently used to describe obesity is the body mass index, or BMI[52], which is actually a very vague measurement for everyday usage and over the years in my experience, the "JC Classification" is much better. It expresses clearly what everyone can see anyway.

Who is the author of this classification, you may ask?

No, not the chap above in the sky, but my wife, (i.e. her initials) and please note, the female gender is usually used when describing (as she does) in this manner, but the classification applies equally to both sexes.

1. Class 1. "She has a weight problem".
   (Moderately polite form of criticism.)
   BMI about 30… i.e. fat.
2. Class 2. "If only she could see her behind in the mirror".

(Difficult, if not an impossibility I realize.)

BMI 30-40… i.e. moderate to severely overweight.

3. Class 3. "Jesus Christ!"

(Not meaning to be blasphemous. Just using the biblical name as an expression of exaggeration. It gets the meaning across.)

BMI 40 plus… i.e. very severe, possibly life-endangering, obesity.

There are numerous and complex causations for this problem and a plethora of articles have been written about the modern epidemic.

The following cases I use as illustrations are all confined to Class 3. above.

Eric, whose nickname was "Hay Rick", was a nice chap who lived alone with his mommy. Not his mother, "my Mommy", as he described her. He was 34 years of age. His father had apparently died years ago of fatty liver disease. I was not surprised. It appeared to be a familial problem.

I had tried to treat his obesity for years always to no avail, and it caused him to drive a huge American car with a column shift because when I asked why, as he explained to me one day…

"It's the only one with a single charabanc seat across the front, that I can fit me arse into Doctor."

Some years previously, soon after his 28th birthday, I had been forced to send him to Woolworth's store in Wolverhampton, where the big red weighing scales in the basement could weigh clients weighing to up 30 stones, when my surgery scales only went up to 24 stones. But as time went on, and his mommy continued to give him huge breakfasts, half a dozen sandwiches for lunch, then an evening meal that would prejudice the *Titanic* ever setting off on its maiden voyage let alone causing it to sink, even these scales became of no use. His weight went up to in excess of 30 stones. I had to find another source of weighing him.

Inspiration. The public weighbridge, just down the road in Ettingshall. I gave him 50p per month, and off he went promising to bring me back the weight chit, and he rigorously did so. Actually he had to do everything rigorously, he was so huge.

One morning my receptionist came into the consulting room, a little perturbed.

"There's a man on the phone from the weighbridge Doctor, about Eric. I don't think I can deal with this. He sounds very worried. I think you ought to speak to him yourself," she said.

Now, my receptionist at our Woodcross branch surgery at that time was my shield, a brick wall if needed, to all and sundry, and if she was worried, I should be worried. I had learned to speak to the caller at her request. I asked her to pass the call through to me then. The weighbridge operator came on the line.

"Sorry t' bother you in surgery, but shit Doctor, sorry f' swearin', but y' know that Eric bloke, y' sent t' see me t'day?" he apologized, swore, apologized, pointed out, and questioned, all in one sentence.

"Yes," I replied.

"It meks y' swear when I talk about 'im y' know. Well 'e come in, in 'is works van t'day and stopped it on the weighbridge. I didn't know that, and 'e 'ad't got out, so I weighed it with 'im in it fust. Then I had t' weigh it again after, when I found out, when 'e got out," he explained, confusingly.

"Well, shit Doctor, sorry f' swearin', guess what?" he continued with.

"What?" I replied. He seemed very worked up.

"By 'imself 'e weighed more than the bloody van 'e was in, with all 'is tools in it as well!" he exclaimed incredulously, continuing to have the usual Black Country problem with his "H"s.

"Yo'll 'ave to do somethin' with 'im Doctor. 'is bally is so big I think either 'e's gonna bost, or the weighbridge is," he finished with, explaining that his worry was that Eric's abdomen was about to burst, or that he was in danger of breaking the weighbridge, something of an exaggeration I thought. Nevertheless, I thanked him for his call, and attempted to reassure him that I would do my best when Eric eventually turned up.

Despite this I am afraid to disclose that despite all my ministrations, Eric continued to be massively obese. I tried advice, *ad nauseam.* I tried short lifestyle chats. I tried long lifestyle chats. I tried dietary advice, NHS dietician referrals and private clinic referrals etc. All to no avail. We did not have bariatric[53] surgery in those days, and Eric continued to enlarge until one day he presented in the surgery when still weighing in excess of 30 stones, he had unusually lost a little weight!

What had happened I enquired?

Well, love had entered his life. At the ripe age of 37 years, he had met his first girlfriend. I suggested that he bring her to see me sometime, which he did so, a delightful young lady, perhaps JC Class 1. or 2. but nothing like Eric, a definite Class 3., possibly a Class 3.-plus. She had clocked on to the problem… "Mommy". We quickly established a rapport, she and I, and we quickly got him off mommy's foodstuffs regime, and on to a care plan to continue him to lose weight, which he did so, and he successfully continued his progression, (all because of love?).

Shortly after this I heard the patter of tiny "Little Erics" running around as well. Bliss!

Eric's real problem was the same that many patients have with lifestyle-induced conditions. He wanted a "quick fix", a simple answer, a pill, when really he needed to change his whole lifestyle, eat less, take more exercise and do all the very obvious things that we all know instinctively about to lose weight and not get fat.

Drug therapy for obesity in the 1970s and 1980s mainly involved the use of so-called "appetite suppressant" amphetamine-like drugs [54] with psychostimulant effects, or "fill you up-like" compounds such as methylcellulose granules which just made you feel full and bloated, a little like overdosing on celery. In the 1970s into the 1980s this led to appetite suppressants being abused, when as well as being used for obesity problems they were subject to use by athletes and sports personalities as physical performance enhancement agents[55], a use often denied.

Methylcellulose in various forms is still prescribable and is in the current (2014) *British National Formulary*. It is advised for use now as a laxative!

That would also cause weight loss, somewhat artificially I suppose.

Despite all this for some reason I have found that many of my Black Country "fatty favourites" were, and still are, like Eric and his spouse, always extremely pleasant and likeable personalities. They are often quite refined, despite a rough working-class exterior, and, they are often, extremely polite and respectful types.

Beryl and Tommy were other good examples.

Beryl attended my antenatal clinic for several periods of care. Each of these resulted in a bouncing baby infant. However, on each occasion it was very difficult to ascertain that she was actually pregnant, as she was the same size when 36 weeks pregnant, as she was when not. Only by physical examination and when ultrasound scanning[56] became available, was one able to ascertain the delivery dates of her babies. Nevertheless, she had no less than four fairly normal deliveries, all infants now grown up, and who are all of somewhat similar circular outline to their mother.

Tommy, her husband, was/is similar, but worse. He was also always as high as he was wide, and had the ruddy cheeks and red nose of what I call the "happily fat" personality. He was a definite Class 3. classification, huge and circular in outline, but with a superadded problem. He was a chef. This made it a little difficult to avoid food. Like all his family, even aunts and uncles, he was big, yet he was (and still is) extremely polite, with impeccable manners, and despite my advice and treatment he has but lost only a little weight over the years.

I received an "urgent" call one day to see him at his home, oddly, from the local fire brigade. "Make sure the Doctor brings his emergency drug bag" my receptionist at Parkfields surgery was advised, and she passed this message on to me with some alacrity. By this time all my staff had been appointed by me, and they were a delightful and very dependable team. This message was passed on with a peculiar smile. Something odd was amiss here. I didn't know what the emergency was, but this family never sent for a frivolous reason. I quickly went along.

I soon found out. There was no sign of fire, but the station chief officer was waiting for me. He explained the emergency, a scenario unlike anything I had previously heard. Apparently Tommy had taken a bath, when due to his huge bulk, normally on finishing his bath as he could not get up and pull out the plug, he did so with his big toe. Unfortunately, of late as he had put on even more weight, as he did so on the day in question, the suction effect as the water escaped, sucked his behind and nether regions down into the base of the metal bath, and he became wedged and unable to move! He was both physically and emotionally embarrassed. The fire brigade were called. It was only a small bathroom and only two at a time, muscular firemen, could get into the room. They were unable to pull him out with their bare hands despite both being amateur weightlifters, and despite having been on manual handling courses, when they hadn't met anyone Tommy's size before. Accordingly, they decided to sacrifice the bath and cut him free. This was a metal bath. At any cutting attempt, heat was developed. Tommy started to cry out in dismay. As well as getting very short of breath, he was getting burns to his distal regions.

I was called thus, to supply analgesia to enable the rescue to proceed.

"Hello Doctor," Tommy cried out in a rather weak voice at my arrival. "I am so sorry to call you out like this, but I am afraid me bum [buttock] 'as got stuck, and these nice firemen blokes cor get me out without settin' fire to me goolies [testicles], I'm afraid. I really would value your 'elp, please," he exclaimed in his usual very polite manner.

Poor chap. Tommy was by then somewhat in emotional distress, but he was also becoming a little blue, around his lips. This blueness, cyanosis, indicates poor oxygenation of the blood, he was so restricted, and I determined thus that this was becoming a true emergency. As in the past then, no particular time for medical precautions other than a simple alcohol swab. A quick wipe. To an exposed part, I shot in a large dose of pethidine, a morphine-like drug, not quite so potent as morphine and not such a respiratory depressant, and he became immediately calmer.

The boys quickly cut the bath open and freed him. He fell to the floor with a huge great crash as the bath fell apart. He was quite distressed but still dopey from the effect of the pethidine, but his cyanosis resolved and his vital signs became all OK.

He had a nasty superficial burn to his "private parts" I could see though.

"That don't matter Doctor. He's alive and well. I'll look after that. Please, you have a nice cup of tea with the boys, and I'll clean all the mess up. You've all done enough, and a good job," Beryl kindly responded with.

We all sat down and Tommy joined us as the drug effects wore off, when Beryl had "kissed me better" he disclosed.

I'm not sure which bit he meant by this, but his rosy cheeks (facial) had returned!

Like many of my encounters, this story had a happy ending. The local authority housing department was contacted and it was explained what had happened. On my recommendations they very understandingly build a downstairs extension to the house, where Tommy had a walk-in bathroom and shower fitted for his future ablutions to be performed.

He never became stuck again. He and Beryl had no more children. He retired early from work, and his family are now grown up and all are delightful and polite mirror images of their parents. Tommy has lost some weight, and he remains a charming man. Whenever I see him about, he is still very grateful to me ever since that day.

References and Author's comment:

52. Obesity. *Davidson's Essentials of Medicine*. 2009. Churchill Livingstone:

Body mass index.

Wikipedia. The free encyclopedia:

Body mass index (BMI) is a numeric account of individual thickness or thinness, a complex formula of body mass based on the height and weight of an individual.

$$BMI = \frac{\text{Weight (kgs or lbs)}}{\text{Height (metres or ins)}^2} \times 703$$

It is usually estimated on a simple chart.

BMI under 18 suggests the individual is underweight (eating disorder or illness).

BMI 20 – 30 is normality.

BMI 30+ means simple obesity.

BMI 40+ is the so-called "morbid obesity" i.e. with a high risk of developing cardiovascular and/or cerebrovascular disease, diabetes etc.

BMI has practical importance in that it is used by insurance companies to assess your liability and acceptability for insurance.

It has many applications in medical practice, in particular it is used by anaesthetists to assess your risk for general anaesthesia. Refusal by anaesthetists and surgeons for non-essential surgery is common, with a BMI of 40+.

53. The National Bariatric Surgery Registry Report. The Royal College of Surgeons of England. April 2011. London WC2A 3PE. www.rcseng.ac.uk/:

Weight loss surgery. NHS Choices.

www.nhs.uk/Conditions/Weight Loss Surgery/:

Bariatric surgery is the name given to various surgical procedures to aid weight reduction. These are either (a) "malabsorption" procedures, bypassing stomach contents into the bowel, or (b) "restrictive" procedures, making the stomach smaller with gastric bands, intragastric balloons etc.

Until recently such surgery was recommended only as a

last resort for dangerous obesity with a BMI over 40, for various reasons, and they are expensive procedures, although they do avoid the later costs of the complications of massive obesity.

Current costing (2013) for a Gastric Banding operation = £5,000-8,000

Gastric Bypass operation = £9,500-15,000

The operations are also complex with complications. Whilst short-term results are impressive with patients loosing half of their excess body weight, they have to continue a rigorous restrictive diet/exercise regime in the long term post-operatively. The operations do not help the psychological symptoms of reactive depression or anxiety that such patients commonly exhibit, and demanding patients should be also be aware and advised that the long-term results on mortality i.e. the death rate, in particular for such procedures, are still unclear.

54. Amphetamines, past and present. The Oxford Journal of Psychopharmacology. 2013. Sage:

The National Centre for Biotechnology Information (U.S.) www.ncbi.nlm.nih.gov/:

The considered importance of the amphetamine (amfetamine) family of highly addictive stimulant drugs was such that they were given only 1/3 of a small page in the 1976-78 *British National Formulary*, on my arrival in general practice.

However, amphetamines were first synthesized in 1887 but they were not used widely until 1934, when introduced as "Benzedrine" a nasal inhaler used for colds and for the relief of nasal congestion. The strips inside were often chewed or put in coffee for their stimulant action, and they were regularly given to members of the armed forces of both sides in the Second World War to fight fatigue e.g. in long-distance bomber flights etc. and to boost morale. Their use became widespread. Near the end of the war, Hitler himself was known to receive daily injections of an amphetamine (Metamphetamine) a drug now known to produce unpredictability and paranoia.

Then later these drugs were given to lorry drivers in the

post-war years to aid them on long-haul deliveries etc.

Around the 1960s though it was begun to be noticed that as well as aiding fatigue, such drugs also induced subjective weight loss, presumably by speeding up metabolism.

In my early days in practice many amphetamine-like drugs were recommended for weight control, and I personally often prescribed such preparations as Tenuate Dospan (diethylpropion) and others, for some years until the profession became aware of the habituation and central nervous stimulant effects such drugs could cause. Another drug, Ponderax (Fenfluramine) was highly recommended by many consultants because of supposedly less stimulatory effect, but then had to be withdrawn as it was discovered to cause fatal pulmonary hypertension in some cases.

The prescribing of such drugs has all now been restricted and is infrequent, although they and similar drugs are still used, even in children for some disorders such as attention deficit hyperactivity disorder (ADHD), or for narcolepsy, a condition that causes intractable sudden daytime somnolence and sleep attacks.

55. A bitter pill to swallow (the career of Willie Johnson). *The Herald* (Scotland). Gaspers. 29/03/2003:

Fencamfamine (British trade name: Reactivan). www.drugbank.ca/drugs:

Reactivan, an amphetamine-like drug was initially introduced in the 1960s as an appetite suppressant drug, and was later recommended as a stimulant to improve physical performance and to aid daytime fatigue and lethargy. Only some years later was it withdrawn due to its dependence-inducing properties.

At the World Cup competition in 1978 in Argentina the Scottish footballer

William "Willie" McClure Johnston (19/12/1946-) who at that time also played for West Bromwich Albion the (almost) Black Country football club, was sent home when found to be using the drug Reactivan. He purported to having been given this by his doctor for his hay fever!

This is a little odd as despite my specialist knowledge of this medical subject and an extensive search of the literature, I have been unable to discover any recommendation for this drug to be used for this or any similar complaint!

Willie was/is quite a character. In 1980 whilst playing for Glasgow Rangers against Aberdeen, an opponent, John McMaster had to be given the "kiss of life" after Johnston stamped on his throat during the match. Willie later justified his actions and apologized by explaining that it was all a mistake. He thought McMaster was Willie Miller, another participant. He got the wrong man!

A quite brilliant footballer, as well as being remembered as one of Scotland's greatest players, he is still thought of very highly in the Black Country. In a poll in 2004 he was voted as one of West Bromwich Albion's 16 greatest players of all time.

56. Ultrasound scan. NHS Choices. www.nhs.uk/Conditions/ UltraSound:

Obituary. John Wild. The British Medical Journal. 26/10/2009. Polestar Ltd:

Ultrasound using very high frequencies (2-18 MHz) above the hearing threshold of humans is now widely used in medicine as an investigative procedure, as well as for physical therapy. It was first used in the Second World War when sonar systems were used in submarines and for navigation purposes, when it was noticed to be killing fish nearby and having a heating effect, a side effect not widely publicized.

The father of ultrasound (diagnostic sonography) was a very inventive Englishman, Dr John Julian Cuttance Wild (11/08/1914-18/09/2009), who after war service in the Royal Army Medical Corps moved to the USA and who in 1949 using an ultrasonic aircraft flight simulator produced images of living tissues, later expanding his work into cancer detection and other modalities. He received many honours for his works even being depicted on a British postage stamp in 1994.

External (investigative) sonography is now used in obstetrics to visualize the foetus in the womb using a simple handheld probe, and it is now used widely in many other specialities. It can also be used internally, via an endoscope, to examine the gullet or chest and other internal body structures.

Physical therapy (treatment) sonography utilizes an ultrasound applicator, a transducer, in direct contact with the patient's skin, alternating in compression/rarefaction waves to be absorbed by soft tissues e.g. ligaments and tendons, or scarred areas, and is widely used to aid tissue healing processes.

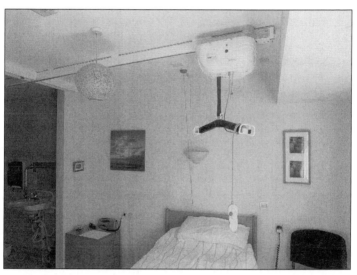

The Bed hoist at the Cheshire Home that had uses other than for what it was intended. See Chapter 13.

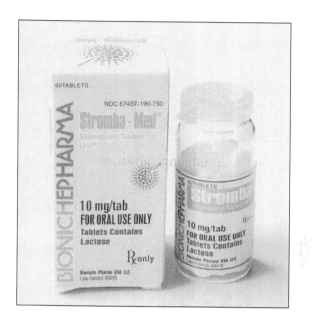

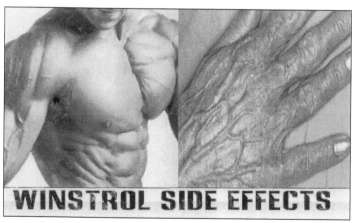

Stanozol (Trade name Stromba or Winstrol), the anabolic steroid formerly given for Chilblains, has wanted and unwanted side effects in both men and women, not always realized by the patient! See Chapter 14.

theguardian

The forgotten story of ... Willie Johnston

Sent home from Argentina '78 and escorted from the pitch at gunpoint   the silky left winger will be remembered for all the wrong reasons

Scottish international Willie Johnston is accompanied by police on his return to the UK from the World Cup finals in Argentina Photograph: PA PA/PA

Scott Murray
Tuesday 23 December 2008 14.30 GMT

No matter how great a player used to be, it seems the bad usually outweighs the good in the memory. Diego Maradona is remembered more for the Hand of God than anything specific he ever did with his feet. Eric Cantona will always be defined by that leap into the crowd at Selhurst Park, catalyst for the modern Manchester United or not. And Graeme Souness, a sublime all round midfielder, perhaps the greatest in British history, is now usually painted as the wild thug who rammed his studs into Steaua Bucharest's Iosif Rotariu's special parcel, rather than the man who delicately set up the 1978 European Cup for Liverpool.

Then there's Willie Johnston, fated to go down in history for one thing: failing a drug test while representing Scotland at the 1978 World Cup. Which is a terrible shame as it misrepresents everything about Johnston mainly because he was one of the fastest and most skilful left wingers of the era, still the only Scottish player to score twice in a European final, but also because the drugs bust, the result of an innocent misunderstanding, skews his status as a bona fide bad boy hero whose scrapes with The Man would become legion and legendary.

Johnston's career started with a bang: in only his fifth first team game for Rangers he was one of the stars in a 2-1 win over Celtic in the 1964-65 League Cup final. Immediately afterwards there were the first signs that Johnston might prove troublesome to handle. The Rangers manager, Scot Symon, had promised his team a £500-per-head bonus if they won the trophy, but Johnston later found there was only an additional £50 in his wage packet. When he approached his boss over the matter, Symon explained that "too much money can turn a boy's head". He also offered him a

Taking the appetite suppressant Reactivan "for hayfever" was not approved, especially for Willie Johnston in the 1978 World Cup in Argentina. See Chapter 15.

The "Russian" linesman Tofiq Bahramov at the 1966 World Cup Final. ?
With future Minister of Health in the background. See Chapter 23.

16. Happy days are here again

The 1980s insidiously heralded a new dawn in the Black Country, as elsewhere in the UK. The colours of life continued to change. It was becoming less black. The last Black Country coal mine closed at Baggeridge (reference no. 4) in March 1968 although other fields such as the Littleton deep mine near Cannock continued working until December in 1992. The massive steelworks complexes at Bilston and Brierley Hill closed in April 1979 and December 1982 respectively, and many foundries and industrial plants also closed. Once the largest foundry in Western Europe, F.H. Lloyds of Darleston closed in the 1980s.

As a result of all this the climate changed. With the loss of the industrial haze, one could climb the hills at the Wren's Nest near Dudley, or Beacon Hill near Sedgley, and facing east see clearly right across the Midland plane to the hills of Barr Beacon on the far side of Walsall near Birmingham. My patients could now put their white washing out to dry on weekdays rather than just Sundays, the atmosphere was so much cleaner.

The health of the patients changed. No longer after a bank holiday was the morning surgery crowded with men wanting a sick note as they could not face up to the return to heavy dreary manual work. No longer did the folk present with a chronic cough showing me a handkerchief stained with sooty or blood-stained sputum. Should we regret the demise of the heavy industries?

The womenfolk likewise began to enjoy better health and became more emancipated in their outlook. It is not widely known but the contraceptive pill was first made available as far back as 1961, albeit on a private prescription, at a subsidized price of 2 shillings per month. The supposedly enlightened minister of health at that time was from the Black Country, yes, none other than the Member of Parliament for Wolverhampton, Mr Enoch Powell[57]! As a result of increased usage of "the pill" by the 1980s women were no longer drawn down by the drudgery of unwanted multiple pregnancies, and the bringing up of many children that they struggled to financially afford.

The children were becoming healthier. Newer and more efficient vaccination regimes meant that the infectious diseases of childhood, measles, mumps and rubella (German measles) and others that I had been seeing cases of every day, began to decrease, eventually to almost disappear. The worse of all was whooping cough, now becoming a rarity.

This disease when seen but once in the acute phase was never forgotten…

Sent for by Granny in the middle of the night, she knows the difference between a "whoop" and a "croup", to see a 3-year-old, twitching with a high temperature, gasping for breath under a poorly lit council house back bedroom 40 watt light bulb, snotty nose streaming, pouring saliva, struggling for life, was so upsetting. Then after the acute illness had settled, in some weeks, if they survived, they coughed for months and were sometimes left with residual shortness of breath forever, for life. The vaccine for whooping cough was only slowly taken up due to side effects and poor publicity. Whilst the vaccine had only "supposed" side effects, a child could definitely die from whooping cough.

I became close to my patients. We shared life's crises together.

About this time then, approaching the end decade of the millennium, the health of the practice and the populace in general was improving, and I was beginning to get the hang of this general practice, that is after about 25 years or so. But suddenly dramatic change occurred. Now in my 50s, I changed ladders. My delightful senior partner had long retired and I fortunately had a younger male and two female partners[58] all very well trained, very competent and well liked by the patients. They were pleasant personalities and excellent and good capable doctors. Out of the blue I received two new job offers almost simultaneously. I was promoted to a new role at hospital in Birmingham, to become a hospital practitioner grade ENT surgeon with increased sessions (another story) and I was offered, and I took, a senior partner post in general practice just a few miles away at Kingswinford, in Dudley, still within the Black Country. By arrangement with the trio of partners in the new practice I was able to continue both my hospital and GP appointments, and I continued in practice in this way for many years thereafter. I quickly discovered that my new patients and my new partners in Kingswinford were no different to those in Wolverhampton, and likewise were as delightful to work with. As a result of my new job(s) about this time my wife began to describe me as a "funny doctor, he's both a GP and a specialist".

She has done so ever since with, emphasis on the word "funny". I continue to think (hope?) that she means that I am "unusual", rather than peculiar or amusing!

References and Author's comment:

57. *Enoch Powell: A Biography*. R. Shepherd. 1996. Hutchinson:
    Enoch Powell. Wikipedia. The free encyclopedia:
    John Enoch Powell MBE (16/06/1912-08/02/1998) was a "Brummie", a sort of honorary Black Country man, a politician, a classical scholar, linguist, writer and soldier. He was at times incredibly bright and enlightened, yet, often held unusual views on life in general. He was always, however, somewhat of an enigma as a person. At King Edward's School Birmingham he was described by a schoolmate, later a friend and colleague of mine (the author) as...
    "A real pain. Incredibly bright and always right. A very, very clever know-it-all."

A classical scholar he became a professor of ancient Greek at the age of 25 years and he spoke 12 languages in all, including being fluent in Latin, Greek and Hebrew. During the Second World War he served in the armed forces obtaining the military OBE, when he became only the second man ever to rise in the ranks from private to become the youngest brigadier in the British Army. His self-opinion was such that at the end of the war he had great aspirations to become Viceroy of India after Lord Mountbatten, and so he learned to speak Urdu in just a few weeks as he thought it would be essential for such a post. He was never required!

In the post-war period he eventually entered politics, and he was elected conservative Member of Parliament for Wolverhampton South East in 1950, where he served until 1974, when he became an Ulster Unionist MP (until 1987).

As well as serving a multiplicity of ministerial and other posts in this period he is mainly remembered for his…

"Rivers of Blood" speech, a term that he actually never used, made against further immigration to the UK in 1968 in Birmingham, which became highly criticized by all parties, and other conservatives such as Michael Heseltine and others, and for which he is still remembered today.

What is not well known, however, is that this speech was based on material and actual events and occurrences from his constituency in Wolverhampton at the time. A clever (crafty?) man, wishing to obtain the maximum publicity for his speech, he made it only after asking the advice of a friend, Clem Jones, then the editor of the *Wolverhampton Express and Star* newspaper, making the speech purposely on a Saturday afternoon, knowing that, "this speech is going up like a rocket Clem".

It was then available to be reported in both the Saturday evening newspapers, the Sunday weeklies and then the Monday daily newspapers in full.

He wanted it remembered and quoted long term. It certainly has been, and by many since that time. (Suckers? Are they doing what he wanted, one may ask?)

When later accused, he felt very strongly that he was not a racist having defended many causes of minorities such as that of the Mau Mau in Kenya in the past, and such as obtaining appointments for West Indian nurses in the NHS, and others.

Following his retirement he was greatly admired by Mrs Margaret Thatcher and he shared many of her political views. He was extremely hostile to any suggestion that the UK join the common European currency etc.

He was also revered and almost adored by some, but not all of the general working-class public, and he still is remembered especially so, in Wolverhampton. This was evidenced when…

On the Andrew Marr show (see reference no. 12) on December 22nd, 2013, the business secretary at that time, Mr Vince Cable, used Mr Powell's "Rivers of Blood" speech as a criticism of the current government's attitudes to immigration.

In reply to this shortly afterwards, on December 31st 2013, in a letter to the editor of the *Wolverhampton Express and Star* newspaper, Mr I. Payne, whose family were immigrants living within Mr Powell's constituency at the time, totally disagreed with Mr Cable, who he felt was using idealism instead of reality, pointing out that Mr Powell was very popular within the local immigrant community, many of whom shared his views, and many of whom still do so!

Whilst his harbinger-of-doom-type prophecy has not occurred, many of his other predictions have proved correct. From the point of view of immigrants having the whip hand, he has been proved very wrong indeed, but still, do the locals know better than those in central government? It is unclear.

Perhaps he should be better remembered for the opening line of the "Rivers of Blood" speech i.e.…

"It is a reminder to those elected by the people, that they are there to make things better and to use their authority and skills to serve their country."

58. *From Cradle to Grave: 65 years of the NHS.* G.C. Rivett. www. nhshistory.net/:

Geoffrey Rivett wrote very comprehensively in his first books in 1998 on the contemporary history of the National Health Service (see reference no. 22). These excellent writings are now kept up to date on the Internet website using the link above.

The articles show that...

In 1948 less than 10% of all doctors in the UK were female.

By 1975 still only 20% of all doctors in the UK were female.

This had increased to 33% by 1998, and if the current medical school intake (2014) continues with 60% plus female students, it is predicted that by 2017 and onwards there will be a majority of female doctors working within the National Health Service in the UK.

17. Animals, "Dags"

My medical training as one would expect was confined to members the human race. I have from time to time in my professional career, however, become "involved" with other species, with animals.

As a junior doctor on emergency room duty I was at one time asked to see…

"A bird with a broken leg, Doctor." It was a pigeon, not a young lady!

I also saw cases of patients being involved with accidents with farm animal in "casualty", as A & E departments were called in those days, but I never anticipated that later in life I might be involved in general practice with animals, in particular a propensity for problems with dogs. I have previously explained my meeting with police dogs and my antipathy towards the "dags" of my gypsy patients. There were others.

Breda was aptly named. A tiny wizened woman, worn thin by multiple pregnancies, and having to look after a tribe of children, often when her husband was away on holiday at "Her Majesty's pleasure" i.e. in Winson Green Prison, at the time concerned. I visited her home early on in my GP years at a postnatal visit following the birth of her 12th child. She had 11 boys. At last, a girl, and all of them lived, without Dad, in a 3-bedroomed council house.

I noticed a message on the side gate…

"Beware of the dog. Survivors will be prosecuted."

Even by Black Country-speak language this was a little odd, so I entered warily via the front door. She was quite well, as was the new babe. I enquired as to the notice regarding the dog.

"Oh, Docta, that's our Cuddles. He's owa guard dog, a bostin wammel [dog] 'e is, as we've 'ad lots a burglars in the street. Wud yo like ta see 'im?" she said, opening the back kitchen door as she spoke, anticipating a positive response from me.

I heard the clunk, clunk, of a heavy chain and looked out to see a rectangular slab of a dog, huge, black and brown and slobbering, saliva dripping off his jaws.

"It's alright Docta. He wo' 'urt ya. He's a big softie really," she explained seeing my reticence to approach him.

"He's one a them guard dogs, a Rottweiler," she explained.

Now I knew that these work dogs were not really meant to be kept as pets, and that they had been used to guard concentration camps in the Second World War.

"Is he? Oh right," I muttered slowly and out loud, but thinking to myself... Is he really here to keep intruders out, or the huge household in? In the 1980s these dogs were uncommon and unusual, hence my alarm, and I left without further ado.

It was about a year later that I returned, again for a postnatal visit. Yes, another girl. I think she was breeding a football team and now she had the physiotherapist and masseuse as well.

I made sure I went in by the front door, not the gate. I could hear the clunks of Cuddles' chains as I approached. I had not been satisfied by Breda's previous reassurances. I checked that all was OK with the birth then and quickly left. I did take the opportunity to offer some contraceptive advice though, I recollect, for two reasons.

Firstly these last two children had been born in quick succession, and as her husband had been in prison these last 3 years, serving "four to five" for grievous bodily harm I thought he might be a bit upset on return, with two new arrivals in his absence! Conjugal visits were not allowed in those days, and whilst he was not very bright and one could have possibly got away with explaining that the first baby was a product of a "protracted pregnancy", he would have to have been as thick as a brick to accept the second one!

Secondly, for my help really, no more babies in future would avoid me having to visit the home and perchance meet up with Cuddles again.

On looking back I feel that I began to learn about animals about this time, and dogs in particular, but only slowly, and with gradual experience. Cuddles made me realize that as well as names, size also was nothing to go on, as regards dogs especially. This was borne out following the occasion when I first had to visit Pearl.

Now poor Pearl, (I've left her title blank as I cannot recollect her marital status) was also a frail little thing, and always a little odd. I think this oddness was accentuated by alcohol as she could daily be seen in the afternoon staggering back home after leaving a local pub, as always wearing bright red lipstick, elevated over her upper lip like an 18th century courtesan, and a fox fur around her neck, even on hot summer days. In the surgery one kept well away from this fox fur as it was known to be, like her, covered in nits[59]. On Christmas Day one year I was called by a caring neighbour as he had just seen her outside at the dustbin, in the cold, just wearing a vest, and nothing else, and I mean just a vest and nothing else!

It really was a white Christmas that year so even though it was Christmas Day I went quickly to the house. I peered through the window to see her indeed, stark naked except for a vest, lying on the floor, writhing-like on the front room carpet!

I entered through the unlocked back door to find poor Pearl, alone in the house, and as confused as hell. She didn't know where she was, who she was, and who I was, and who anybody was. It was freezing cold in the house with no heating on, and she was hypothermic and dehydrated and I could find no food in the house other than a half-eaten tin of Kennomeat[60] dog food on the table. She had been eating that, in her confusion.

I got her dressed and warmed her slowly up in some blankets. I then managed to obtain some turkey and other food from her caring neighbours and we gave her a hot drink. I threw the Kennomeat away. She slowly returned to her normal mildly odd self, explaining that her female impersonator son was away working and that she was alone in the house for the whole of Christmas. She seemed back to normal, whatever that was for her, and so I simply arranged for a follow-up visit the next day, Boxing Day, for reassessment by my senior partner, a sweetie of a man. It was his day on call then, and so I left the house.

48hrs later, the day after Boxing Day I arrived at the surgery early before surgery to read the morning mail and deal with any problems that had arisen over the holiday period, to find my partner there already, limping about, and with his one foot all wrapped up.

"What's the matter with your foot?" I queried.

"Your bloody Pearl," he cried out. "I went as you asked yesterday. She was OK but eating the Kennomeat again, so I went and chucked it all in the bin, I did. As I did so and I turned around a dog, her dog, bloody reared up and bit me he did. Savaged me," he disclosed, cursing further as he spoke, unusual for him, a very mildly tempered man.

"I had t' fight him off I did, he was so upset at me t'rowing his dinner away," he cried in his Northern Ireland brogue.

"What sort of dog was it then?" I queried, noticing that he just had a bandage around his foot. What was this ferocious type of dog then?

"A bloody chihuahua thing, huge it was, it was," he cried. "Ripped me to bits it did," he added with indignation.

I think there was a little bit of overexaggeration here. Consolation calmed him down. He made a full recovery. Pearl remained as normal as ever, for her. I never discovered what happened to the dog, who must have been out the back when I attended. I learned that day though, with a chuckle, that size in dogs is not always directly proportional to aggressiveness.

I have had meetings with many animals in my practice. I've had a cat bite me and scratch me so severely that I needed dressings. I've had a cockatoo try and eat my shoelaces, but it is with interest that I have noted how some dog owners especially, like parents with malcontent children, often see no wrong in their offspring or their pets, in their actions and behaviour much of the time.

This attitude is seen in all walks of society. Lady Timson was a prime example.

In my later practice we had many outlying patients who lived in large homes, estates in some cases, even titled folk, who lived out in the Severn Valley, away from the Black Country. Lady Timson was one such patient.

She was of "Black Country nobility" stock, her deceased husband being an iron and steel industrial magnate. She lived in a Georgian-style house in the grounds of a large private estate, and I visited her on occasions and met her collection, a veritable herd, of dogs that she doted on. Whilst I had no problems dealing with her, a delightful lady of "the old school", and her ailments, I also had to deal from time to time with problems with her dogs, who were a complete pain.

Rudyard was a little dachshund, a yappy but otherwise docile little fellow. He never did much else. Byron was a medium-sized indeterminate terrier-type who just got in your way. The largest, however, was William, an Irish wolfhound who could do no wrong, he was the troublesome one.

Odd names though for dogs one can see. All named after writers of one sort or another, so I thought. Rudyard and Byron were easy, so one day I asked as to the origin of "William" as he could have had a multiplicity of poetic namesakes.

Oddly I discovered that he was named after Bill, the head gardener for some reason or another. Perhaps a previous liaison here. Some other reason? Lady T never disclosed.

I should point out that we were always semiformal, Her Ladyship and I. She always addressed me as "Doctor E", and I addressed her as "Lady T".

"Look at him, Doctor E," Lady T would say as she saw me off after my visit at the door, as I watched William cock his leg up and piddle up the rear wheel of my car, having already watered the front wing on my arrival. Cheeky thing.

"He loves to play about, and mark his patch you know," she said.

Mark his patch, I mused. I'd like to mark him personally for doing my car every time I visit, I thought. Fetching the paint off, he was.

Well I solved the problem with William, or rather he did, on one of my visits.

I arrived one afternoon to be called by Lady T on to the terrace at the side of the house where she was seated drinking her afternoon tea and admiring the view across to Dudley and Sedgley on the horizon in the distance. I bent down and turned to open the small metal entrance gate. As I did so… woof, woof, woof, right in my face, two front paws on my chest, and snarling teeth and tongue inches from my face! Slavering and snotty he was. A violent assault. William.

"What the '," I cried out, dropping my bag and stepping back, scared the life out of me he did.

I was much shaken, initially, but only initially. I was brought up in Dudley. I never even heard of the word conciliation until (divorce and) middle age. Retaliation was what I knew about, and instantaneous in type it was.

"Turn your body towards your opponent, boy. Aim the blow at full arm extent to obtain the best leverage. Put your shoulder, then all your body weight behind it lad," demanded my mentor at the grammar school boxing club.

Well I did. Without thinking, I was so scared. William got one. 14 and a half stone it was. An instantaneous straight arm job, smack on the end of his conk, his snoz, his nose! Snot, saliva and other bodily fluids sprayed out in all directions.

I know from my anatomy days that the nose and the "smell brain", the rhinencephalon[61], in a dog is a much more sensitive and a much more important organ than it is in us humans. I am afraid that William got a big unexpected stimulus to his organ and system that day that he found difficult to cope with. He ran off and away, with his tail between his legs. Whine, whine, whine he cried, shaking his head and violently sneezing to clear the overload just received by his olfactory organ and system.

Lady T pleasingly never saw this, and when she enquired as to why he was running off and sneezing, I explained (lied) that…

"Oh, he's just had a bit of a shock to his nose. Sniffed on a sharp stone or something, I think." She just accepted this, but the dog and I, we established an instant rapport. He had a good memory. He never came near me again, and when I arrived in the future, he kept well away, and never "marked his patch" on my car or "played about" near me again.

I couldn't say the same of Mrs Large's dog. He didn't play about. He was serious. He didn't like me and I didn't like him from the word go. We had mutual loathing of each other, always. Like Lady T, Mrs Large could see no wrong in her animal. Razor his name, which like his owner's surname to her, was very appropriate to him, a slim and sharp, pseudo-greyhound, a whippet. Mrs large lived in council property and always had home visits as she was so obese, 18 stone plus, with leg ulcers and a multijoint arthropathy so that she just could not get out of the house to go anywhere unaided, let alone visit a doctor's surgery. When seen in the living room the dog was always present and messing with my doctor's bag instantly when my back was turned as I consulted with his owner.

"Look Doctor, he's playing with your telescope again. Cheeky doggie," she cried as the canine swine chewed through my £36 spare Littmann stethoscope yet again, and messed up all my other examination equipment and notepaper! Cheeky?

Repeatedly he did this despite ever being chastised by his mistress, time and time again. In time he went through (ate) three stethoscopes, one auroscope (the instrument for looking down and examining the ear and its canals) and several notebooks, and all the various straps and locks on two of my doctor's bags.

I was becoming "perturbed". I couldn't at all afford this.

However, circumstances changed. When I first visited her one gained access to the house by reaching through the letter box to obtain the front door key that was inside on a piece of string, and thence obtain entry. This system worked well for ages until some local gyppos discovered the key also and entered the house one day and went and stripped all the lead off the back roof for scrap, so the key entry was abandoned. Razor was then tied up, out the back, in guard dog fashion so to speak. So then when one arrived, entrance was obtained round the back, when one was then confronted by a mad and fed up animal jumping and slashing, all teeth and claws showing usually, tied up to the clothes line prop. He was not a happy dog and was always very upset to see me, and likewise me to see him, the nasty little beast. I could never calm him down, despite repeatedly trying doggy conciliation (I knew the word then, post-divorce. I knew it never worked.) A new method of approach was required.

Oddly he was tied up with a long piece of square elastic. This enabled him to shoot through the air and jump at you, scaring the life out of you, and any gyppo or other intruders that might visit, then he twanged back as the elastic retracted.

I discovered one day that the yard was six slabs wide, and if you walked in a straight line along the sixth slab, the elastic only extended him to the fifth slab when he was violently jerked backwards again, after he leaped at you. Now most folks did this quickly, and shot into the house to avoid further confrontation. I discovered though, if one just stood one's ground… twang, he was jerked back and smacked his bag of bones-type body against the wall. Undeterred he immediately got up and flew at me again. In a doggy stupor he was. Smack, back against the wall he went. Up he got again, and so on and so on. Smack again, and again. Now all this went on for several minutes until he realized even with his dopey doggy intellect that I was "partaking of the Michael" and that he was getting nowhere and becoming quite exhausted and quite knocked about. He calmed down. His attitude changed. Whilst not actually subservient, he just quietly sneered, and almost regarded me with disdain and a tight-lipped snarl. We established that day a new relationship i.e. antipathy, a mutual loathing, but from his point of view, never a full understanding. Accordingly this all went on time and time again when I visited.

He never gave up. He never learned. Smack, against the wall he went, smack, several times, before I entered the house. I tended to enter slowly, but it made no difference. He never learned.

Never mind, my drug bag recovered. Mrs Large remained medically unaltered.

I have used dogs in my stories as examples as I remember them so well, but over the years I have learned that as a GP one has to be able to cope with all animals and pets, as well as the foibles, feelings, and phobias of folk, when visiting at home to address their medical problems.

We were never taught this at medical school.

References and Author's comments:

59. The Biology of Pediculus humanus. P.A. Buxton. 1947 2nd Edition. Edwin Arnold:

Head lice. NHS Choices. www.nhs.uk/Conditions/Head-lice:

Re-appointment of school "Nit Nurses". The Telegraph article. 24/04/2011:

Author's advice: be warned. Some readers might find this reference rewardingly informative, but others somewhat a little distasteful, ladies especially.

"Nits" are not head lice insects themselves, but the hair-attached eggshell cases of the hatched out human head louse (Pediculus humanus capitis). The lice themselves are unusual in that they spend all their life only on their host, mainly the head, but also other hairy bits as well, as they cannot jump or fly because of their body shape and short legs, unlike fleas and other infestations who can live elsewhere!

They are a completely different species from the body-living and disease-carrying

body louse (Pediculus humanus humanus) and the pubic area-living pubic crab louse (Pthirus pubis).

It has been postulated that the human head louse plays a

part in aiding the development of human immunity to these other disease-carrying relatives!

Human head lice are transmitted by personal contact (i.e. they can't jump!) not as a result of poor personal hygiene, and they are completely harmless other than causing great parental concern. They are seen more and more in general practice since the demise of the school "Nit Nurse" and in some areas parents have signed petitions asking local authorities for such valued nurses to be reappointed.

60. Kennomeat. Wikipedia. The free encyclopedia:

The Food Standards Agency. London.WC2B 6NH:

Food pets die for. A.N. Martin. 2003. New Sage Press:

Kennomeat was a dog food, and Kattomeat a cat food, manufactured originally by Robert Wilson and Sons in the 1930s, later taken over by Spillers Ltd. then Nestle, with closure of production in 1998.

Despite intensive literature and other searches made, I have found it impossible to ascertain the actual and accurate content of this very popular pet food, and its modern contemporaries. Manufacturers are so very secretive.

After the First World War much commercial animal food contained horsemeat supposedly due to the abundance of horses originally raised for the war effort, but even then, as now, the meat content was vary variable and the amount contained still is a debatable issue. The type of meat content of animal food is often described as "human grade" but includes parts of animals that humans would not consider as edible. In addition, certain harmful chemical contents to e.g. dogs, have now been identified, such as theobromine found in chocolate, sulfoxides in grapes, and others in onions and garlic etc. which have at times been added.

Furthermore, it has been alleged by some sources that controversially some dog and cat pet foods are purported to contain material from veterinary surgery sourced carcasses of euthanasia-killed dogs and cats themselves!

61. The Rhinencephalon. *Anatomy Regional and Applied*. R. J. Last. 8th Edition. 1990. Churchill Livingstone:
Physiology of Domestic Animals. Sjaastad, Sand and Hove. 2nd Edition 2010. Scanvet Press. www.scanvetpress.com/:

That part of the brain concerned with the perception of smell (olfaction) is known as the "smell brain" or rhinencephalon, that takes impulses from sensory nerve cells in the nose. Humans have approximately 5-10 million of these sensory nerve cells whilst other species, such as dogs, are known to have 125 million cells or more. Rather than just the simple perception of odours, this means that the dog brain is enabled to have many more complex and multiple connections with other areas of the brain, such as those responsible for emotion, pleasure and memory. This in turn means that a much greater proportion of the total dog brain overall is concerned with smell and that the canine smell centres have millions more abilities than the human equivalent.

Such increased abilities are not only found particularly in certain mammals such as dogs, deer or whales, but in other species such as fish, insects and even plants.

Yes, certain plants can detect organic volatile compounds!

On the other hand some species e.g. most birds, have a poor or almost no sense of smell, with only a few exceptions such as albatrosses or vultures.

18. Night workers

Nowadays when the *hoi polloi* exit the newly built huge and shimmering glass and glittering showrooms into Raby Street near the centre of Wolverhampton, in their shiny and new BMW and Audi saloons, little do they know what this place was like just over 30 years ago.

When I first visited then, as ever, it was 2 o'clock in the morning when I received the call, to what I later ascribed as one of my "night workers".

"Can you come straight away Doctor? Our Teresa Aziz 'as lost the babi, 'er fust, an' 'er's only 18," was the call, although not made in a terribly concerned voice, as if she had seen it all before. She had.

I went straight away nevertheless, to number 4 – back of 6, Raby Street. I'd never been to this street before, it was very dark. No street lights. I couldn't see the numbers so I went down the supposed second entry. Just a dark cavern in front of me, when I was immediately grabbed by a strong pairs of hands, and yanked back into the semi-darkness of the street. They had been waiting there, I realized.

"Where do you think yo'm a goin'?" said the strong arm of the law, two of them.

I could see their buttons shining on their uniforms in the dim moonlight. Black Country policemen by their accents.

I explained that I was the doctor, looking to visit a Teresa Aziz, an urgent call.

"Oh, 'er's 'ad a miscarriage," was the reply. "It's the knockin' shop, next entry down Doc. All the street lights here am bostid [broken], an' the public telephones. They rung from the station down the road. We knew yo wuz comin'," the voice said, hands now let go of me.

I never did see their faces, as they escorted me to the house, the next entry down, where I went into the cavernous darkness again.

It was almost a Dickensian experience. The small room down stairs was illuminated by a roaring coal fire, and a 60 watt light bulb. Sitting half on a chair by the fire, was an Asian gentleman rubbing his hands to warm, but the room was mainly filled by a couple of voluminous red-headed ladies standing with tattooed arms folded, and a small single bed, filled with what I assumed was Teresa, up in the corner.

"She's had a miss Doctor, just at 12 weeks, 'er fust. It's complete and she's stopped loosin' since we rung," redhead no. 1 explained.

"Abdul, gerrup and get some boilin' werter f' the doctor, quick," redhead no. 2 demanded, and bawled, all in a single breath.

I was taken aback a little by all this, but proceeded with my history and examination. It was some 30 years ago now. I don't remember too much about the case other than Teresa was OK and that the ladies present had dealt completely with the medical details, but I do still recollect that I found it very odd when I pulled the bedclothes back to examine Teresa, that I discovered a dog in bed with her as well!

This was nothing though compared to my other remembrance of this night, her tattoo. On the inside of her thigh was a large arrow pointing up her leg, with the caption… "Follow this arrow"!

I remember that I left somewhat bemused after this.

Next day in the surgery my partner explained that Raby Street was the centre of the well-known red-light area, and that in the Flynn household that I had visited, all the adult females were either "on the game", or "had been on the game," and that Mr Aziz was "a convenience Mr" to satisfy the immigration laws of the time.

"Did you notice the crucifixes over all the beds?" he asked.

"They sure need them in that house, and did you see the kids?"

"Well, no," I replied, "it was 2 o'clock in the morning and I assumed that they were all in bed somewhere," I explained.

"They are a real liquorice allsorts lot they are," he announced. "All shapes and sizes and colours they are. There are ginger-headed West Indian-type kids and

Chinese-type blue-eyed kids. All as a result of the family employment. The lady bosses, the Flynns, came over from Ireland in the 1960s and started the set-up that they have run ever since. However, the whole place is spotless and the kids are all well looked after and well behaved. The girls all go to the VD clinic, for their regular check-ups, and they are all polite and no trouble to anybody, except when the booze gets into them, which is most Fridays and Saturdays and Sundays. And weekdays, sometimes, as well," he added.

I thus got to know Teresa, a bright and bubbly red-headed character, early in my career and we became well acquainted, over the years following my visit.

I remember seeing her further in the surgery for the results of some tests just a few years later, when I somewhat sarcastically remarked…

"Congratulations Teresa, it's your 21st."

"Fuck me, sorry f' swearin', but no Doctor, no, but thank you very much. It ain't me birthday yet," she replied.

You might be offended by the language, but by this time I had become used to patients, even very young ones, swearing in conversation with me. I was neither affronted nor offended. It had almost become a sign of confidentiality, of an established closeness. In the Black Country I had begun to realize that you can only swear at your friends or folk that you like, without causing offence.

"I ain't 21 until a wik on Wednesday," she disclosed.

185

"No, Teresa," I went on to clarify. "I didn't mean your birthday, although I see that it is due. Reading your notes and looking at your hospital attendance letters, these new results show that today is the 21st time that you have had "the clap", again," I revealed!

Yes, at (almost) reaching the age of 21 years, she attended surgery for the 21st time with the diagnosis and for treatment of venereal disease i.e. "VD" in those days. Sexually transmitted disease or STD so-called nowadays. Try as I may, repeatedly I failed to get her out of her "occupation" with all the risks it involved.

She was one of the first patients that I met who demonstrated how young girls easily accepted and entered a lifestyle of prostitution[62]. Virginia was another...

Crash, bang, wallop! Virginia (somewhat inappropriately named this time, perhaps) was projected into my surgery consulting room, precipitated like this and other cases I'd seen, by a boot; her mother's.

"S'down," snarled her mother, Mrs Thicket, pointing to my examination chair.

Now I knew Virginia from previous consultations as a bright and quite pretty dark-haired 18-year-old, very unlike her mother, a rather worn middle-aged lady who had unfortunately terribly thick spectacle lenses that made her look a little as if wearing diving glasses. You know, the type of lens that if you look straight on to, you see concentric circle reflections. I never quite knew if she could see me clearly as she peered and squinted at me in conversation.

"I want you to examine her Doctor, and tell me if she is alright", she said, peering towards me as normal. "Me and George [Mr Thicket] came 'ome from the club last night. Early we was, so seeing the lights on and we went round the back to get in, we did," she continued. "Well, as we opened the gate, guess what, a black chap jumped out of the kitchen window and run off, up the garden and over the fence he did?

We went inside and there she was, in the living room,

pulling her clothes down and her drawers up," she explained. "She's engaged and due to be married soon to a lovely white chap who's in the army and we want to be sure she's OK Doctor," she finished with, not explaining what she meant by "OK", but I got what she meant by all this.

I thus examined Virginia, who swore that she had not been up to any "hanky-panky" (Black Country speak for "dubious behaviour", in this case, of a sexual nature), with her coloured friend, and I was able to reassure her mother that although she was not *virgo intacta* so to speak, I could find no signs of any injury or assault etc. I advised that they should return in the future should they have any later concerns. They did, 7 months later...

I was writing up the last patient's notes when they entered, more normally this time, and I only glanced up. Mrs Thicket explained that although Virginia was well, she was worried about her putting weight on lately, and that it was important, as she was due to be married in a couple of weeks time, and could I have another look at her daughter and advise, please. I thus suggested an examination, without really looking up, and asked her just to jump on the couch. I looked up...

Well, I know Mrs Thicket had poor eyesight, but until then I had not realized how bad it really was. Even from a distance one could see an abdominal profile that was very suggestive, and not just wind. Quick questions were required.

"Are your bowels OK Virginia?" I asked, starting as always in a roundabout way. "What about your waterworks and your periods perhaps. Are they all normal?" I asked.

"All normal Doctor. Completely normal. Going normally, not missed a thing," Virginia replied, with a sort of wry grin.

Well "completely normal" was not what my examination revealed. Despite supposedly having normal menses, she was having what appeared to be a quite normal pregnancy, of about 28 weeks i.e. 7 months, gestation!

I explained this to them both, to nobody's real surprise it seemed.

"That's it. Yo' 'll 'ave t' bring the weddin' forward to your soldier chap's next leave," Mrs Thicket explained, and off they both went, to tell George.

Following this Virginia proceeded to attend my antenatal clinic regularly and she had a quite normal pregnancy up to term despite having no vitamin or iron supplements or other previous care, and "oddly" she had no further periods after the day of my examination! How unusual?

Nothing much further happened until...

"Come right away please Doctor. We have complications with Virginia," was the call from the midwife, in the middle of the night from Ward A2, the GP Delivery Suite at New Cross Hospital. I went straight along. Something was amiss I saw on my arrival in the car park. Police cars with lights flashing at the main entrance and the unit door.

Chaos reigned inside. On entering I found George sitting outside in the delivery suite corridor, with a surgical towel covered in blood around his head, being looked after by nurses, who beckoned me to go into the delivery suite to see Virginia, and the new baby. There was other shouting and noise from elsewhere in the background. Chairs and stools were knocked over. The place was in a mess.

I rushed in. Virginia was sitting up in bed holding the new wrapped up infant, looking very disturbed, not the usual exhausted smile of the new mother, and Mrs Thicket was growling over in the corner.

"Look at the babi Doctor, look. Look at 'er. Tell us what yo think," she cried.

So I did.

The reason for her consternation was very apparent. The beautiful new infant had dark eyes and a full head of curly black hair, very brown skin colour, and was obviously of mixed racial parentage! Very brown.

She was not at all like Virginia's new husband, the chap in the army, apparently blue-eyed and blond, who I actually never met, and who was still on the premises.

He had attended the birth, and like everyone else (except Virginia perhaps?) he was amazed by the appearance of the new infant. An argument with Virginia had resulted across the delivery bed, which evolved into a fight with George, who had by then arrived at the scene. Things had become very violent and George had been hit over the head with a chair. The police had the soldier now in custody on the premises still, and were considering a charge.

I quickly examined Virginia and the new babe who were both disgustingly well, and then took a look at George. He was more interested in the baby's origin than his injury, which required him being sent off to A & E for treatment, and he was quite aghast with his daughter, when with clarification all was explained to him.

He openly disowned her, there and then, swearing that she would never set foot in his household again, ignoring the fact that just a few minutes ago he had been defending her honour. I attempted to calm all down, and I eventually left the scene.

George, a Black Country man, was true to his word. He had physical and visual problems for life following his head injury but that did not deter him in his regard for his daughter. I followed the family up for many years. Whilst the baby was doted on by both George and Mrs Thicket, and grew up into a beautiful almond-eyed girl, Virginia was excluded from their house forever.

She never returned to the family home, and went down the social scale. She lived for a short while with her coloured friend and was divorced by her new husband.

She was "on the game" full-time by the time she was 30 years old with several criminal convictions, and by the time she was 40 years old she was running an establishment herself. A rather sad story of how without close parental guidance, young women especially can easily enter the sometimes so-called "honourable" profession.

It is quite amazing on thinking back how naïve I was in my early GP days. I knew nothing about the sex industry, a fact that landed me in trouble on several occasions…

I had to visit a lovely lady, Mrs Meg with whom I was on first names terms, who shortly after getting married to a local publican in middle age, had become unwell, and she had just moved into his public house, The Royal Exchange, in Bilston. She now resided there with her new husband, the long-term licensee. The receptionists at the surgery were a little odd, I recollect, and all giggled and gave furtive looks when I explained that I had to visit.

"Go round to the back Doctor, not through the bar. Just knock the back door, and go up the stairs," I was instructed, so I duly did so, as I was told.

I went down the side entry and up the back stairs. On arrival in the upstairs back living room I was a little surprised to be met by several rather pretty young ladies, somewhat bleary-eyed, in semi-undress, stocking, suspenders, negligees etc.

Night clothes, a little unusual I thought, as it was about 1 o'clock at lunchtime, but I was cheerfully met with…

"Hello Doctor, go on through, Mrs Meg's in the bedroom," it was explained. "We've all just got up."

So I did, again, as instructed. I saw my patient, and left after a while, down the back stairs, thinking nothing of all this. They just appeared to get up late here, I thought.

The next week I had to do a follow-up visit. The same thing. Up the back stairs, young ladies in nightclothes and undress again, cheerful, eating what seemed to be their breakfast, and I saw my lady patient.

This time though I made enquiry of her…

"Who are the young ladies outside Meg?" I asked after dealing with her medical problem.

"Oh, er, they are just Les's, my new husband's nieces, staying with us for a while Doctor," she said with a frown. "I've only been here a week as you know, and I found them here when I arrived. I'm getting rid of them though in the near future, don't you worry," she explained with a firm shake of her head, and I left thinking nothing of all this, a little pleased that she appeared better with my treatment.

That Saturday night I went for a drink to the steelworks social club just down the road from the pub, where I met my father, having a drink with his close friends, Bob Allardyce, a retired police sergeant, (whose son at that time was a professional football player and who later on became a Premier League manager) and Dennis Turner, a local councillor at that time (later to become an MP and member of the House of Lords, and already mentioned in Chapter 8). A pretty knowledgeable trio.

"Hello gents," I began with, knowing them all quite well. "Would you like a drink? Pints of bitter?" I continued, knowing all their preferences.

Unfortunately, I also added… "I had to visit a pub where they sold Holden's beer the other day, up in the High Street nearby."

"Which one Edward?" Dennis asked with a frown on his brow. He knew a lot about beer, Dennis did, and Bob. They'd drunk enough with my father.

"Oh, The Royal Exchange," I innocently revealed. "I had to visit a lady there," I explained. "They don't seem to get up very early in that place, do they?" I asked.

Well, the reaction was incredible. Raised eyebrows. White faces. They all looked around over their shoulders aghast, to see if anyone had heard what I had said. All three of them!

"What the '," cried out my dad. He couldn't speak otherwise.

"Early, get up early? Bloody hell Edward. That's "the Trumpet"[63] you are talking about," Bob whispered, with a kindly arm around my shoulders. "It's famous for various reasons, not just the jazz music that's played there. I've had many clients who have visited there professionally. It's been a "knockin' shop" for years. Everybody in Bilston knows the place. They work nights there they do, and weekends and bank holidays. Usually horizontally. They do tend to get up late then I suppose," he quietly explained. He was such a nice man.

My father was distraught. "Don't let on in here that you've seen anybody from there," he confided. "Especially y' mother."

Dennis thought it all hilarious. He just grinned at me. He knew what the place was as well. I was somewhat abashed, but I quickly recovered with the dawn of realization. I didn't ever mention my visits again, in polite company that is.

Later on when Mrs Meg had improved, she came to the surgery one day.

"I'm much better Doctor, getting about well now, as you can see, and I've got rid of all of Les's relatives," she explained, with a glint in her eye, nod, nod, wink, wink, explaining with expression at the same time.

I had begun to learn about "night workers". They were not all women though.

It was odd when I was called to Mrs Riley one day. A widow for some years she struggled to the surgery even when unwell, normally, so I went along expecting to find her somewhat ill in bed. I was surprised then to find her in the living room of her cold post-war uninsulated, typical council house that had been thrown up in the 1940s and that many of my patients still lived in. Damp. Condensation. Mould on the walls. Metal-framed windows etc. She was sat on the settee crying.

"Oh, Mrs Riley, what's the matter?" I asked.

"I'm glad it's yo Doctor. Yo'll understand. Yo'm local. It's me son, Riley," she tearfully replied.

I must explain here, that Mr Riley, deceased, had really liked his surname, and as after the birth of their firstborn, Mrs Riley had had to have an emergency caesarean section and then a hysterectomy, effectively ending the family line, he had decided to propagate the name. Hence their son was named Riley Riley... it isn't a spelling mistake! Unfortunately Mr Riley senior died in a steelworks accident when his son was very young, leaving Mrs Riley to bring up her son alone. As a result, as is often seen with no male role model as parent, Riley junior had become a bit of a problem child with behavioural disorders at school and elsewhere. He was plagued with a lifelong skin problem, psoriasis, for which he would constantly forget his prescription for his smelly ointment, Ung ZALPCB[64] and of which he was very self-conscious. He was always in trouble as a child, and this went on to his adult life.

Mrs Riley went on to explain her upset. She had heard that we had been burgled one night at the surgery the previous week. We had. Very oddly also. The place was trashed. A real mess had been made. The receptionist's toaster (a wreck), used for their tea breaks, had been taken and even the old electric sterilizer had been stolen, although it was so useless and out of date I had not been very upset. Dr Gupta, who shared the premises, had had the door kicked off his consulting room, including the frame and his room smashed. Oddly, my room had not been touched.

Mrs Riley explained... It had been her son and she wanted to apologize. She took me upstairs to see in the loft. It was full of TVs, cookers, radios, and every electrical appliance that one could think of, up there. The floor was creaking with the load. All Riley's ill-gotten gains. She was overwhelmingly embarrassed and apologized profusely for our burglary, and offered to pay for any damage that he had caused. She offered a brilliant new toaster, somebody else's, but hadn't got a sterilizer.

That was not necessary, I explained, our insurance covered any damage costs, but I thanked her very for her disclosure, and I insisted that she tried to make him come and see me sometime, to discuss all this. He apparently liked me, so hadn't damaged my room at all! Nice of him. Nevertheless, I was landed with quite an ethical dilemma. Although patient confidentiality had to be considered, Riley had been committing criminal acts, and I needed to consider reporting this to the police, perhaps.

To my relief, future events spontaneously resolved my dilemma.

Wilburn was a big, big chap. 18 stones and 6 foot 4 inches tall. All muscle. All the family were the same, even Mom and Dad, who came to the UK in the 1950s from Jamaica. He, however, limped into the surgery this time, his foot in a plaster splint.

"Why Wilburn, what's happened to you?" I asked.

"Well you see Doc, it's long story," he went on. "I'm in real trouble," he explained.

Apparently he had come home early from his night shift (heavy) job as a moulder early one morning, to his high-rise flat in Blakenhall, in Wolverhampton, where he lived with his wife. His wife worked nights as well. As he came out of the lift, who should he meet, coming out of his own flat, but a white chap, who subsequently turned out to be Riley Riley, struggling with a cooker in his arms.

"Wow, Wilburn what did you do?" I asked.

"Well I didn't lose me temper. I just used me loaf Doc," he explained.

Apparently, he just said "Hello" and went on upstairs to his brother Jerome's flat where he borrowed his shotgun and then came downstairs again!

Riley by this time was just leaving the flat, now with a TV in his arms.

"Heck, Wilburn you didn't shoot him, did you?" I asked with alarm.

"No, no Doc. I told you. I used me loaf. I just gid 'im a sharp tap in the bollocks wid the gun you know," he replied. "Just a sharp tap, with the wooden butt end you know. Not the metal bit. I didn't want t' 'urt 'im much," he said. "Squealed like a stuck pig he did. Just a sharp tap as well it was. Then, as 'e was goin' down so to speak, I gid 'im another, not a sharp tap even, just a knock this time, on 'is head you know, just t' slow 'im down a bit," he finished quite blandly!

"Why then is your foot in plaster and why are you in trouble now?" I asked somewhat perturbed by all this.

"Well you see Doc, the po-leece were called as expected, and they 'ave charged me with hassault they 'ave, 'cos apparently 'e now 'ave a fractured skull, and it was only just a knock I gid 'im, you know. I tink 'e's a bit soft in the head you know," was his medical explanation.

"Oh, so that's why you are in trouble," I replied at his apparent clarification.

"No, no, Doc, that ain't why I's in trouble. I ain't bothered by no po-leece. They was very nice, you know t' me. They know this

Riley Riley chap very well and when 'e comes out of 'ospital they's goin' t' put 'im in jail, you know, they are. Me, I'm in trouble at home it is you know. When I 'it 'im, he dropped the bloody television on me big toe, and broke it he did you know. They tell me I can't go t' work for tree weeks because of it now wid my heavy job, and the missus is now furious wid me an' all because of I can't go t' work, and as 'e dropped it, 'e broke the tele as well," he disclosed. "It was a new tele, an' she is very unhappy you see now then. Can I have a sick note please?"

How could I refuse?

Whilst all this solved my dilemma, it was of no help to Riley. He eventually went to jail where he met other members of the criminal fraternity. By the time I left the practice when he was then in his 40s, he lived alone, his mother had died, and he had had several further holidays, at Her Majesty's pleasure!

Furthermore, these stories sadly go to show how even from good family backgrounds, a life of social degradation and criminality can easily develop, and although Black Country attitudes are changing, and the public is more aware and beginning to complain[65] (sometimes for very odd reasons: see the reference) more and more about criminality and prostitution, there are salutatory lessons for us all to be learned for the care of our children.

References and Author's comment:

62. Prostitution. John Philip Jenkins. 2013. *Encyclopaedia Britannica*. www.britannica.com:

Prostitution in the United Kingdom. Wikipedia. The free encyclopaedia:

Prostitution is the practice of engaging in indiscriminate, both heterosexual or homosexual activity, generally with someone who is not a spouse or friend, in exchange for payment in money or valuables.

Prostitution in the United Kingdom (in 2014) is legal!

Only related activity such as kerb-crawling, soliciting in a public place, owning or managing a brothel etc. is illegal. It is also illegal to buy sex from a person younger than 18 years of age, although the age of consent for non-commercial sex is 16 years.

Despite an extensive search of the literature, including incidence figures from the Office of National Statistics etc. accurate numbers of persons engaged in the sex industry are not known and are difficult to assess. Nevertheless, in 2009 the total number of prostitutes in the UK was approximately estimated to be 100,000, and these somewhat incredibly contributed approximately £5.3 billion to the UK economy as a whole. Yes, £5.3 billion!

63. *Hitchmough's Black Country Pubs, 2nd Edition.* Tony Hitchmough. 2014. Longpull:
www.trumpetjazz.org.uk:

The Trumpet, so called since 2006, is a now famous (infamous?) Black Country pub specializing both in impromptu jazz music and comedy, and frequented by such well-known figures as members of the pop group Slade and others in the music fraternity. The comedy at times is known to be somewhat risqué and even worse, as were "other night-time activities" that took place in the past. The pub sells a variety of local Holden's Black Country Ales (cf. Mr Holden, the author's mentor, Chapter 5) and supposedly has speciality pint glasses for women.

Formerly called The Royal Exchange, it was originally a butcher's shop and was granted a licence to sell ale and beer by the Duke of Wellington's Beer House Act of Parliament in 1830. Later it was used by the state as a source of tax exchange revenue by HM Collector of Taxes, hence its name. It is now so well known and respected, that it even has its own website. It is quite a respectable joint.

When I first visited there was no special rear entrance with arched nameplate as now. It was quite a surreptitious rear entry in those days!

64. *British National Formulary* (BNF). The British Medical

Association and the Pharmaceutical Society of Great Britain. 1966. Hazel and Watson:

Wolverhampton Area Health Authority Dermatological Formulary.

Dr P. J. Ashurst. 1981:

Psoriasis is a common skin disease characterized by thickening plaques of the outer skin layer (epidermis) commonly involving many of the body extensor surfaces, unlike eczema which commonly involves flexural surfaces, and it can involve the scalp, the nails and elsewhere. It has many complications, extraordinarily even such as acute tonsillitis, as seen by me, the author, many times (I have never been able to establish the causative connection), and it can lead to many other problems such as joint disease involvement and severe deformity etc.

The cause is unknown, but flare-ups are thought to be related to multiple environmental factors and stress reactions etc. (Riley certainly had all these.)

For many years it was treated with a variety of preparations containing coal tar, although of late this has been found to be of limited benefit, and local corticosteroid preparations are now advocated for more useful effect. Coal tar solution (Liquor picis carbonis) is an alcoholic solution made from prepared coal tar, a by-product of the carbonization process of making coal into coke or gas. It is used in many ointments, soaps and shampoos. As well as being quite smelly, it stains clothing and can cause other unpleasant side effects such as sunlight sensitivity, not the sort of side effects to give to patients who are often self-conscious and concerned regarding their unpleasant looking rash!

Ung ZALPCB is a preparation (advocated by the eminent dermatologist

Dr P. J. Ashurst of Wolverhampton) which is smelly, because of the coal tar, and very sticky, marking the patient's clothes, but with a corticosteroid combination.

It was widely used for psoriasis in the Black Country and Birmingham with great success for many years, although it is now no longer available as a prescribable item.

It had to be freshly prepared and contained...

ZALPCB ointment (Ung ZALPCB):

Solution of Coal Tar...	8.0%
Betnovate (corticosteroid) ointment...	5.0%
Zinc Oxide...	12.5%
Starch...	12.5%
White Soft Paraffin...	to 100%

65. Punter Complaints to West Midlands Police. 999 call. 11/06/2013.

www.expressandstar.com/news/crime:

One of the most "unusual" complaints ever received by the West Midlands Police, about criminality was published in the *Wolverhampton Express and Star* newspaper in June 2013. The audible recording of this 999 telephone call complaint can be heard by searching on the reference above, and was made when a man complained that a prostitute that he had met in Walsall was so distasteful, compared to an advertisement that she had made, that she should be charged for breaching the Sale of Goods Act for making herself out to be better looking than she actually was in real life!

As the call was thought to be so spurious, the emergency line was shortly terminated by the police operative, much to the man's upset, and so he then rang back!

He even offered to come to the police station to discuss the matter.

It was eventually pointed out to him by the police, that it was his action in soliciting for sex that was illegal, and that he could be charged with wasting police time, an offence that carries a penalty of up to 6 months imprisonment in jail, rather than the lady, who had committed no offence!

19. My narrative fallacy?

Death is a rather permanent condition.

It, is not difficult to confirm, but it can be difficult to give a causative diagnosis.

On reflection in the mirror of my mind I now realize that there were some conditions and circumstances that I always had difficulty with, especially those in my early practice. This was very much evidenced in my experience of cases of sudden and unexpected death.

However, as I grew more experienced, into middle age, I began to think I knew most things. Could I diagnose everything, I asked?

Well I persuaded myself that I could, even retrospectively, to find a simplistic explanation for many events, illnesses, diagnoses and even deaths that had randomly occurred.

Only later did I recognize my fallacy.

It was a lovely but cold winter's afternoon, early in my career when I was called by a concerned neighbour to see a male patient, Mr Edward "Teddy" Black, found in a collapsed state at his home. When I arrived the police were already in attendance, a young officer, with the neighbour, Mrs Gold, who had called. She was golden by nature as well as by name. She was quite distressed to see me.

"Hello Doctor," she cried. "Thank you for coming. I went in t' give Mr Black, me friend, 'is dinner, but 'e 's collapsed on the fire. I think 'e 's jed yo'll find. A lovely mon, 'e was, but 'e 's bin very down of late since 'is wife died," she explained.

I didn't know him well, but his notes had shown that he indeed had been somewhat… "A bit down Doctor," since his wife had died some 3 months previously, and he had been to see my partner who had given him a supply of night sedation to take, as he only purported to have not been sleeping very well. He had had no other significant complaints.

He was lying on the floor in the living room of his spotlessly kept semi-detached council house, unfortunately across the hearth, with his head partially in the embers of what appeared to be last night's coal fire. He was very cold with no vital signs, pulses or respirations, and he had obviously been dead some time.

I rolled him over to examine him, and to my surprise I found a pool of dried blood beneath, and a knife in his hand tucked under him that had penetrated his chest. His head and hair were also partially burnt away because of exposure to the fire. There was a large poker lying alongside his body as well. I looked around. The room was otherwise undisturbed, with nothing amiss or abnormal to see, other than what I discovered then was an empty bottle of my partner's sleeping pills that he had been given when seen previously.

He had not been seen for over a month at the surgery. I could not give a definite diagnosis of the cause of death here, so I thought this case needed to be referred to the coroner for opinion. I was about to do so when the young police officer came out with…

"Does this need to be reported to the coroner Doctor? Can you give an obvious cause of death as there are no suspicious circumstances here, d' y' think? You don't think it was intentional, perhaps, do you?" he asked, sort of gave his opinion, and questioned me all in one go.

Obvious cause of death? No suspicious circumstances?

Well other than he could have stabbed himself, or perhaps been stabbed by someone else, or been hit with the poker by an intruder as the house was unlocked, he could have died as a result of burns and smoke inhalation from falling in the fire.

Then he could possibly have just had a heart attack or a stroke and fallen with any of the previously mentioned problems, after also having overdosed on his medications. There was nothing very obvious to me here. There were a multiplicity of potential diagnoses and causations. With some alacrity I gave a short reply...

"It is a little difficult to give a diagnosis here."

Up to that time in my career I don't think I had previously seen a more suspicious and unexplained death, and I knew that if this was to be reported to the coroner, as I eventually did so, it meant that the young officer would have to stay in attendance with the deceased, even though he was approaching the end of his work shift. Then until the coroner's officer gave his permission e.g. for further examination of all the circumstances of the death to be investigated, only then could he, the officer, leave, and the body be removed. The young man was not happy, but he realized that this was the correct procedure to follow, and he accordingly performed his appropriate duty.

I left soon after, with Mrs Gold.

The cause of death you may ask?

I wasn't sure as to the true diagnosis, but I had my suspicions. Only after post-mortem and toxicology examinations were completed, was it discovered that Teddy had taken a huge drug overdose that had caused him to collapse and die. He was a bright individual with no memory disturbance etc. so it was highly likely that this was an intended case of suicide. Both my partner and I were both distressed that we had never managed to ascertain the depth of Teddy being just "a bit down Doctor".

This was my first exposure to a true suicide.

Cases of so-called "attempted suicide", however, were different. They were not normally so difficult to evaluate... or so I began to think.

This was so in the case of Bruno, who true to his name was both of dark complexion and of dark psyche. I always felt that he was a peculiar character, I know not why. In consultations in the surgery his mood was always black and he often talked of death or dying. He married late in life and had no children, and because of anger problems, he had difficulty in coping long term with any sort of job, and close to the incident, he had recently become unemployed again. He spent much of his time away from folk, reading etc. A loner. Ever he was always miserable, rowing and arguing with his long-suffering wife, threatening her with harm, while never harming himself, and this all came to a head one summer's day.

Apparently following an argument, he had violently assaulted his wife, when he had oddly chosen to hit her with a wooden toilet seat, which knocked her out, into deep unconsciousness, and she was so unarousable that she had already been taken off to hospital by ambulance, by the time I arrived at the house, when called by a concerned next-door neighbour. Bruno, it appeared, thinking he had killed his wife, had then run out of the house into the road outside and jumped in front of a passing truck, when the very awake driver had managed to brake violently, and only just lightly knock him down. He had then got himself up and run back inside the house, to cause himself further damage.

The police arrived at the same time as myself.

He was being held down by several neighbours when we arrived, especially as he was attempting to bash himself on the head with a lump hammer! I could see that his scalp already had several abrasions and bruises from this, and quite a worrying frontal dent to his forehead was evident as well!

Clearly visible also were multiple wrist slashing that one could see, which he had apparently inflicted on himself with a knife, before I was assured that he had also, "Stabbed 'imself in the chest Doctor, 'e did, an' 'e ay jed yet," someone said.

He was quite enabled enough though to reply...

"I am dyin', I am," he gasped as he raised himself up at this. "I've stabbed meself in me 'eart, and 'as nothin' werked yet I've took a bucket full of tablets an orl, an' yo cor stop them werkin', so thea," he shouted for all to hear, very out of breath, naturally as he had just attempted to stab himself in his heart.

Then whilst he was still being restrained, another team of ambulance men suddenly arrived, sent for by somebody. The place was getting pretty crowded.

Seeing what was going on they immediately requested my advice as where to take him, once we had got him permanently subdued.

Referral. This was a difficult problem...

He had various knocks and bruises, but no evidence of serious injury or fracture as a result of his road traffic accident. He had slashed and gaping wrists. Sedate him then, and send him to normal A & E perhaps? Any competent A & E could deal with these problems.

No. His apparent depressed skull fracture caused by the hammer would indicate an intracranial injury and sedation might arrest his breathing. A neurosurgical referral then, perhaps?

No. His chest stab wound? He had somehow managed to miss his heart, by stabbing himself in the right side of his chest! (What a dope.) I suspected that he had a collapsed lung on this side, hence his shortness of breath and impaired breathing. A pneumothorax? This was serious, and would necessitate an urgent thoracic surgical referral. A very specialist opinion, not available at all hospitals.

But, hang on. His purported drug overdose meant that he required to be seen by a specialist medical team as well, maybe have his stomach washed out, and could they then get a psychiatrist to see him in view of all of this, I thought?

Multiple opinions were required. Where on earth should the ambulance take him?

I solved the problem. I rang a colleague, a local Casualty Department chief, and on his advice sent him along, to his care. This was outside my field of expertise. Let someone more senior decide on his ultimate management.

We bundled him into the ambulance with restraining devices and accompanying helpers and sent him quickly off to hospital.

At his leaving, I felt relief, then, whilst tidying up my bag, someone asked…

"Was it intentional? D' y' think he really meant it Doctor, or was he just trying to get attention?"

This was a little like the question from the policeman regarding Mr Black, and his suicide, I never realized then, that in my career I was to be asked this particular question time and again with cases of self-harm, often the questioner somewhat missing the obvious.

Carmine was another attempted suicide case in point. I remember that he was what many folk would just describe as being "a little odd". A bit obsessional. He lived alone and had been seeing me for a number of years for a multiplicity of "non-organic problems" when I noticed a change in his behaviour. Often religion would crop up, the afterlife and death. Even existentialism was discussed, difficult as it was to me, to comprehend as a doctor of modern medicine, "How a person can be the self-determining agent responsible for one's own life choices in the modern yet meaningless universe"! Wow. Complex? Yes.

Then on one occasion he announced that he was changing his name. I didn't enquire further, but on leaving I recollect that he closed the interview with… "God be with you".

Just his increasing oddness, I thought, nothing particularly alarming.

It was even more peculiar to get an urgent call shortly afterwards to visit him, from the ambulance service, which was in attendance at his home following a 999 call, from himself. Unusual. I had never been requested to visit his home before, and so as with all such calls I quickly went along.

I was met at the door by an ambulance man with a wry grin on his face.

"Do you know this chap Doctor?" he asked. "He says he's got a new name, it's Jesus, he says," he explained. "He won't let us near him Doctor. He says we are not clean enough to touch him," he followed with, with raised eyebrows, questioning.

I was not prepared for what I met inside…

The house was bare. No pictures or colour. Mundane décor and furnishing. Carmine himself was lying on the floor in his living room, in just a sort of loincloth. He had somehow managed to assemble two large pieces of wood in a cross-like crucifix fashion and was lying spread out on top of these.

He had also somehow managed to cross his feet and then had hammered a 6 inch nail through them, fixing himself to his cross!

After this, with arm outstretched and holding a nail in his hand, he had then hammered another nail through the palm of his left hand, he was right-handed, and then became stuck! He couldn't finish his self-crucifixion.

Mind you, he had gone the whole way, as far as he could. Around his head was a self-made crown of thorns, a piece of barbed wire, and he had a sharpened stick in his side that he had stabbed himself with that looked a little alarming, and with all this, the whole place smelt strongly of vinegar. He had a large bowl of it, on his right-hand side, but I don't think that the Sorbo rubber sponge that he had intended to use would had been invented in Jesus Christ's time.

Apparently, after putting the second nail in, he had gathered that he had reached an impasse. What to do? Well, remarkably he had been able to reach out and grab a nearby telephone, and dial for help, and we had now all arrived.

I was for some reason, acceptable to him. He allowed me to touch him and make a physical examination, and give him some analgesic pain relief, but I dared not pull out his nails. The fire service was sent for, and we managed to get him off to hospital in a drowsy state, still with his feet crossed and his left hand nailed to pieces of wood, and a piece of his spear still in his side. All for A & E to deal with, and a psychiatric opinion to be obtained at a later date.

The question came… I was getting used to this…

"D' y' think he meant it Doctor?" from the fire officer.

I shook my head. Lots of injuries, yes. But no, no. It was too convenient that telephone, nearby on the floor, near to his only useful hand, I thought.

I came to the conclusion then that like other cases that I had seen up to that time in my early experience, these "oddballs" like Carmine and Bruno, were predictable. Their repeated aberrant behaviour led to acts of attempted, but not actual suicide. They were attention seeking, perhaps? Were these just cries for attention?

In my early years I began to feel that I could spot these oddball cases. Their unpredictability was predictable.

I had forgotten Teddy.

Fuchsia was not an oddball though. She was decidedly normal, or so I thought. She was an unmarried middle-aged lady, prematurely retired from her post as a primary school music teacher due to local authority cutbacks. She had lived alone for many years, remaining single after disclosing to me of an unhappy love affair with a married colleague early in her career, when being a staunch Roman Catholic she had ended the affair, as children were involved, and she purported to have put this behind her for many years. Only occasionally in consultations had she mentioned the old story.

She had few friends or social contacts and following loss of her job she spent much of her time browsing the Internet, alone at home, on her home computer.

She came to see me on one occasion only with what I labelled as a "tiredness syndrome", with lethargy and a feeling of being unable to socialize and mix even less than she normally did. She had slight appetite loss, mild anorexic symptoms, and some sleep disturbance but no significant symptoms of psychological or psychiatric upset otherwise, other than being upset by her neighbours who had complained of her practising on her French horn from time to time. Now having lived myself next to a French horn player at one time I could understand her neighbours being perturbed and hence her upset, but certainly there was no suggestion of depression or dying, and there were no abnormalities to find on physical examination.

I wondered then if there was possibly a delayed menopausal

or other endocrine problem here, so I gave her my reassurance of no physical illness and instituted a few screening investigations and arranged follow-up. I never realized that as she left the consultation room looking as deflated as she ever did, that this was the last time I was to see her.

The rest of her story I later obtained from her next-door neighbour...

It would appear that she left my surgery premises, and went straight home.

She then went into her garden, then down into her garden shed from which she emerged drinking a full bottle of neat creosote!

Creosote[66] is extremely toxic when taken by mouth, and this was observed by her next-door neighbour, who saw her do this whilst working in the garden that day.

He called out to her... "Stop, stop. What the ', yo' doin' Fuchsia?" apparently to no avail.

"'er looked a bit mithered [perplexed] Doctor, but 'er still drunk the lot," he said. "I run round the 'ouse an' lamped [thumped] 'er on the back, but it was t' late," he explained. "'er 'ad swallowed the lot. 'er was a bostin', lovely wench yo' know, despite playin' that bloody trumpet all the time," he said with tears in his eyes, clearly being terribly upset by her behaviour and of being unable to help.

She had collapsed almost immediately and the emergency services were called and had promptly arrived. She had been taken immediately to the local A & E department at New Cross Hospital, Wolverhampton in great distress by now, where despite attempted resuscitation she died shortly after arrival. The consultant in charge later described to me in detail her clinical picture on arrival, and the absolute agony that she was in, when that all he could do was give massive doses of sedation, as well as perform other measures, all of which were unfortunately unsuccessful, it evolved.

No reason for this deliberate act was ever found, despite careful and full investigation of her life and social circumstances by the police, the social services and the coroner. The precipitating cause of her suicide was never ascertained. I attended her inquest both in a professional capacity as her physician and in a personal capacity as a friend as she had but few relatives. For some time after I recollect feelings of inadequacy, in that I never realized that she had a depression quite so severe.

Myrtle likewise never struck me as depressed. She was a vivacious and pretty middle-aged woman, with a large and lovely home, an expensive sports car, a wealthy property developer husband and a charming son. She was seen in the surgery for a number of years by various partners always with "chronic anxiety symptoms". She tended to openly berate her husband for not giving her enough attention that she felt that she deserved, he being tied up with his business all the time, she complained, and she also felt somewhat let down by her son. She felt that he was a bright lad that should have been in grammar school education, but because he had always been given too much money by his father, he never felt the need to attempt any high academic standard, and was just coasting along in private education. She complained for years of being tense and anxious. Of being ratty and short tempered, uptight and being a poor sleeper, not helped by sedation, only much alcohol, at night. She was seen repeatedly by my female partners, but never took their advice re treatment or counselling. She wanted a cure. A quick fix. A pill.

Her behaviour became more disturbing with time, and I wondered if she was drinking too much, despite her denials. Certainly her liver function and other haematological investigations indicated borderline results. Could this be an alcoholic psychosis developing, I thought?

Feeling a little disingenuous towards her though, eventually I persuaded her to see a consultant psychiatrist, only "via a private referral, well out of the area", would she accept. She couldn't (wouldn't?) accept the stigma of friends finding out about a psychiatric problem and would only go far afield away from prying eyes so to speak.

"I wouldn't dream of seeing any Tom, Dick or Harry under

the NHS round here," she decried. "What if my friends found out?"

Thus she accepted my referral to a consultant psychiatrist at All Saints Hospital, Birmingham where I knew they had a unit specializing in alcohol and addiction-related psychiatric problems. I never dared tell her of its previous name, the Birmingham Borough Mental Asylum! She would have been much deterred.

I heard nothing else of her case for a while after my referral, until I received a letter from the doctor to whom I had made the referral. He described her illness and thought that "perhaps she has an underlying depressive disorder". Oddly though, after another while, in further letters he described her improvement, but then for "ethical reasons" he was passing her care over to a colleague of his. I thought this was a little unusual especially as she was a private and fee-paying patient, but she seemed to be in competent hands.

I didn't find out what this ethical problem was until one day her husband came to surgery for an unrelated matter. When I asked as to his wife's welfare, he astounded me by disclosing that his wife had left the marital home, was then living with the consultant that I had referred her to, and she had left both him and his son, "home alone" so to speak! He did not appear terribly perturbed by this. And following the affair, apparently she had applied for a divorce, to which after a time he agreed and he had made a full and generous financial offer to her as settlement of the marriage. I expressed my utmost dismay at all this, but he was in no way upset. I realized then that he was glad to be finished with the marriage, and he explained how he and his son had become even closer and happier since her leaving.

It seemed a sad end, but all was not finished, yet.

Months went by. She turned up in surgery again. Her affair had broken down and she had returned to live locally in a flat, alone, following her divorce. She was, not unnaturally I thought, pretty down, but generally was back to her normal self, bitterly complaining about her now ex-husband, her son, and the doctor that she had the affair with. Life was all against her, she had had a big social comedown and so we discussed further coping strategies. She still wanted a quick fix, another pill to cure all, but I did not think this would be of help. I also asked all the relevant questions about self-harm and suicide[67] in view of the now suspected diagnosis of depression. No real abnormalities were found or suspicions aroused. Finally I suggested a counselling referral and she agreed to think about it and return.

Apparently she did so return after a few weeks and saw another partner, who gave similar advice, but she didn't like my advice I suspect, and never returned to see me.

I was called as an emergency. She had been found in a "collapsed state Doctor" at her flat. I found her in the bath, she had been dead some time!

There was a note left behind stating how she felt… "Hopeless and life had no further meaning". She had taken a full bottle of antidepressant drugs given to her by the hospital, with a full bottle of Scotch whisky. She had taken a nice, very hot bath, and presumably as a terminal act had slashed her wrists, although there was not much blood loss or injury to see.

This time I did not get "D' y' think she meant it", from the callers.

Her meaning was very obvious to all.

As a result of such cases as Fuchsia and Myrtle, in middle age I began to feel an empathy of sorts with my patients. Despite knowing that suicide was a social issue, I felt saddened that I could not spot and help to prevent their demise, despite all my medical training and education. I began to conclude that no matter whatever their personal characteristics, oddballs or not, whatever questions one asked, investigations one made or referrals one arranged, it was quite impossible to foresee or pre-diagnose cases of self-harm or suicide.

I began to despair somewhat with such cases.

Only now, on reflection in later life on putting all this together and writing these stories, do I realize my mistake, the narrative fallacy[68] of my previous conclusions. I developed simplistic and totally contrasting ideas. I thought I could predict, then I couldn't predict suicides. I made contrasting conclusions based on random and unpredictable events retrospectively, all after they had occurred.

I now realize that with all cases of psychological or psychiatric symptomatology whatever their personality, characteristics, social circumstances, age or sex etc. suicide and/or self-harm should always be discussed and or suspected in such cases. This is especially so in the case of those folk who can be described as being "socially deprived"[69].

My conclusions now are that as a doctor, I did not and will not ever know everything. Despite trying to do so, I could not pre-diagnose all.

References and Author's comment:

66. Creosote toxicity. The National Poisons Information Service, Birmingham Centre. City Hospital, Dudley Rd. Birmingham B18 7QH:

www.hse.gov.uk/biocides/copr/creosote:

Creosote is a caustic mixture of chemical products obtained from the distillation of tar, and there are two main types i.e. coal tar creosote and wood tar creosote.

Coal tar creosote is the most toxic to humans and has mainly been used for wood preservative since 1716 in Britain, when a patent was granted for its use to protect ships' wood "from decay and worms". Wood tar creosote has also been used for wood and meat preservation and has medical uses, to burn away malignant skin tissues, in dentistry to prevent necrosis etc. Even today some by-products are still prescribed e.g. in proprietary cough medicines such as Benylin, and others, but generally its use has declined because of both toxic and carcinogenic effects. It has been used as a cattle wash and sheep dip, and even small doses have been given to animals by mouth to kill internal parasites.

Readers should also note that the burning of any wood fire causes the accumulation of carbon and creosote inside an unswept chimney, a common cause of chimney fires.

Since April 2003 retailers can no longer sell creosote to the general public in Great Britain, and its use has been further curtailed in the EU when as from May 2013 all advertisement, usage, sale and storage has to be pre-authorized under the Control of Pesticides Regulations.

67. Suicide – Warning signs. www.nhs.uk/Conditions/Suicide:
Struggling against suicide. D. De Leo. 2002. Crisis:
The warning signs of suicide are
1. Threats of self-harm or suicide.
2. Talking of death or suicide.
3. Actively looking at methods of killing e.g. stockpiling drugs etc.

The NHS website and De Leo's book expands on all this and gives advice both to patients and observers when suicide is anticipated.

Advice is given on emergency contacts and resolution teams etc.

Furthermore, and quite correctly in my opinion, it is stated that whilst here may be obvious signs of suicide risk in some patients, as in my experience, this is not always the case!

68. *The Black Swan Theory.* N.N. Taleb. 2007. Allen Lane (UK):
In his book the essayist, scholar and statistician N. N. Taleb describes the human tendency to find "simplistic explanations" for random, rare and unpredictable events, even when these repeated explanations are often contradictory. His theory, "The Impact of the Highly Improbable" is known as the Black Swan Theory and in his book and later editions it is expanded on into many walks of life, especially politics, banking and the financial world, when he cites in particular how banks and trading firms are vulnerable to Black Swan events and are exposed to losses beyond those predicted by their defective financial models.
He gives rise to the term "narrative fallacy".

Other and simple examples of this are e.g.:

1. Pop culture was changed forever by the decision of Decca records to turn down recording four unknown teenagers, who were later taken on by EMI. No one now has a logical explanation for this decision taken by EMI, and then why the Beatles ever became as big as they did.

2. After September 2001 it was said in the national press after the 9/11 events in New York that, "Countries are either with us, or against us, in the fight against terrorism", when countries can be very much against terrorism, yet not an ally of the US.

3. "We must attack Iraq or Saddam Hussain will develop weapons of mass destruction (WMD)." Other options of monitoring or containment were just illogically and flatly discounted, even whilst he was being closely observed.

In this chapter I give a medical example of narrative fallacy, constructing an idea around facts i.e. how to recognize intended suicide, then later constructing another entirely opposite idea around very similar facts, not noticing the quite obvious contradiction of my conclusions made at the time.

I suspect this is a phenomenon found in many doctors in middle age, who later go on to realize this and who with experience change their minds.

It should not be confused with the delusions of grandeur of the Hubris Syndrome found in many leaders and politicians. (Discussed later in reference no. 88.)

69. Suicide Statistics Report. Elizabeth Scocroft. 2014. Samaritans: Men and Suicide. Jacqui Thornton. 2014. Samaritans. The Upper Mill, Kingston Rd Ewell.KT17 2AF. www.samaritans.org: Suicides in the United Kingdom 2012. 18/02/2014. Office for National Statistics:

In her article Elizabeth Scocroft discloses that in the UK as a whole, consistently the rate of suicide in men of all ages is approximately 3 ½ times greater than the rate in women, which is confirmed by the figures of the Office for National Statistics.

The comprehensive report of Jacqui Thornton further discloses that the incidence of suicide is 10 times greater in those in the lowest social classes living in deprived areas, and this is due to many factors, social background, personality traits, relationship breakdowns, masculinity etc. all of which are discussed in some detail. Men let their distress build up to a breaking point. There is a well-known link in men between unemployment and suicide risk especially, that is seen to increase during difficult economic times and recession.

In 2012 there were no less than 5,981 suicides registered in the UK in all adults over the age of 15 years!

This enormous figure, not well known to the general public, is comparable to the much publicized death rates found in many other studies of major diseases and/or trauma. Suicide in 2014 is still a big problem.

20. Confidence. Confidentiality

Confidence implies trust or reliability, of a person or thing, of a hypothesis or a prediction. Confidentiality, the medical term, is that mutual private and secret trust between a doctor and his patient.

Confidentiality is an important duty, but it is not absolute and many patients are not aware that a doctor can disclose personal information if:

1. It is required by law.
2. The patient consents either implicitly or expressly for the sake of their own care.
3. It is in the public interest.

Guidelines for confidentiality[70] are issued to doctors and the public by the General Medical Council, as well as those for "good medical practice", the code that doctors should abide by, and that all doctors have a duty to keep up to date and observe, as well as current legislation, common law, and data protection requirements. Failure to do so can result in removal from the General Medical Register and loss of Licence to Practice.

This seems fairly straightforward it would appear, but I found that in my real life practice, things were not so clear cut. Who for example was to define what is "In the public interest".

Indeed, on reflection back into my career, confidentiality issues led to some of the most difficult problems that I ever had to manage. Some of these were pretty clear cut. Others were not so easy, and even now, after many years, the reader may find the disclosures quite controversial.

Ginger's problem was more of confidence that confidentiality. It is known that some ladies have an unusual but understandable preference not to see a female doctor. What is not widely known is that this sexual preference also applies to men, perhaps more so. When he, Ginger, came to see me one time I could see from the appointment system that he had been to the surgery some five times in the previous month, and cancelled appointments to see lady partner doctors, when normally he only was seen on occasion once every year or so. Something was afoot.

"Am I glad t' see yo' Doctor," he began to explain. "Arn got the serm problem as me missus had," he went on. "She couldn't hold her werter an' I'm getting' the serm. I 'ave t' gerrup five times a night, an' when I do so it wo come out. I used t' be able to hit that wall from 'ere," he said, pointing to the opposite side of the consulting room. "But now, I piddle on me shoes, an' afta ar'n bin, ar dribble down me trouser leg as well. I really doe like it very much. My missus 'ad the same, an' yo sent 'er to a specialist, one of them gynacolumists, who gor 'er better, so I'ne come to see yo about it, an' I doe want yo t' discuss it any ferther with anybody else now, please," he said.

Sounded pretty easy diagnosis, a middle-aged man's simple prostatic obstruction, but why hadn't he disclosed this previously I asked?

"What?" he exclaimed. "I ay torkin to no wimen doctor about werter work problems. It doe feel right y' know t' talk t' a woman about such things, an' yo know what that young mon doctor said t' me when I tode 'im about it?" he asked, questioningly, regarding the male doctor he had previously seen.

"No," I replied.

"Well, 'e said I needed an examination, an' 'e was gooin' t' 'ave t' stick 'is finger up me bum!" he said with disdain in his voice. "I ay a doctor, but I ay saft an orl, an' I know there's nothin' wrong with that part a me. I goo as regular as clockwork in that department I do. It's me werter works that the problem. I ay 'avin' nobody stick their finger up my bum, I ay, that is if yo doe think I need it Doctor?" he explained to me and questioned me at the same time, as Black Country patients often do.

"And, whatever yo think and do, I doe want yo t' tel me wife about it, an orl. It's between me and yo," he added.

It all became clear. He refused to discuss with a female doctor or even his wife, with what to him was a very private problem, and he did not understand the need for a rectal examination or such, as intended by my male partner.

I simply explained the very necessary need for, and the method of examination, required in his case to obtain a diagnosis, and he went on then to allow me to perform such, although even then he was not very keen. Following this I referred him off to a local urologist for further opinion and the required treatment.

Ginger's problem was a matter of confidence in me, rather than confidentiality, and it reflected the level of understanding and closeness that I was beginning to achieve with my patients. It was a form of flattery in a way that I have always felt a little embarrassed to accept. I met it from all ages and it was often very unexpected and often in response to what I thought was my just normal duty. Ron and Ruby were a younger example of this.

They came to see me together, a young recently married and charming couple, and members of our local Jehovah's Witness community. They explained that since their marriage despite being well and having no relationship problems, she had been unsuccessfully trying to conceive for over 6 months now.

At physical examination I found no abnormality of either she or he, and a later sperm count of his showed only normality. Supplying her with a medical thermometer[71] likewise showed that she was ovulating normally and regularly at the correct time of her monthly cycle, all normality.

I broached then the actual physical act of intercourse.

"Were there any problems or hang-ups here?" I asked.

217

"No, no Doctor," Ron replied, with Ruby nodding her head in agreement at the same time. "The only thing I am not happy with, and I think my wife will agree, is that we both do not get much satisfaction from doing it," he explained a little sadly, Ruby again nodding her head in agreement.

That's odd at their age it seemed. I needed to go into this a little deeper. And so I did.

What the ' I thought at their reply! Their explanation astounded me, but I had to look nonplussed.

It was difficult.

Ron explained how after a period of normal sexual foreplay, he eventually ended up masturbating to a climax, in her umbilicus, her belly button! Not a difficult job, but unfulfilling, and they had been doing this for over 6 months since their wedding!

No wonder they felt a little dissatisfied. I had to have a think here.

"I am pretty sure I can get an answer to your problem," I said, knowing full well that at that time I didn't. "I'll try and get you some further information and ask you then to come back to see me," I went on with, and they left the surgery thus, as always with a smile.

It took me a week to sort out an answer... Dave. There were no psychosexual counsellors available in the NHS in those days, but Dave. He was my hospital theatre ODA, the operating department assistant. A bright chap. Very understanding. He was the chief anaesthetic assistant at my hospital operating session. He was always talking about blue videos that he had or had seen, so I talked to Dave.

He very kindly loaned to me several of his "The berst berlue of berlue videos, Doc",

he was a Brummie, and I discreetly passed them on to Ron, with the instruction...

"Look at them yourself first Ron, and if you think suitable, then pass them on to your wife," I said, with the instructions... "Note, they are purely for your medical education, not for others or recreational purposes."

WHAT THE ' - REFLECTIONS OF A BLACK COUNTRY

Off he went with a little smile on his face, again.

Surprise. Eight weeks later Ruby turned up in surgery. Rosy cheeks and a grin.

Somewhat unabashed she disclosed, "I looked at those videos Doctor, with Ron. We were astounded, but then we had a go. After a little practise I think we have got quite good at it, and we persevered, and we quite like it, and now I would be grateful if I could have one of those new pregnancy tests please Doctor, I'm late?" she politely explained with a very big smile now.

Wonderful, after only a few weeks "practise", I thought.

This story had a happy ending as you might expect, although on thinking back now, Dave never got his videos back. I wonder what happened to them?

The reason for including this tale, is that Ron and Ruby were unbelievably grateful to me, following her successful pregnancy. We established a lifelong friendship, and, when we meet socially, or just in the street as we still do, we always exchange a smile and politenesses, and a little grin as to the intimacy of what we had shared together.

When I moved practices in later life they found out, and followed me to the new premises which were several miles away, where they remained as patients until my retirement.

Their confidence shared, has been a confidence for life.

These were examples of the easy cases.

Mr Buff's case on the other hand was not easy, and he was not grateful to me. His case involved the matter of confidentiality not confidence.

I was asked to see him, Mr Buff, one day by my senior receptionist who had been in the practice for many years and knew all the patients intimately. She explained that she was a little worried as he had turned up at the front desk requesting a repeat prescription, when he had received a renewal of his regular drugs just a week previously, and she disclosed that he had also collided with another patient's car in the surgery car park on his arrival.

"He's not himself Doctor," she said. "He's riffy dirty and very mithered [unwashed and very perplexed] and he doesn't really know where he is. He's been like this for a while now since his wife died, you know, and I've took it on myself to tell him that he must come and have a consultation with you," she went on to explain.

Contrary to their public image, I have always found my all ancillary staff extremely kind and caring folk, despite their poor reputation with the general public, and this despite their awkward and often not very well paid job. She was a middle-aged married lady with grown up children, and knew what she was talking about.

I thus saw Mr Buff immediately at her request.

He was unkempt and dishevelled, although well nourished, and appeared generally very unlike his usual smart self. His cardiovascular problems were under control with his drugs, but he had quite marked short-term memory loss evident, and was unsteady on his feet and had a marked tremor of his hands suggestive of considerable cerebrovascular circulatory problems. When I went to examine his gait it was so bad, I discovered, that he had poor limb control and he fell over both getting on to, and off, my examination couch!

He was clearly unfit to drive and I told him so, in a kindly way, much to his dismay. He flatly refused to accept my advice regarding his disabilities and to contemplate giving up his driving. Thus, following his leaving the premises I decided to contact his daughter by telephone, and she confirmed all my suspicions, telling me further of his increasing inabilities at home and of several minor road traffic accidents that he had had whilst driving, in the last month alone. I don't think he had deliberately not disclosed these accidents to me. They had just been forgotten.

There was only one thing to do here. As he was both a danger to himself and to the general public, I had a duty of care and I breached my confidentiality. I reported his case to the medical officer at the DVLA and sadly his driving licence was revoked. Then I arranged to see him further, together with his daughter and my practice health visitor regarding his future care.

This was the first time I had knowingly breached confidentiality with a patient, and although it was very necessary and in his best interest, I personally felt it was quite sad to have to do so.

Over the years with an ageing practice population and because of increasing life expectancy, there was an increase in the number of elderly and disabled drivers in my practice like this, and unfortunately I had later to repeat this action on further occasions.

In addition, I didn't realize it at the time, being concerned only with day-to-day affairs, but on reflection it has become apparent that I found matters of confidentiality occurred with all ages, not just the elderly, and of these, without doubt the most difficult cases I ever had to deal with were those involving youngsters and the diagnosis of sudden infant death syndrome (SIDS), often known as infantile cot death syndrome[72].

It is only now, some 25 years later do I feel free to make disclosure regarding such cases.

Scarlet and Simon were a case in point, a devoted and young newly married couple that I had known most of their lives. They both came from hard-working, working–class, stable family backgrounds, and it was to everyone's delight about 18 months after their marriage that she turned up in my antenatal clinic, eventually to have delivery of an exceedingly normal infant. All was well for several months, and they moved into a small council semi in Lanesfield, close to all amenities, and to their attendant families. We were all distraught then in the practice to hear the news, one Monday morning close to their first Christmas as a family, that the baby had been found in bed in a collapsed state over the weekend, and even after emergency hospitalization, the infant had subsequently died. A complete tragedy.

They required much comfort and sympathy and a diagnosis was eventually given as "cot death" after subsequent investigation from the hospital. My health visitor and I had to see them both for consolation etc. for some time following this.

About a year later Scarlet turned up pregnant again in the antenatal clinic. This time, however, she had lost her bloom, her *joie de vivre.* She should have been delighted. Something was amiss, it was easy to tell and in view of the previous cot death I had to broach the subject carefully.

It was only then on carefully mentioning the previous baby did she disclose to me very quietly, that following a celebration night out, she and her husband had returned home for the first time after leaving the child in the care of a babysitter, i.e. her Mum, and that they had both gone to bed after this, somewhat worse for wear due to drink and much alcohol. They had gone to bed with the baby in their bed, lying between them both, and it was only on awaking next morning had they realized that the little fellow had slipped beneath them both under the blankets and was in an unarousable state, both of them lying on top of him. The emergency services had been called, but it was too late. He had been taken to hospital etc. to no avail.

She disclosed that really the baby had suffocated beneath them and that they had been too embarrassed and distraught to disclose this previously to anyone. It was only now, with her second pregnancy and still feeling very guilty, did she feel it was possible to disclose the nightmare that both she and her husband had gone through and were still experiencing. We sat together for many minutes or so, with my hand on her shoulder. We did not, neither of us, say a word. There was no need.

I remember now, after all the years gone by, still of my incredible sorrow at this disclosure, but I had to rally. She and Simon both needed my help.

I saw them together and spoke to my partners and to a consultant paediatrician and a senior police officer colleague. They gave advice, but left the final decision up to me. Other than the verbal admissions given by the parents, there was no definitive medical or other evidence causing the need to change the previous diagnosis of cot death, and so it was decided that no further other action would be taken.

I explained this "in confidence" to them both, and how with

the help of my health visitor and a local social services friend, that we would need to carefully monitor them in the future, and the new forthcoming pregnancy, which we did. And it all went along successfully. Their second child was a delight and grew up doted on by Scarlet and Simon. I never thought or wished at that time that I would ever see such a situation and have to make a similar decision.

It was 8 years before it happened. Again!

Fawn presented as a 19-year-old unmarried mother, because she refused to terminate her pregnancy despite being abandoned by the father of the child. She had been thrown out of the family home and with help from my health visitor had managed to obtain a small first-floor council flat near to our branch surgery in Woodcross. It has been a long time since but what I do remember of her flat was how cold it was, and the incredibly steep stairs that one had difficulty in negotiating especially in the night when visiting. They were so narrow that it was difficult to carry just a small doctor's bag with the required gear. They were typical post-war brick built uninsulated rooms, with exposed two-bar electric fire heating and single-glazed metal window frames etc. I shudder still thinking about them. However, it was the best that could be obtained at the time, for her.

Despite this Fawn was a compliant patient. She attended all antenatal clinics and educational classes and she went on to a normal hospital delivery of a healthy baby girl. Things seemed to be going OK in the postnatal period and she was seen and followed up regularly.

That was also until around Christmas time, when the babe was about 3 months old.

Again, one morning at the surgery we were informed by the hospital authorities, again New Cross Hospital, Wolverhampton, of a sad event that had occurred over the weekend previous. Following a sudden collapse the baby had been brought into the A & E department as an emergency, but was found to be unresponsive on arrival, and was deceased despite attempted resuscitation.

Later investigation and inquest revealed a diagnosis of sudden infant death syndrome, a cot death, with no definitive other causation. It wasn't the only child death we had in those pretty awful flats (still the same today, 2014).

Fawn required much help, from us and social services for a protracted period at the time, she never returned to her parental home after this, and we became close, I suspect because of the attention given by all the members of the practice.

It was then with a little surprise one day many months later when she came to see me, with a minor problem that I now forget what, that suddenly she poured out almost a confession.

"Doctor, I need t' tell somebody about what happened with the babi," she disclosed. "I couldn't tell the lady doctors in case they tell me Mom 'n Dad, but I know I can talk t' yo, an' share a secret," she said.

I just nodded. I turned my head and thought... Oh no, not again. I think I know where this is leading.

"Well, it wasn't a cot death doctor, with the babi. I was going downstairs all alone, on me tod I was, t' lock the front door, down them bloody steep stairs, when I tripped an' fell. Halfway down I fell, I did Doctor, with 'er in me arms I did. Somethin' flicked 'er 'ed back an bostid it against the wall, an' er stopped breathin' right away. That's when I sent for the ambulance an' they took 'er away they did. I am pretty sure it was that fall that killed 'er. Not one of them cot death things you know. I was too scared t' tell anybody, an' I've bin thinkin' about it ever since you know. I am ever so mithered [perplexed], I 'ad t' tell somebody. Can yo keep a secret Doctor? I wouldn't want t' get yo or anybody else into trouble you know," she said, almost effusing out her story, in tears by now.

This poor young woman was afraid and lonely. She needed aid and guidance, not admonishment, especially after disclosing to me such a confidence.

I helped her out again, just as in the previous case. I took professional advice and again eventually all was left to my decision. There was no need for any administrative procedure. I arranged counselling and further care. It was a long process and I became emotionally drained but there was a happy conclusion.

We became lifelong confidants. When it was all over I remember at the time thinking out loud… "The second one. At least it will never happen again".

It did!

Many years had passed by. I had moved on to practice in Kingswinford, in Dudley.

Pleasingly, I had seen only a few more infant deaths, but there were some, and some were "cot deaths", so labelled. These were always a terrible problem for parents to be faced with. The uncertainty of it all, no known causation, it caused them so much grief.

Veronica's baby, 6 months old was supposedly one of these.

I had almost forgotten, it was in the new millennium now. It was 10 years since Veronica and the family had been devastated by a "cot death", but all the worry of that time had now resolved. Her psychiatric disorder, her schizophrenia, was well under control on her regular and newly developed drugs, and her home life and care was supervised by a community psychiatric nurse (CPN), a new type of nurse grade, introduced and incredibly beneficial for patients and their home supervision. They had not been "invented" in my early practice days.

She turned up then one day in surgery for her routine follow-up, when I congratulated her on her improvement and her well-being, and now relatively normal family life, when she suddenly came out with…

"Doctor we've been together now for many years you know, and we have become friends," she stated. "Looking back to when I was mad, [Psychiatric patients I have heard many times describe the acute phases of their illness as their "mad phase". They can tell the difference. I was not alarmed.] there is something that I need to get off my chest," she explained. "I have never even told my husband or my hospital consultants about this, but I think I need to confide in somebody now and feel that I can tell you," she said.

225

Pleased at this, I didn't realize what was coming. I had forgotten days gone by.

"You know my baby that died?" she said. "Well it wasn't a cot death as the hospital and the coroner said. It was me. I killed the baby. My voices [i.e. to her audible auditory hallucinations] at the time told me he was threat, he was going to come between me and my husband. And they went on and on and on about it, and I needed to kill him, to stop this. So I did. One night, I gently smothered him with a pillow, and I left his body knowing that my husband would find him, and he then called the emergency ambulance," she went on to explain. "I know I was ill at the time and I am OK now, and I don't have the voices any more, so I realize that I need to tell someone, and especially my husband. Can you advise me, what to do?" she asked, with a kindly and "calling for help" type voice.

Although incredibly surprised, as I had met this all before, I knew what I had to do. Again. Firstly I responded kindly and quietly and arranged a joint meet with her husband, to explain… he was brilliant. He loved his wife dearly, and he accepted her story without recrimination or malice. Then, as previous, I had had to discuss this with several other colleagues and professionals, especially as they had by now other healthy children who could have been at risk, but no further action was needed or was taken. She was carefully followed up by the hospital and her CPN.

It was, as before, a confidence shared, and oddly all due to the same medical condition.

Following these confidence and confidentiality disclosures you may ask, what happened to all the folk involved?

Well, it is with great satisfaction that I look back to reply…

My Jehovah's Witness couple now have a grown-up family and are happily entering middle age together. Our mutual confidences remain.

Mr Buff became slowly more and more confused, but was devotedly cared for by his daughter with a "Home Care Package" of home help ladies etc. at his bungalow for several years. I saw him at home from time to time and his prescription drugs were delivered to and administered by his daughter, until his death at a later date. He had completely forgotten my breaking of his confidence, so this was never a problem, but others later arose. (See the next chapter for the sequelae of his case.)

Scarlet and Simon are now the middle-aged parents of delightfully polite and very preciously loved healthy teenagers, and Fawn has matured into a lovely young adult woman and re-established the relationship with both her ex-boyfriend and her parents. She is likewise happily married with teenage children.

Veronica remains stable and well, and is now a grandmother, much to her delight, her children having all now left the family home.

The "cot death" incidents have all been forgotten.

We all remain great friends, with secrets of confidence and confidentiality shared.

P.S. I never did get those videos back you know.

References and Author's comment:

70. The General Medical Council. Regents Place. 350 Euston Rd. London NW1 3JN. www.gmc-uk.org/guidance/confidentiality:

The GMC is a charitable but statutory body set up to supervise and regulate the Health Service and the medical profession, setting out standards of care and good practice, and the educational requirements of doctors and medical staff. It covers the whole of the UK and has regional branches. It maintains a register of all medically qualified practitioners, and issues a Licence to Practice to all doctors enabling them to work within the UK.

It is accessible to both the medical profession and the general public.

71. *Pocket Gynaecology.* 10th Edition. S. Clayton and J.R. Newton. 1983. Churchill Livingstone:
    www.babycentre.co.uk:

During a woman's hormonal cycle, ovulation, the release of an egg (the ovum), from the ovary, tends to occur at about the 14th day, and the ovum takes approximately a further 10 days to descend down her (fallopian) tube to become embedded in the lining of the uterus. Just before release there is often a slight fall in basal body temperature i.e. body temperature on first awaking after 3 hours of uninterrupted sleep, and then a spiked rise of 0.2 to 0.5 degrees C that persists for several days.

The most fertile time for fertilization is at about the time of the temperature spike which can be measured on a basal thermometer, which has a finer scale than that of a normal thermometer, and supply of which can be obtained from a GP.

Regular charting of basal body temperature should be taken and charted over a period of three cycles or so, with readings being best taken before arising and taken at the same time each day, to obtain a clear confirmation that regular ovulation is taking place.

72. *Lecture Notes on Paediatrics.* 7th Edition. S.R. Meadow and R.W. Smithells. 2001. Wiley-Blackwell:
www.nhs.uk/Conditions/Sudden-infant-death-syndrome:
www.lullabytrust.org.uk:

Sudden infant death syndrome (SIDS) also known as cot death, is the sudden unexpected and unexplained death of an apparently fit and healthy child.

The definitive cause still remains unknown, with approximately 300 cases per year (2014) still occurring in the UK, although UK and worldwide figures are decreasing. There were 22,000 deaths worldwide attributed to SIDS in 2010, down from 30,000 in 1990, but it is nevertheless still an all too frequent an occurrence.

Most deaths occur in the first 6 months of life when the baby is asleep, but it has been known to happen whilst they are awake.

The cause is thought to be multifactorial, in a vulnerable type of child sensitive to stress, with low birth weight or prematurity, with other environmental factors implicated such as exposure to tobacco smoke, minor respiratory illness, bottle rather than breastfeeding etc.

Professor Meadow, the author of my reference book, has been implicated in much controversy regarding the diagnosis of this disorder, and for further explanation of this see the later reference no. 76.

As a preventative measure parents are now advised that it is thought best to place the baby on its back to sleep, in a cot within the parental bedroom, avoiding sleeping with the infant in the same bed. Also advising not letting the baby become too hot or too cold, making attempts to keep the child's airway unobstructed by clothes or bedding etc. is thought to have led to a decrease in the incidence of this problem.

A thorough investigation into how and why SIDS occurred, including post-mortem examination is necessary in all cases, and the police and the health-care professional team needs to work closely together in each case, especially as the family generally requires much help and psychological support.

The Lullaby Trust proves such help for bereaved families, and can be contacted on their UK helpline 0808 802 6868.

Medical statistics and disease incidence figures can be wrong. Infanticide and child abuse cases may be misdiagnosed as SIDS due to lack of evidence. As in my quoted experiences, other causes of death such as accidental suffocation or injury, only sometimes come to light at a much later stage, and I learned that parents, as with all cases of child death whatever the cause, need to be treated with the utmost sympathy and kindness.

21. Court cases. Nutcases

Memories in this chapter involve cases of skulduggery and murder most foul.

Readers who wish to avoid such are accordingly advised to skip to the next chapter, although I do realize that disclosing this might cause most even more avid attention.

On joining general practice I found many aspects of my education that were inadequate that I have previously mentioned. Medicolegal training in the 1960s was another of these, when I was ill-prepared for both the complexity of legal problems that I was to be involved with, the changing times of violence and abuse in society, and the sheer number of cases that I was eventually to meet.

One of the earliest cases I was involved with was that following the death of confused Mr Buff, mentioned in the previous chapter, when I received a witness subpoena to attend court one day. It was a case on behalf of Mr Buff's daughter against somebody. After consulting my defence union, I rang her up to enlighten me as to what it was all about.

Poor Mr Buff was grief-stricken at his wife's sudden death and never got over the shock, despite much care and devotion from his only daughter, as mentioned previously. Apparently even when he had lost his driving licence he still managed to walk to the Sedgley Beacon Cemetery on a weekly basis to visit and attend to her grave. However, over time his health, both physically and mentally, had deteriorated and despite a great deal of home care from his daughter and a "Home Care Package" of aid instituted by the local social services department, eventually he died at home.

I knew all this. However, his daughter went on to tell me that a reading of his will was arranged by his solicitor, coincidentally my own practice solicitor, and she duly turned up on the date arranged, surprisingly to find another lady, a complete stranger, in attendance as well. She was even more surprised when details of a relatively new will were disclosed, when it was revealed that Mr Buff had left his complete and entire estate to this unknown lady, including all monies, his bungalow that he lived in, and all the contents etc. Hence, eventually I and others were called to Dudley County Court when his daughter disputed the outcome of this new will.

On the day I recollect how odd it was to appear in a case on the opposite side to my own solicitor. Details were disclosed that Mr Buff had attended the solicitor's office in Wolverhampton town centre, travelling there by bus, being accompanied by his new friend, to an appointment, the time and day and the appointment all having arranged by her. The new lady friend it was disclosed had acquired his friendship and struck up an acquaintance when meeting him several times alone at the cemetery only, and on no other social occasions. She had never socialized anywhere else with him. She had provided no care for him. She had never visited him at home. She was totally unknown to both his daughter, family and all others, and at no time prior to the making of the will had she contacted anyone, other than Mr Buff himself. It was all "a bit sniffy".

I was called to give evidence, and accompanied by his medical notes used in evidence I revealed his history of cerebrovascular disease etc. and I told of his confused state and poor memory, and in my opinion, his inability of being capable of making rational decisions on a day-to-day basis.

The solicitor and his clerk, the will signature witness, gave evidence of the making of the will, and his condition on the day that the will was made.

His daughter and others all added to the story.

It was a lengthy proceeding and lasted all day. However after just a very short period of contemplation the judge gave his decision…

"The contents of the will are valid and I find against the appeal!"

His decision, he went on to explain, was made because on the actual day of making the will, neither myself, his daughter or anyone else involved with his care, had actually seen him. Therefore, no opinion of irrationality could be made on

Mr Buff that particular day, and as he was capable of making his own way to make the will, albeit accompanied only by the only recipient, and he was supposedly capable of rationally signing the document in front of witnesses, it could not be disproved that he was *compos mentis* that day, and the will stood.

All these factors gave conclusion to the decision.

We all thus went home somewhat deflated, even my own solicitor, a kindly man, who offered the daughter his condolences. These were times when the law was literally enforced to the word, although I doubt very much in these more liberal times, such a decision would have been made.

His daughter's languorous response was to disclose…

"Although I feel snayped [snubbed or outraged] the result was all due to the fact that me Dad, a bostin, lovely mon Doctor, was saft in the yed and as nutty as a fruit cerk[73] for months before he died."

A typical Black Country woman's acceptance of inevitability.

But times were changing, as was society, and I never realized the seriousness of the actual crimes I was to become involved with. In the late 1980s I had the sad duty of aiding the police in obtaining a witness statement from a 12-year-old. My first murder case, when she had witnessed, and graphically described to me, the effect of seeing her father plunge a knife into her mother's chest during a violent family argument over a minor disagreement...

"The point of the knife cum out through my Mom's back Doctor," she wept.

At the time I never thought I would see such pain again. I did, and worse.

In earlier chapters I described my meeting with prostitutes as patients. Their world was on the edge of normal society, and they were often subject to violence, even murder[74] with several local deaths, so that by the 1990s I think I had almost become inured to violence. It had become the normality of acceptance when in 1996 a local nursery school assistant was attacked by a disturbed man and severely injured protecting the children[75] in her care.

This was just a few months after the most disturbing case of my career.

I clearly remember the young man who presented one evening surgery with his 4-year-old stepson, complaining of a short history of sickness and diarrhoea, but little else at that time. The child was unwell, but did not appear terribly ill on examination, and I merely prescribed "starve him of all solids and push fluids" etc. the routine treatment of a gastrointestinal viral upset.

He apparently improved a little, and I was surprised then when a week later he presented with similar symptoms, again being brought by his now quite concerned stepfather on return from his work. No one else at home had similar symptoms and again he was not terribly unwell, although as a precaution I now prescribed some fluid replacement therapy. I suggested follow-up if he did not improve, and this would have been easy as they lived but a few yards from the surgery.

Note, again he was brought by his stepfather. I did not realize the significance.

At this time I was working some of my days in hospital and my next contact with the case was when I received a dramatic telephone call from a consultant paediatrician colleague from New Cross Hospital, 72 hours later. She enquired as to what I had prescribed for the child as the stepfather like many patients in distress could not coherently and accurately explain the history. The child had been admitted on the previous day, overnight (when I was working in hospital), and was now in extremis, with suspected renal failure! I was astonished.

The paediatrician explained that when the child's serum sodium (the level of sodium in his blood) sample was taken to the biochemistry lab on admission, the reading was so high that the biochemist on duty thought that the testing machine was faulty and they had recalibrated the whole apparatus! Only to get the same figure when the test was repeated.

Sadly as a result of all this the child died later that day!

In the practice where he had been seen in my absence, we were all distraught.

The whole episode had spiralled out of control we felt. But something was a little odd. He had never seemed so terribly ill when seen by us, to cause alarm. On the occasions I had seen him with his stepfather, he was not terribly unwell, but quiet ("Beware the quiet child", I always taught medical students)... But he was always quiet, and there was never any suggestion given of suspected foul play at home.

It was only later then, were we astounded further by contact from the hospital, when it was disclosed that his mother was being charged with his killing, having supposedly poisoned him by giving him salt, and laced it into his drinks, repeatedly!

A court case was prepared, and eventually myself and my partners and other medical witnesses appeared at Stafford County Court. I recollect feeling very apprehensive on the day, when although I had given a statement of my involvement in the case, I had been unable to find comprehensive medical information regarding salt overdosage and I felt an unease at the thought of being cross-examined on the subject. I was also unfamiliar with court protocol and procedure especially in such a high-profile case. However, it was not to be. The mother up to the morning of the hearing pleaded "Not guilty" to all charges, only at the very last moment of onset of the case to change her plea to that of "Guilty of manslaughter", on the grounds of diminished responsibility. She was later sentenced to life imprisonment, with the diagnosis of the severe personality disorder "Munchausen syndrome by proxy"[76] that would be supposedly untreatable in hospital!

When I look back to this sad episode, one of the lowest of my career, I realize that whilst there were difficulties and possible mistakes made in this child's management, and it is easy to say that, with that brilliant medical instrument,

"The retrospectoscope", I doubt very much if this case could have had any other final outcome. It was impossible to obtain the diagnosis on clinical signs and history alone, and indeed, on arrival in a specialist hospital department a diagnosis was only obtained after repeated biochemical investigation.

What I have never previously disclosed was that on hearing of the diagnosis, I was so disturbed by this, that unknown to all but my wife, I came into the surgery on weekend nights and went through all the notes of all the patients seen in that week by all the doctors in the practice, and the practice nurses and health visitors.

We had seen in total that week nine similar age group patients with similar symptoms and from similar social classes. They all were treated at home and all made a recovery without complications. If we had sent all these into hospital we could have been accused of malpractice and of blocking hospital beds. Nevertheless, somehow we failed in our duty of care to this child, but even now I do not know what we could have done further to help him and avoid his ultimate death.

I was intensively antagonistic and critical of the mother

initially following the conclusion of this case, but on reflection and in conciliation one has to accept that she was suffering from an illness, albeit a psychiatric disorder, and so my attitude towards her, albeit gradually, has changed.

My attitude to the case of Graham and his Granny has never changed…

I cannot remember when Gray (the name used by his family) went to live with his grandparents, a working-class Black Country family, but he was a troubled teenager. His grandparents were the retired wardens of Woodcross Boys Home, a local authority residential home for delinquent boys, superbly run by the couple for a number of years, she providing the kindliness that many of them had never seen, and he, an ex-naval petty officer, providing the strength of character and discipline that likewise they had never met. For some years my partner and I were the responsible medical officers, and it was a delight to see many of the initially very disturbed lads become mature and responsible citizens, often returning to, and at times even marrying into, the local community. Gray became just the same, a reformed lad, under their care, and the man of the house when his grandfather died.

I was called to the family home in Sedgley one day for an odd reason. Gray's granny, Iris, had been in a road traffic accident as a front seat passenger whilst out for a drive with him, and had sustained a fracture of her lower leg, which had been manipulated and immobilized in a full-length plaster of Paris splint. She also had suffered a large laceration to the top of her scalp that had been sutured in hospital. I was to review that she was progressing satisfactorily following this, and to remove her sutures. Iris was her bright normal self, uncomplaining of both her injuries and of his home care, and indeed, she was very complimentary about Gray's looking after her, of how he was already encouraging her mobility, changing her dressings etc. and she was proud of his lifestyle in general. All was progressing well. I performed my duties accordingly and left.

Three weeks later to the day that she had been in the accident, I received a call in the evening from Gray...

"What the ' shall I do Doctor? Me granny 'as 'ad a funny rash for a few days, and now 'as suddenly collapsed and her cor get 'er breath and 'ers gone blue," he cried out in alarm on the telephone.

Now he was a sensible lad, not easily alarmed, and blueness, cyanosis, indicated a marked impairing of pulmonary oxygenation. A serious emergency, possibly requiring resuscitation. I was already at another home visit dealing with an urgent call. There was no time to lose. I had a direct telephone line number to Ambulance Control, the operatives of whom knew me well. One of those new paramedics and an emergency ambulance was sent out straight away to his address.

It was thus with some dismay that I later learned that despite being still alive but in severe shock when the paramedics arrived, and being taken as an emergency to A & E, that Iris had died despite all the proper care being taken. It was understandable, she was a frail little thing, now into her late 70s, but it was unusual to obtain the eventual diagnosis from the hospital following a post-mortem...

"Pulmonary embolism secondary to fat embolism with cardiorespiratory failure, all due to fracture of the tibia", a condition whereby fat contents from the site of the fracture had become lodged in her lungs, causing blood clotting then respiratory failure and her death. This was most unusual as this condition usually occurs within a short time of a fracture, and it was rare to occur some weeks after the injury, as in Granny's case. Immobility, especially in the elderly, predisposes them to the condition.

I was even more dismayed some time later to receive a request from a solicitor to appear in court on Gray's behalf, as he had subsequently been charged by the Crown Prosecution

Service with "Causing Death by Dangerous Driving", i.e. the death of his own grandmother, a charge which at that time could carry a custodial sentence of up to 2 years in jail.

When I saw him he was distraught. Not by the threat of a fine or a jail sentence, it was the personal dishonour, that he had been accused of causing the death of the most loved person in his life, he had little other family and few close friends.

Despite reassurance, he was inconsolable. The case went ahead though.

I turned up at court, Stafford County Court again, and gave my evidence as to Iris's injuries, and to her and Gray's characters. It was about this time that I had started to take a deeper interest in medicolegal matters and practice, and with my now 20 years of hospital speciality experience, I had become very familiar with the diagnosis and treatment of facial and head and neck trauma cases. Furthermore, with my general practice experience I had also become familiar with the social aspects of such injury, the psychological effects, effects on employment etc. It was with great interest then that I was allowed by the judge to stay on in court and listen to the technical evidence of the case given by an accident investigator.

It was described to the court how when taking a left-hand bend on the main Sedgley to Dudley road (that I knew very well), that Gray had "lost it" on the bend, not particularly due to excessive speed, and collided with a vehicle travelling in the opposite direction. In addition, the prosecution council alleged that Gray had been negligent in his duty and had allowed Granny not to wear a seat belt, a fact denied by him, causing severe worsening of her subsequent injuries and another reason for the charge being made. A photograph was shown taken from inside the car, showing the damage to the vehicle dashboard, all bashed in, and the windscreen, a nice oval hole in the glass window, caused by her head, etc.

I paused. What the '.

I had one of those "*2001: A Space Odyssey* man-monkey

238

moments"[77], the dawn of realization hit me!

I whispered in counsel's ear. I was allowed back into the witness box.

It was explained by counsel to the judge that this time my testimony was to be made as a relative "expert" in the case, and my qualification for this. He accepted and allowed this, pleasingly.

I explained how the prosecution technical evidence, that I had not seen previously, showed that at the point of impact it was highly likely that Iris was wearing a seat belt, but it was worn in an improper fashion i.e. she had taken her arm out of the diagonal portion of the belt, which would not have been visible to the driver, and this meant that she was restrained in a lap belt-type of restraint only. At the point of impact then she would have momentarily been flexed into a jackknife position, thus throwing up her legs and causing the dashboard damage and her leg fracture, and with her head flexed forward she had made the oval hole in the windscreen, and thence sustained the laceration on top of her scalp. This explained why her injuries were different than one would normally expect in a relatively low speed accident, and why she had no facial injury from hitting the windscreen or any chest wall injury such as that caused by diagonal seat belt restraint.

The judge halted the case, and called all counsel for consultation.

The charge was changed to "Driving Without due Care and Attention" and the claim of not wearing a seat belt was dropped.

Gray pleaded guilty, and accepted a driving ban and a fine.

He must have been the most delighted man ever to accept such a sentence.

His honour was restored. That was the main thing. He was a Black Country man.

One would have thought that I would go home after the last cases quoted with some sense of elation. This was not so. I felt I had let my patients down and my testimony to me was inadequate, as in Mr Buff's and "the salt" cases, and I was very late in helping in Gray's case. Despite my years of experience since qualification, at this time I felt uneasy and unfamiliar with court cases and procedures and the legal terminology involved. I had to do something about this.

Remember, I was approaching middle age and it was about the time that I moved practices, I changed ladders. I took a long look thus at my education and knowledge. I needed to take a more active interest in postgraduate education, IT, newer procedures and research etc. I needed a revamp.

Accordingly I went on many courses and upgrades, with the permission of my new partners, and I modernized my knowledge, I adapted. I settled into learning again, updated my clinical medicine and enlarged on more modern medicolegal practice. As well as medical courses at university I particularly remember courses run by barristers and those regarding Lord Woolf's 1998 reform of Civil Procedure Rules that enabled me to handle court cases in a much better fashion. There were many others. I think it took me some 5 years before I felt settled again, happy with my life and the service I was giving to my patients in my later practice years.

References and Author's comment:

73. Neurosyphilis. *Davidson's Essentials of Medicine.* 2009 Churchill-Livingstone:

The Way we Live Now. *New York Times.* (Article on language). 08/10/2003.

www.nytimes.com:

Neurosyphilis is a late-stage complication of the sexually transmitted disease syphilis. It can include bouts of irrationality, tremor and paralysis and frank dementia etc. Symptoms can include the syndrome known as "General Paralysis of the Insane".

The phrase "nutty as a fruitcake" is supposed to have originated from the description given in 1939 by the gangster Jake (Greasy Thumb) Guzik when describing his long-time boss Big Al (Alphonse) Capone, who was suffering from this complication in his later life, although the phrase had been used previously.

Many in history were supposed to have suffered from this disease, including such well-known figures as Delius the composer, and Tolstoy the writer.

It is purported and disputed that the dictators Adolf Hitler and Idi Amin, also suffered from this complaint.

In the 1960s in America, the term "fruitcake" began to be used to describe an effeminate male homosexual. In government and debate it has even been used as a obloquy e.g. in the US Congress, to heighten the sense of offence.

74. *Britain's Ten Most Wanted.* Vanessa Howard. 2009. J. Blake:

Crime writer Vanessa Howard in her book describes the death (and others) of Gail Whitehouse, a prostitute found murdered in the bushes behind The Moulders Arms pub, Wolverhampton, known locally as "the Monkey House", a notorious public house just 1 mile from my surgery at the time, and frequented by many of my patients. Her killer has never been found but, her death has been implicated as being caused by the same unknown and possible serial killer (now behind bars) who violently murdered another local prostitute, Janine Downes, just 1 year later.

75. *Behind the Smile.* Lisa Potts. 1998. Hodder and Stoughton.

In 1996 Lisa Potts a nursery assistant at St Luke's Primary School, Blakenhall, Wolverhampton, not far from my surgery, was severely injured by a machete-wielding paranoid schizophrenic man whilst protecting the children in her care.

She sustained severe injuries and multiple lacerations, almost severing one of her arms, and as a consequence, a great deal of psychological trauma.

Her attacker, later found hiding nearby was sent indefinitely to a secure mental hospital ward.

The award of the George Medal for her bravery is widely known.

What is not widely known is that for all her injuries, including scarring, depression, and post-traumatic stress disorder etc. compared to others awarded compensation for similar injuries, she was awarded the almost derisory amount of £68,000!

She subsequently wrote her autobiography, with a foreword by the ex-prime minister's wife, Cherie Blair, and became a noted counsellor and charity worker.

76. Munchausen's Syndrome. R.A.J. Asher. *The Lancet* 10/02/51. Elsevier:

Munchausen Syndrome by Proxy, The Hinterland of Child abuse. S.R. Meadow. *The Lancet* 13/08/77. Elsevier:

The Independent article. Kate Watson Smith. 18/06/1997:

The Daily Mail article. Sarah Chalmers. 25/06/1997:

UNICEF Child Homicides UK report. 2014. 30a Great Sutton Street,

London EC1V 0DU

Baron Karl Friedrich Hieronymus Freiherr von Münchhausen 1720-1797, was a German nobleman working in the Russian army who told and wrote extensively of fantastic and impossible stories of himself.

In 1951 Dr R.A.J. Asher, an endocrinologist, first described a syndrome of fabricated medical history, including self-harm and disguised signs and symptoms of disease that he labelled as "Munchausen syndrome".

This was enlarged on by Prof. S.R. Meadow in 1977 to include the behaviour of a care person to fabricate, exaggerate or induce a health problem in those in their care, and which was then labelled as "Munchausen syndrome by proxy".

The medical profession was initially sceptical of the "proxy" diagnosis, and the syndrome only slowly gained acceptance.

Although now widely accepted, there has been much confusion regarding terminology of the condition up to date. The World Health Organization adopted the name "factitious disorder by proxy" in 1996, and the Royal College of Paediatrics and Child Health UK adopted the name "Fabricated or Induced

Illness by Carers" in 2002, etc.

Meadow himself later controversially implicated many cases of sudden infant death syndrome in this diagnosis, alleging that many such diagnoses were actually due to physical abuse, accident or even murder. However, following several high-profile cases of what proved to be eventual wrongful conviction involving his evidence and opinion, he was struck off the medical register by the General Medical Council in 2005, only to be reinstated the following year on High Court appeal.

I saw my first case of Munchausen syndrome as a junior doctor, when I operated on a man in Birmingham who had had 14 laparotomies i.e. surgical explorations of his abdomen, in a multiplicity of centres, when no disease was ever found, and his diagnosis was only made retrospectively!

My only other experience, is the case as quoted in this chapter, and as stated previously, it is easy to criticize in retrospect the management of such cases which are irregular in type and extremely infrequent in occurrence, and possibly never seen by most doctors.

In this, my only general practice case seen in over 40 years of practice, the later press releases such as those in *The Independent* and *The Daily Mail* newspapers, were inaccurate, they offered no solutions, and they questioned the care given to this child by all agencies. Oddly though, the case was never discussed with me at any length or depth by anyone other than my partners, neither by the legal profession, the police, nor journalists involved with the case, despite such publicized criticism.

I knew this mother very well for some time before this sad incident occurred, and I knew many other details of her, and the case that were never disclosed.

Furthermore, my experience of the diagnosis of sudden infant death syndrome (SIDS) or cot death, only now disclosed some 20 years on, leads me to reveal that whilst the vast majority of cases of cot death I have seen have been of unknown causation with impeccable parental management, and I cannot quote statistically significant figures, the cases of misdiagnosis as quoted in the previous chapter go some way to agreeing with Meadow's postulate!

77. *2001: A Space Odyssey* (film). Stanley Kubrick. 1968. Metro-Goldwyn-Mayer:

This science fiction film was produced and directed by Stanley Kubrick, and was inspired by an Arthur Clarke story "The Sentinel".

Although only slowly recognized, it is now regarded as one of the greatest and most influential films of all time.

In the act depicting "The Dawn of Man" a group of man-apes realize and learn to use a tool, a bone, eventually used to kill other man-apes. Not quite the same, but hence the "the dawn of realization" term that I adopted in this chapter.

22. Visiting the sick

GPs do not generally like making home visits.

This is a controversial statement, a sweeping generalization perhaps, or a even a terminological inexactitude, descriptive terms first introduced (in 1906) in a parliamentary speech by Winston Churchill. But in everyday life it is true.

This is nothing personal regarding the patient concerned, or the necessity or urgency of the visit, but home visits in the daytime disrupt their very full daily regular schedule and timetable. Most practices do not routinely have dedicated time for the practice "doctor on call" and so daytime visits often means the doctor visiting in an already busy and fully scheduled day. Resultant lateness then in commencing evening surgery, causes a delay in treatment and annoyance to waiting patients who are unaware of where the doctor has been, and a delay to the doctor him or herself in finishing surgery later in the day. This is the abnormal medical time world doctors work in, with invariable delays as normality, and difficulty in getting home to normal family life.

In my time, daytime visits were often to patients with relatively minor self-limiting conditions, or socio-medical visits to the elderly or to the disabled. This was and still is how the NHS operates.

Night-time or out of hours visits, however, were and still are very different. Whilst again they can be to acute self-limiting problems, in my experience the real medical problems invariably occurred at this time. This was when one got to know one's patients. This was where a GP and his patients got to bond and share life's crises together. I had my suspicions when GPs were allowed to opt out of being on call in the so-called "New Contract" that they were obliged (compelled?) to take up in 2004, that there would be a breakdown of this bonding, to the detriment of both patient and doctors alike… Unfortunately, I suspect that today in 2014, these suspicions have proved to be correct.

Whatever or whenever the visit though, I quickly learned on arrival in practice, one invariably never knows what you are going to see, until you actually get there and see… the patient.

Ronald Charles Pratt always sent for me on my night on call at the end of evening surgery, to see his wife, Champagne. She was a downtrodden, meagre little thing traumatized by awkward obstetric[78] problems, the bringing up of four children by the age of 30 years and dealing with her overbearing and dominating husband. He knew everything, you couldn't tell him anything, and he knew especially when to call the doctor. She suffered from various stress-induced problems including indigestion and gastric hyperacidity and on the several occasions that I visited her in the evening he, not her, insisted that I dispense antacid medicines from my medical bag for a problem that could have been easily dealt with earlier in the day.

I asked my senior partner for advice with such a case.

"Patient education. That's the problem Ed," he advised. "You'll never teach this chap illness self-management. He needs running about a bit. He'll get the hint."

I took his advice the next time Mr Pratt called. It was a wet January evening when once again at the end of a late evening surgery about 8 p.m. my receptionist came in looking perturbed.

"That Mr Pratt demands a visit for his poor wife again Doctor. The same problem as always I'm afraid," she stated with disdain in her voice. A kind, caring lady she had been upset by his somewhat rude and demanding tone on the telephone as ever, and she knew of his bullying of his wife. After my chat with my partner this time I went along thus forearmed with an idea.

When I arrived, as usual it was indigestion, and as I examined Champagne on the couch in the living room, he was in the kitchen having his dinner, she leaned over to my ear...

"I didn't want t' send Doctor," she said, "but he was very queer [Black Country speak for "angry", not "odd" or "gay"] when his dinner wasn't ready t'nite. It's me stomach again an' it's worse cos 'e insisted on 'avin a vindaloo at the wikend," she whispered quietly as an explanation, and to not let him hear her words.

I quietly nodded an "I understand", and I returned to the kitchen, and waited.

"Well Mr Pratt," I explained when he had finished his dinner, "this gastroenterological problem with protracted symptomatology is so recurrent, although subacute, yet somewhat persistent and theoretically intractable, that an alternative therapeutic agent such as a proton pump inhibitor, (see reference. no. 28) another formulation of pharmaceutical medication is indicated, and it should be definitively commenced as an urgency tonight," I declared, blinding him with big words as I spoke.

"Yes, yes, of course," Mr "Know-it-all" replied, somewhat vaguely for once.

I knew he hadn't a clue what I was talking about and I knew he hadn't got a car.

I offered my help.

"Come on let's go quickly, I'll give you a lift to the chemist's. It's a quarter past 8 o'clock and we will just make the Central Pharmacy in town before they shut, if we go right away," I said, writing out a prescription quickly as I said all this, and handing it to him. He came outside and we got into my car, he still in his shirtsleeves. It was raining cats and dogs, a real dirty, cold, sleety night, and we sped quickly off into the dark, into the town centre. We made the chemist's just in time.

I leaned across and opened the door for him. He got out, script in hand and made for the nearby door. As he turned and looked back, rather wet from just his short trip, I waved...

"Good night old chap. Hope you get on OK," I called out.

"But, but, but," he whimpered, realizing what was about to happen.

"Yes," I called. "I'm off now. I only offered a lift to the chemist's!" stressing the "to" of my reply. I slammed the door. I drove off home. My dinner was overcooked again, but it was worth it.

I later gathered from the local grapevine gossip that he returned home looking like a drowned rat. I never had any more late calls from him. Champagne recovered, she came to the surgery herself in future, hopefully avoiding further vindaloos.

Mind you, it was not always the patient, him or herself, one had problems with when visiting at home.

Lavender asked me to call one day as there was a problem with Burgess, her husband, which was not surprising, as Burgess, a quite delightful man, had suffered with asthma since arriving in the UK from the West Indies in the 1950s. His respiratory disorder had been further aggravated by his job as a boiler cleaner, an appointment that involved getting in through an inspection manhole and cleaning out the dirty insides of boilers, and as a result he eventually had sudden severe attacks of so-called "brittle" type of the disease resulting in many hospitalizations. He had not worked for some years when I was called to his house, and he had tried a multiplicity of treatment combinations. He was very interested in alternative medicines and diet etc. and the last time I had seen him he told me that he was now drinking only goat's milk and avoiding other milk sources. Unlike today when there are a variety of milk alternatives available, in the 1980s this was not easy to do as goat's milk was not readily available. Knowing the family well I went quickly along.

They lived in Parkfield Crescent, just a stone's throw from the surgery. It was in the autumn when I arrived outside. All the neighbours' gardens and lawns looked good. The whole place was very tidy, not overgrown or leaf covered as one often saw. I took little notice and went on in inside.

What the ', I thought, but this time my expletive was due to something different.

A smell. What a stink. It wasn't lavender!

As I walked through the door to be greeted by Lavender herself, the smell of this normally pristine household almost knocked me over. Burgess was there in the sitting room, as wheezy as ever but not terribly distressed, by his standards. His wife stood alongside. Her face was like thunder. There had obviously been a dispute.

"What on earth is the problem Lavender?" I cried.

"Well, youse know Doc that he has got hit into 'is 'ed that this goat's milk is the stuff f' 'im," she explained, "and 'e is tryin' to make some money. 'e 'as gone and got us an hanimal that 'e is hirin' out t' all the neighbours. All the gardens now look very nice don't they?" she asked. "Well, that's OK for them, heatin' all the grass and the leaves and such, but I'ze sick of hit all, hi am," she cried getting angry, in almost a weepy voice. "I'ze sick of it all," she said. "An' 'e hain't no better drinkin' the bloody goat's milk anyways, 'e hain't," she added firmly. "What cans I do Doc? I'ze at me wits' end, the end a me tether, I iz?" she asked.

I'd never met this problem before and I was a little taken aback, but the smell. Why the smell. It was overwhelming. I couldn't think straight. I was confused here I remember.

I must have looked confused, as seeing my difficulty, Lavender took the initiative.

"'ere, come and you see Doc, come and see," she said, opening the back door into the rear kitchen.

I looked in, in astonishment, but the smell made it difficult. I could see a couple of adult-sized goats munching away a something under the sink, with several little ones running around bleating and sniffing at the piles of muck and shit and contaminated straw strung all over the floor.

It was like a farm animal shed, and in the kitchen of a council house!

It all became clear. The source of Burgess's goat's milk, and his entrepreneurial spirit in helping himself out monetarily, whilst at the same time helping out his elderly neighbours. The goats had been cutting all the lawns and eating garden rubbish, and he had been getting paid for them doing so, all whilst getting himself a supply of his milk. No wonder Parkfield Crescent looked so smart.

I can't all these years later remember how I actually sorted out all this problem, but I do remember explaining to Burgess that he had to get the animals out of the house for public health reasons, which he did, and I got the local authority to go in and advise about whether or not he could keep goats at the property.

His wife was placated I know, and after speaking to some of his locals, I think alternative accommodation somewhere for the goats was found.

His asthma never got any better, lifelong.

Not all calls though are of such a spurious nature. They can be the exact opposite. Take the case of old Laurel.

Laurel described himself as… "One of yoa Grandad's lads, Doctor." This despite the fact that he was over 80 years of age, a retired coal miner from Baggeridge pit. He was tall and slender, a fit man for his age, that had managed to live longer than the average miner, and being still a young man when the pit closed he never had the chance to develop silicosis that choked the breath out of the older men, like my grandfather. He was happy to have survived. He was not a complainer. It was unusual to receive an odd call thus from his wife one day stating that…

"'e 'urt 'is leg yestady Doctor, only just peggin' the washin' out, an' 'e wo do a thing now, lazy bugger. Can yo please come an see 'im an' sort 'im out Doctor, cos I cor? Lazy 'e is," she said.

Odd this call I thought, so I duly went along to their old NCB house in Lower Gornal where many of the old miners still lived, on the edge of my practice. On entry, I found Laurel in an armchair in the back living room seated with his legs both stretched out in front of him. Sitting very still. He did look a little unwell.

"Mornin' Doctor. Sorry t' get yo out, but I've 'urt me leg. I dropped the clothes line on it, an' although I walked on it at fust, I cor stand on it now. I bay as tough as I used t' be yo know," he disclosed a little abashed at sending for me.

Odd this I thought. I'd better examine him, and so I did.

"Tell me, where is this clothes line?" I asked a little aghast after my examination.

I was shown the clothes line, and the 8 foot tall metal reinforced concrete post fastened on to it, that had dropped on his leg the previous day. Apparently he had been on a small stool pegging out the washing the day before, when he slipped, and as he grabbed the clothes line as he fell, he had pulled the quarter of a ton concrete post on top of himself.

His wife explained to me…"Yo should 'ave seen the mess 'e med a the clothes Doctor. I 'ad to waash them all again. Lazy bloke. 'e ain't done a thing since. Slept in that chair all night 'e 'as since, an' all."

I explained to her, carefully, that a mid-shaft fracture of both his tibia and fibula was a pretty good reason to be lazy, and not to bother about the dirty washing, and I sent him off to hospital by ambulance fairly briskly! I never did discover how he got from the garden into the house with a complete fracture of his lower leg that required operative surgical plating and internal fixation, and that took months to heal.

When I saw him next, well healed, he explained his recovery.

"I'm a bionic mon now Doctor. I'n gorra metal plert in me leg. Sorry f' sendin' f' yo that day y' know. If I'd a knowed it was broke, I'd a took meself down t' the 'osptal, yo know," he explained. How he had intended to do this does not bear contemplation, and I will never know. Thank goodness.

Many of my visits were like this. Odd story given to visit. A genuine problem found only on arrival. Often one had to deal with the Black Country mindset, such as Mr and Mrs Laurel above. Mind you, the reasons for home visits could be very variable. None was as unusual as the time I was out running.

It was about the time that "the middle-aged marathon runner's epidemic" started. I had caught the disease. It was a fine Sunday morning and I was coming through the private housing estate near to where we lived, near to the end of a 10 miler, in all the gear. Lightweight, long-distance, grossly expensive running shoes, with muddy socks, a thin reflective top, and very, very short shorts. Covered in sweat. Smelling like a vulture's armpit, I looked and smelt the part. Then as I went up the road suddenly Mrs Rackley, one of my young mum patients ran out of a house as I was passing.

"Doctor, Doctor, quick," she cried. "It's little Harry my son. He's choking. Come in. Come in quick. We sent for the ambulance, but you'll do," she said, volunteering my services!

(It is amazing in life how many times, others have volunteered my services in life. Cf. my brother in chapter 4. But it is a fact of life for a doctor that in an emergency situation quite often one's services are volunteered by others, patients, friends and relatives, usually without recourse or request.)

But I didn't mind on this occasion, she looked really distressed, and I knew her well. She didn't normally panic unnecessarily. She grabbed my arm and almost dragged me inside, partially undressed and smelly as I was. She didn't care. Her son was her concern.

I went into the kitchen where her husband had little Harry in his arms desperately holding the child. The boy was in extremis. He was semi-conscious, making violent inspiratory gasps to breathe, and was turning blue. They explained that Mum was making dinner, and a salad, when he climbed on to the kitchen dresser and started to eat some of the ingredients. Suddenly he had collapsed choking, unable to speak, gasping for breath, and then he quickly became unconscious.

He had a regular but weak pulse and was flaccid and unarousable. A quick examination with a torch and a dessertspoon bent over like a laryngoscope blade showed nothing in his mouth. His upper airway was clear, despite his gasps. He had something further down, in his windpipe. He had inhaled something. He was dying, there was no time to lose.

There are very few real emergencies i.e. what doctors consider as real immediate emergency medical problems. This was one of them… "Acute airway obstruction".

I tried violent rear chest wall thumps, no effect.

I tried shaking him upside down, just holding his ankles, violently, all to no avail.

I had performed emergency resuscitations many times. I had performed emergency tracheostomies and even major artery ligations in my hospital job. This was the first and only time in my whole career, and still is, up to date, that I have ever performed the Heimlich manoeuvre[79]... a technique whereby with clenched fists, sitting at the rear of the patient, a forced jerk backwards into the upper abdomen is made, and this in turn causes a violent expiration, hopefully clearing the airway. You have to be careful doing this I knew, as the operator could cause serious internal injury to the patient. I didn't tell Mom or Dad of this. There was no time. I got Harry on to my lap, Dad was holding his head up.

Thump! I jerked my clenched fists into the little chap's belly.

First time, no effect. He still remained grossly obstructed.

The second time. Thump!

An even more powerful jerk this time. No good.

Third time lucky, I thought. This was getting very dangerous... but I did it again.

A violent cough ensued and a large 2-inch long green chilli shot across the room!

Harry coughed and choked, and within a few seconds he was awake and crying loudly (good sign) and he returned to a normal colour.

Within 5 minutes he was his normal chirpy self and up and about on his feet again, albeit a little weepy.

I got a kiss from Mom and a nice glass of shandy. We cancelled the ambulance and I arranged follow-up in surgery. I went on my jog home.

On arrival my wife complained as to my lateness and Sunday lunch was waiting and overcooked, again. I explained that I had just stopped off to save a child's life, then had come straight on home.

She looked at me with disbelief and shook her head saying,

"Yes, yes, and pigs will fly. I don't suppose you have just been down the pub with Trevor your running mate, perhaps."

She's got a really good nose my wife. She could smell just the small amount of the beer I'd drunk. For years she never believed me at any time when the subject was mentioned, she shook just her head in disbelief.

Then last year, some 20 years since all this happened I obtained my vindication, at last. It was a Sunday, again. We had by now moved miles away from our previous home and the practice, and we were going for a "dog walk" with a group of friends, and their dogs. Well, who should turn up, but Mr and Mrs Rackley who I hadn't met for many years?

"Doctor, hello," she cried out as I got a kiss. "He saved my son's life all those years ago," she explained to my wife and all the others present. "We were so grateful."

She told everybody all that had happened, the story of the chilli just as I had explained, much to my embarrassment, and that her son was now a grown up and healthy young man! It took 20 years for my wife to admit that she had erroneously accused me of lying to her.

The story of this unusual home visit has a further brilliant ending, well I think so. After the "dog walk" was over and the dogs taken home, we all adjourned to the local pub for liquid rehydration. It was not for all the walking we had done, but all the talking. Little Harry, now a strapping and good-looking young man turned up at the pub himself, summoned by his mum, and he was also extremely complimentary. He was so complimentary that he insisted on buying me a large double whisky as an expression of his thanks, and to further aid my rehydration and recovery from our afternoon walk.

Some of my memories of home visiting have really good endings.

But sadly not all.

After 10 years or so in general practice I began to know my patients. After 25 years or so, they began to know me, we began to know each other. After 40 years we were as one.

It was an odd realization. I could learn just from their demeanour when something of importance was amiss. Hospital doctors often criticize patients for the handling of their complaint, but I slowly began to learn that one needs to see the home environment to obtain a true picture of the problem. After a time there were families that on request I went to visit unhesitatingly, whatever the explanation for the call. I learned to discover the real reason for the visit only when I attended and saw the true situation. A call to see old Violet was such a case in point.

Violet was 90 years of age. She had outlived her husband with whom she had brought up six children, after working in a munitions factory during the Second World War. She worked as a cleaner until she was 80 years old and she still lived in her cold three-bedroomed post-war council house semi, with a couple of her grandchildren and their family. She was a true grande dame ruling the family still with a rod of iron. She was only rarely seen in surgery and when she did she knew the diagnosis and what was required for it. It was unusual then to get an evening request to visit her, from her grandson.

"Doctor, sorry t' bother you," he began with an apology. "It's Granny. She ain't been well for wiks now and weem worried t' death about her. We cor put a finger on it really Doctor as she spends all the time in her room these days and 'er's stopped bossin' us about. She must be bad to do that," he said. "Your new young lady doctor visited 'er this mornin' but 'er wouldn't let 'er examine 'er. We doe know what t' do. I wonder if you could advise us please?" he said.

This was all very unusual and needed investigation. I had never received calls like this, from this family. I went along as a precaution.

Violet was in her room. She was not happy that I had been sent for. I got the diagnosis as soon as I walked into the room.

The smell! I had smelt it twice before. It is like a poignant memory, never forgotten. She also looked pale and thinner than when seen in the past.

"Come on Violet, let's examine you," I said, almost demandingly.

"Alright," she grudgingly agreed, and added. "Yo sent that new woman doctor t'day to see me. I ay avin' no young woman examine me," she explained.

The young woman in question was a very caring and considerate and bright lady partner that had joined me and my other male partner. She was described as "new and young" despite being in the practice some years now, and married with a family of her own. My old senior partner was long retired. I was the old man now, and it is an odd feature of some women, old or young, but sometimes if it is an especially distressing condition, they do not wish to be seen by another woman. It affronts their joint femininity.

She allowed me to examine her... it was not a pretty sight.

She had no left breast. It had been eroded by a fungating lesion extending from just below her collarbone almost to her waist, sticking to her clothes, an obvious malignancy! It was roughly the size of a dustbin lid. Horrendous.

The smell had alerted me. Doctors are trained to be aware of signs and symptoms.

I had already added this to my repertoire, when teaching students.

"Yo know what it is, doe yo Doctor?" she questioned.

"Yes Violet, I do," I gently replied.

"Well I tell yo now, I ain't goin' t' see any specialist and I ain't goin' t' ospital neither," she stated firmly. She was not for turning this type of lady.

"Well in that case we will have to treat you at home," I explained. "You know what it is, of course, don't you? It's a growth, it's a cancer. You've been covering it up, so not to upset the family, haven't you, and how long have you had it?" I asked.

"Yes Doctor, yo 'm right about the family, but I've only 'ad it about 12 months," she said, "and it's not painful but it's mekin me very tired I'm afraid," she added, nodding her head and agreeing with my diagnosis.

We had a hug and a kiss. She got dressed. I gave her a light sedative and left making a gentle explanation to the family. I couldn't speak to my wife when I returned home. I just had a lonely bath. It took hours for my sadness to settle and to work out what to do next. I often found a hot bath a good hideaway, to think.

The next day I discussed her case with my partners and telephoned my local oncologist[80] and explained the situation. He advised that the history was very suggestive of a slow-growing type of tumour that might respond to oral drugs. I also arranged for my district nursing senior sister to attend to her dressing and her general home care.

Violet lived with good quality of life for another 4 years on only oral "tamoxifen"[81] and a bottle of Harveys Bristol Cream sherry every day, looked after at home by her doting family and the nurses. No other drugs. No painkilling analgesia, she didn't need it with all that sherry. No specialist treatment. She died peacefully in her sleep one night, relatively comfortably I am pleased to say.

This encroaching nearness to my patients was not confined to the elderly alone. The youth of today have often been accused of being irresponsible, uncaring and of having lost their sense of social values. Whilst this may be true in some cases, generally speaking I have found that this is not true when it comes to life's real crises. This is illustrated by Merlyn's case.

Merlyn was not a magician. He left school in the post-war 1950s, a tall lean but muscular man. He only ever had one job straight from school, a furnace man shovelling coal, 6 to 8 hours a day. He was encouraged to smoke Woodbines[82] to help him to cough, to clear his chest, and by the time that I met him in the late 1970s he coughed "the black stuff" up constantly and was on 30 or more cigarettes a day. He never had much money despite working a 50-hour week from 6 a.m. in the morning. He never even had a car. He had well brought up, very polite children, and his wife Susan went out to work, a cleaner at New Cross Hospital, to help keep these. He was rarely seen in surgery except for the very odd complaint of adult acne, worsened by his sweaty job I suppose, a trait that he has passed on to his offspring. It was a little unusual thus to see him in one morning surgery.

"Good morning Doctor, I'm pleased to see you, I trust you are well?" as always was his polite introduction. "I've gorra bit of a problem," he said. "Y' know I've coughed the black stuff up like everybody does, for years now Doctor, but lately it's changed. I've started t' bring bits a blood up with it as well," he explained.

Bloodstained sputum amongst the heavy iron and steel industrial workers was not an uncommon symptom years ago, with many bronchitic patients with recurrent chest infections, but this was the 1990s now. I pricked up my ears. I couldn't hear any abnormality with my stethoscope and he looked well, but my suspicions were aroused. I gave him a short course of antibiotics nevertheless and I sent him off for a chest X-ray. He returned the following week for the results, still bringing up small amounts of fresh, red blood, he said.

"Well Merlyn I'm afraid that your chest X-ray is abnormal," I explained. "It shows a shadow in the centre of your lungs that is a little suspicious to me, and I am arranging for you to see a chest specialist as an urgency," I went on. "There's no other treatment indicated at this stage, and I'll get you sorted as soon as possible, but I suspect that it is serious, unfortunately," indicating my anxiety and attempting not to alarm him too much, all in one go. "Have you any questions to ask?" I added thinking he had his own suspicions already.

"I know wa'r it could be Doctor, so doe tell the wife anythin' at this stage," he said to my surprise. "If 'er wants t' know we'll just say it's a shada on me lung, f' the time bein', ay? And I doe want any time off work if I can 'elp it," he said, asking a question of me at the same time.

"Yes OK, we will say it's just a shadow for the time being, if need be," I agreed, and off he went leaving both of us feeling somewhat downhearted.

A phone call. I got him seen by our local chest physician in just a few days. The telephone leapfrogged all waiting lists then, after seeing him my consultant friend rang me back shortly to explain. His tumour was occupying much of the mediastinum, in the centre of his chest, involving the lungs on both sides. It was a highly malignant type of lung cancer[83] proven by microscopic examination of cells in his sputum and surgery was out of the question. You cannot have both lungs removed for such a disease. Radiotherapy was the only treatment of choice for this type of growth, but the prognosis, the predictable outcome, even with treatment was very poor. He had explained all to Merlyn, and his wife who had accompanied him to outpatients and so now knew the diagnosis, and the course of radiotherapy treatment had been initiated.

I never saw Merlyn again, alive. He never came for any sick note to stay off work throughout what must have been an unpleasant time on his course of treatment. He never complained. He never came for any help or advice. Then, in the night, some weeks later I received a call.

"Hello Doctor, sorry to bother you it's Maxwell, Merlyn's son. I'm afraid me Dad's took a turn for the worse Doctor. He's on the floor in the bathroom in a right mess. Could you come right away please? I doe want me Mom t' see 'im like this, please, please," he almost pleadingly requested.

You will have seen throughout this book how Black Country folk repeat themselves as a form of emphasis. One "please" is just being polite. Two "pleases" shows a degree of alarm. But three "pleases" as in this case, indicates a dire emergency, a real *cri de cœur*. I got dressed and sped to the house in the night over sets of red traffic lights. I was there in a few minutes. Susan opened the door, still in her nightie, clinging tightly to Maxwell's younger sister.

"Come in, come in Doctor. Go right upstairs t' the bathroom. He got out a the bed ever s' quickly choking. All I've 'eard is a bang and me lad says 'e doe want t' see me yet," she explained. I went quickly upstairs to the bathroom.

What the '!

I was stopped dead in my tracks. Even now, after 40 years

of medicine nothing prepared me for the sight I was to see that night. It was like a butcher's shop. Merlyn was unconscious, motionless on the bathroom floor, accompanied by Maxwell alone, his tall, thin son. Blood everywhere. On the floor, in the sink, in the bath and on the walls. He and his son were covered in it!

He had had an obvious massive haemoptysis, a pulmonary haemorrhage. Examination revealed no peripheral pulses, no measurable blood pressure. He was unarousable, even to pain… I almost tore his earlobe off, pinching it, trying to get a reaction. He was cold and clammy with fixed, dilated pupils indicating death or near death. He was such a fine man even then resuscitation was in my mind nevertheless, just as a possibility.

"How long since he last responded, spoke or moved Maxwell?" I questioned.

"Not for about 10 minutes or more Doctor since I called you," he replied answering my query in a tremulous voice.

It would have been impossible even with paramedic assistance, and would it be really ethical I questioned myself? Sometimes you have to make instantaneous decisions. This was one time. I got up slowly from the floor where I had been examining him, and turned to the young man. We faced each other in silence for a few seconds. I put both hands on his shoulders as he stood arms by his side.

"He's gone Maxwell I'm afraid." I paused to let this absorb. Then slowly, "There's nothing anyone can do, but us. We need to do something for him. We can't let your Mom see him like this," I gently stated.

The sadness and despair in his eyes as his lids drooped was indescribable. So sad. He couldn't speak. He simply nodded in agreement.

We washed the tiles. We swilled out the bath. We washed the sink. We washed the floor. We used three rolls of toilet paper, all flushed down the loo. We used towels that were so soaked that I put them in a plastic bag with Merlyn's pyjamas and I took all of them home in my bag to hide. I destroyed them later. We cleaned

Merlyn up completely and combed his hair. With a struggle we got him back on to his bed and laid him out in a pair of shorts and his best white shirt. He looked very peaceful. The girls were allowed up to see him. We had been so long they knew what had happened. They were almost exsanguinated in their quiet grief all together.

"I guessed what 'ad 'appened Doctor," Susan said, and added. "Can we leave 'im 'ere at 'ome t'night? That's wa' he'd want," she requested, and I nodded my head in agreement.

"We 'ad a good life together and 'e was a good 'usband t' me and the children," she disclosed. "We werked 'ard. We was always 'appy and we will never f'get 'im," she stated with resignation in her sad voice.

We went downstairs, all of us, and had a quiet cup of tea together. No one spoke until I explained how I would arrange for the funeral director to call after 7 a.m. This avoids paying a night visit fee that not all can afford. I didn't tell them that. I simply arranged to deliver the certificate required for the registrar of births and deaths the next day. As I left after saying my goodnights, Maxwell came to the door to see me out, as instructed by his mother.

He gave me a meaningful and polite nod and said, "Thank you very much for coming t'nite Doctor and for all you've done, and f' not letting me Mom see that tonight. I don't know what I'd have done if you hadn't been there..." all with a weak smile.

I left after patting his shoulder.

We had a secret shared that I have never disclosed until now.

Maxwell was 19 years of age!

References and Author's comment:

78. Obstetrics. *Dictionary of Medicine*. R.M. Youngson. 1992. Harper Collins. www.collinsdictionary.com:

The word "obstetrics" is derived from the Latin word "obstare", meaning to stand by. An obstetrician is a doctor specializing in the medical practice of pregnancy care, childbirth and postnatal care after delivery. A gynaecologist is a doctor specializing in the practice of care of the female reproductive system. There is a great overlap of the subjects and in the United Kingdom most practitioners combine both specialities.

There is a counterpart specializing in andrology, the care of the male reproductive system, although in the United Kingdom this is usually seen as a branch of urology, the speciality dealing with care and disease of the male and female urinary tract.

79. Pop Goes the Café Coronary. H.J. Heimlich. American Journal of Emergency Medicine. June 1974. www.jem-journal. com:

Henry Judah Heimlich (03/02/1920) first described the Heimlich manoeuvre in an informal article in the American Journal of Emergency Medicine in 1974. This is an emergency procedure to unblock the airway that should not be the first method employed. It involves standing/sitting behind an obstructed patient after other attempts to clear the airway have failed, and with clenched fists together, making a forced upper abdominal violent thrust. This causes a violent expiration, ejecting any foreign body or obstruction from the airway. It should not be taken lightly as it can cause internal organ damage and fracture to the chest wall, but when successful, it is invariably life-saving.

Heimlich, an American thoracic surgeon, is a somewhat controversial individual, also advocating this manoeuvre for drowning victims, which is as yet unproven, and advocating other debatable treatments for other conditions such as "Malariotherapy" i.e. when patients are deliberately infected with malaria, to treat cancer, Lyme disease and even HIV disorder.

His manoeuvre is described as being possible to self-perform, although I have never seen this, and if I have not seen it nowadays, it means it is indeed a rare occurrence.

80. Oncologist. *Dictionary of Medicine*. R.M. Youngson. 1992. Harper Collins:

www.cancer.net:

An "oncologist" is a specialist in the causes, the features and the treatment of cancer.

The word is derived from the Ancient Greek word "oncos" meaning bulk, mass, or tumour, and the word "ology" meaning the study of.

This speciality has arisen in my medical lifetime and there now are specific specialist medical, surgical and radiological oncologists. Although the patient may be under the care of a single oncologist doctor or a single consultant in other specialities, many hospitals in the UK now have regular multidisciplinary teams of doctors, nurses and allied specialists etc. who meet to discuss and review complex cases of malignancy and other diseases. A treatment regime decision is now not commonly made by a single person. A scenario of which the patient is often unaware.

81. Tamoxifen. *British National Formulary*. Edition No.64. 2012. GGP Media Gmbh:

A Trial of Tamoxifen at Two Dose Levels. H.W.C. Ward. The British Medical Journal. 06/01/1973. Polestar Ltd:

The National Centre for Biotechnology Information (U.S.) www.ncbi.nlm.nih.gov/:

Tamoxifen (British trade name Nolvadex, and others) was one of the first drugs to be introduced that had an effect on breast cancer. It was first synthesized in 1966 by Dora Richardson working for the UK division of Imperial Chemical Industries, (now AstraZeneca) in the hope of developing a "morning-after" contraceptive pill. Clinical trials did not begin until 1971, and its usage only became widespread following a trial in 1973 by Dr H.W.C. Ward at the Queen Elizabeth Hospital, Birmingham, on Birmingham and the Black Country patients.

Since that time it has become the most widely used drug worldwide for this disease.

It is an antagonist of the oestrogen receptors in breast tissue and is used in the treatment of the so-called "Oestrogen Receptor

Positive" (ER+) type, early and advanced breast cancer.

The drug now has other uses, including prophylactic protection treatment in deemed "high risk" cancer individuals, it is used for infertility and breast pain (mastalgia), and it is commonly used in the treatment of the unusual and more rare cases of male breast cancer disease.

82. Woodbine cigarettes. Graces guide to British Industrial History.

www.gracesguide.co.uk/:

ASH (Action on Smoking and Health) Smoking Statistics. New House. 67-68 Hatton Garden, London EC1N 8JY. www.ash. org.uk/:

"Wills Wild Woodbines" were a brand of strong unfiltered cigarettes made in England from 1888 to 1998, by W.D. and H.O. Wills Tobacco Company, and they were originally named after a wild flower, Lonicera of the honeysuckle family.

They were the cheap so-called "working man's cigarette" and with Player's Navy Cut they were the most commonly smoked cigarettes in the UK up to the 1960s. The Wills family were interesting. The first and possibly the only British drug barons they had a philanthropic ethos and attitude to their workers. They introduced works pension schemes, paid holidays, and workers canteens. Female workers who got married were expected to leave to become housewives, but could request to continue their employment if they later wished to do so. Male clerks were interviewed by a manager and advised against marriage if their salary scale had not reached a certain level. These practices continued up to the 1960s!

Research in the 1950s eventually showed the connection between smoking and the incidence of lung cancer, when low-tar content and filtered cigarettes were introduced. This resulted in the ultimate cessation of production of Woodbines.

The risk of developing lung cancer is dose related, when longer duration and heavier cigarette consumption increases the likelihood of developing the disease. Overall, light smokers (10 to 15 per day) are 10 times more likely to die of the disease than non-smokers. Heavy smokers (25+ per day) are 15-20 times more likely to die of the disease. However, any smoking, at all, significantly increases the chances of lung and cardiovascular disease.

It was estimated in 1948 that approximately 82% of all adult males in the UK smoked. This figure had fallen to 21% by 2010, and although falling still, it was estimated that there were still approximately 10 million adult smokers in the UK in 2014.

83. Lung Cancer. *Davidson's Essentials of Medicine.* 2009. Churchill Livingstone:

Cancer Research UK. Angel Building. 407 St. John St. London EC1V 4AD.

www.cancerresearchuk.org/:

Cancer is defined as a "growth of tissue caused by cells growing uncontrollably usually to the detriment of the person".

The term is often confused with the word "tumour" which is a growth or swelling, but not always to the detriment of the person e.g. a simple skin sebaceous cyst, or even the swelling of an inflamed finger is a tumour.

Cancers are defined as being "benign" just growing locally, or "malignant" growing and invading both locally and spreading elsewhere in the body. They are usually also described as to their tissue of origin and by other descriptions and so there are numerous types of cancers that occur overall in the human body. Cancer is not just a single disease.

Lung cancer is almost the forgotten cancer these days. It is the commonest cancer worldwide still, with incredibly 1.2 million cases annually in the year 2000.

Although the incidence of this disease is decreasing in the UK, in 2010 it was still the second commonest cancer in men with more than 23,000 new cases. Prostatic cancer having the highest incidence described in that year.

Likewise next to breast cancer, it was the second commonest cancer in women in the UK in 2010, with more than 18,000 new cases.

Only when comparing these figures with road traffic accident deaths of 1,857 per year and HIV disease deaths of approximately 500 per year of both sexes in the UK in the same year, does one realize the significance of this disease.

With all forms of up-to-date therapy and modern treatments worldwide the prognosis, the ultimate outcome, of lung cancer disease is still very poor mainly due to late presentation. It has barely altered in my lifetime.

Only 30% of cases survive 1 year, and only 6-8% of cases survive 5 years!

23. Today. Reflections. Conclusions

I commenced medical practice on the first of January 1966.

I retired fully from medical practice, on the first of January 2013.

After 46 years, to the very day, it was not easy to relinquish my Licence to Practice, but being occupied by the everyday confrontation of a working medical practice it was difficult to perceive, if anything, had been achieved in the intervening years.

It was as if all this time passed, as but a moment.

To look back now, is like looking through the early morning mist over a lake… all one initially sees is indistinct and unclear, but with persistence the mist clears, memories come flooding back like reflections on the surface of the water.

Has anything changed? Are the people better off, have my patients benefited over all this time, I ask myself?

The babies, I wonder?

Antenatal care in the first 20 years of the National Health Service was little changed from the time of the inception of the NHS, as far as I could see, when I arrived on the medical scene in the mid 1960s. Care was provided by independent midwives and GPs with little or no shared care for deliveries, and specialist consultant obstetric opinion for difficult or abnormal deliveries was away in hospital with little or no connection to the community. Many deliveries still took place at home, with just a district midwife, and for the vast majority this system worked well. It was not until the late 1960s early 1970s did GPs start to have practice-attached joint midwifery clinics, with midwife-run, GP–supervised, short-stay units being set up in hospitals for normal deliveries. Then, if complications arose during delivery, specialized consultant-led care was quickly available. This system has been remarkably improved on today with better antenatal investigation and screening techniques available, but despite this, recent surveys[84] show that Birmingham and the Black Country still in 2014 has the highest rate of infant mortality figures in the country, when overall life expectancy in the country continues to improve.

Gone are the days though now when I would be called out in the night, (why always at 2 o'clock in the morning did babies arrive, I know not? I write this with clenched teeth) to perform a forceps assisted delivery and the fine-looking, but wet, bloody little person that emerged would require several shakes and mouth-to-mouth "kisses" before a sudden gasp and a cry announced his or her arrival into the world. The little person had dents in the side of his or her head for days where I had grasped with the forceps to get the rest of their body out!

I intentionally use the word "person" here, not "baby". Until I had my own child I never realized that first look that a newborn gives to its mother or father, they know who you are. Just that first look. No sound. Just the look. It is weird. All parents will know what I mean. You have to perform a delivery and have your own child to understand what I am talking about. They are immediately "a person". Instantaneous coupling. It is not in the textbooks.

In the early days of my practice we had very few diagnostic aids such as ultrasound scans etc. and the only "specialist" equipment in the home that we had was a bottle of ether[85] for the mother to gasp on for pain relief, and a mouth-operated suction tube to clear the airway of the babe on arrival, (the content of which you often got a mouthful of if you were not experienced in its usage). There was no cardiopulmonary resuscitation equipment available for either the mother or the infant, in the home situation.

Now the available equipment and diagnostic techniques have incredibly improved. Midwives, GPs and specialist opinions are freely available and to hand, and home deliveries, still with some risk, have gone out of fashion.

It sounds like another era that I think of in my reflections, but this was only 30 to 40 years ago. Childbirth generally is unbelievably improved.

"But what about the children? The kids?" I ask myself. "Paediatrics."

Well, paediatrics, the medical care of infants, of children and adolescents has undergone an almost astronomical improvement as well. Hospital care, investigation, diagnosis and treatment has improved beyond all expectations.

The greatest difference, however, to Black Country childcare in my time without doubt has been the almost total eradication of the infectious diseases of childhood. Measles, mumps, rubella have almost, but not totally disappeared, and some such as smallpox have been supposedly eradicated altogether, (I have seen smallpox, but only in my hospital practice).

I used to see a case of one of these infectious diseases every single day in the 1970s and into the 1980s. But it wasn't just the acute phase of the disease which was the problem, it was the complications, chest infections, long-term deafness and discharging ears, subsequent educational problems etc. which were most distressing. Measles I saw the most of, but I also saw birth defects and later deafness due to rubella ("German measles"), with school-leavers a previously undiagnosed totally deaf ear on one side, having been through all their school years with hearing in perhaps just one ear! I would also see grown-up men (15% of cases) and sometimes women (2.5% of cases), with some form of fertility problem in later life after having childhood mumps. The worst of all, however, was "whooping cough", pertussis, an acute chest infective-type illness that even when the initial pyrexial and whoop stage had settled in 6 weeks or so, then went on to months and months and months of a chronic phase. Snotty running nose, and eyes, coughing sputum, a frail and thin wasted child.

The eradication of all these has been greatly aided by the introduction of modern IT-based computerized systems for general practice, to aid comprehensive vaccination, as well as the introduction of health visitors and community-based paediatric care to chase up clients and poor attenders. We must nevertheless continue to be vigilant in the future, and not allow public opinion against wholesale vaccination to be influenced by outside non-medical opinions and agencies, as has been known to happen in some areas of the country. They have all virtually disappeared now. Good riddance to these diseases. Well done the NHS.

Further views through the mist of memory. The grown-ups?

In the Black Country the coal mines and steel works have all gone. The foundries are now but few. Gone are the days when 65-year-old men retired, worn out by years of heavy manual work and industrial disease and pollution.

The women no longer reach the menopause looking 20 years older than their chronological age, debilitated by multiple pregnancies and the bringing up of large families that they could financially ill-afford, in poor housing conditions.

In Dudley and Wolverhampton the post-war boom council houses, of cold and uninsulated brick walls, with just a single bar electric fire in the bedroom, and metal-framed windows, have all been modernized with central heating and double glazing and good insulation now installed. The post-1950s "high-rise flats", the even worse vertical slums, that replaced the post-Industrial Revolution horizontal slums have either ceased to be built or have been destroyed, and have been modernized with the social interaction of "inmates" encouraged.

In addition to all these social changes, general medical change has been enormous. When I first commenced practice very little investigative medicine was available to a GP in the whole of the Black Country and Birmingham, and the only available investigative test a GP could obtain without an appointment, was a chest X-ray, and that was at the local specialist chest clinic. By the time of my retirement, I could obtain virtually any investigation or test, even a surgical biopsy or an MRI scan, as if I was working in a consultant-led hospital outpatient department, for my patients. Most of these improvements were slow and insidious, introduced by gradual medical research and modern technology. Some were sudden and quick. All this has been achieved despite repeated political interference, one new government of the day after another, again and again arriving to utter the dreaded words...

"We intend to reform the Health Service!"

It is interesting how some of these reforms above others stick in my mind.

All change was slow in my early years, until a certain Mrs Thatcher arrived. Things started to move though, albeit slowly at the start with, just more NHS funding, and then came the introduction of the "Internal Market" that everybody now knows about. I recall the introduction of the Limited Prescribing List in 1984, when out of the blue with little or no discussion with the profession, many long-standing established preparations that patients were dependent upon, were removed from the prescribing list of a GP, to "rationalize prescribing" it was said. "Rationalize" a word used then, and still used by politicians, as a euphemism for "cost reduction". It meant that many simple preparations such as cough medicines, tonics, mild painkillers and laxatives were no longer prescribable by the doctor. You could only buy them over the counter as a proprietary preparation if you wished. This was expensive for many patients, especially the elderly. Politicians didn't seem to realize this. By de-prescribing them, it didn't stop the patients wanting or needing them!

I recollect a feeling of being affronted by this prescribing change, at the time, as did many of my colleagues.

How politicians, not doctors, dare tell me what I could or could not prescribe, I thought. But gradually though, it dawned on me that I was wrong. It was the beginning of patients being made aware of some responsibility for their own health, rather than just... "G' t' the doctor's. He'll give yo summat for anythin'. It's free, this National 'ealth Service," the attitude of dependence that many patients had at that time.

But then the politicians began to become even more involved (another of their euphemisms...? Involved, means interfere) with clinical management of conditions itself, not just drug administration. I think back to 1990 when the "New GP Contract" came into force. (Yes, another "New" GP contract! Today's politicians please note.) Instructions came that all patients over the age of 70 years must be offered a yearly home visit to enquire as to their general health, with instructions to measure their height and weight, to enquire as to their diet etc.

This was even if they were up and about and well and attended surgery. They had to be offered a visit. Some of my elderly were quite indignant about this when sent for, they considered it a slight on themselves.

We in our practice were by then one of the few practices at the time that had a computer already installed, essential to initiate this system, when daily some patients reached the age of 70 years, some moved, some died. It was an administrative nightmare to perform, of little or no benefit to the patient, and completely political in ideal. Interestingly, as I recollect all this, I realize that the then minister of state for health at that time, a certain Mr Kenneth Clarke[86], is still in Parliament in the new millennium (2014), his "reform of the Health Service" and all the work and expense it entailed totally forgotten!

Not all the hindrances were due to political figures though. On taking a longer look back at my experiences it is only now do I see, that like many of my profession I myself adopted a conservative attitude, a resistance to change in my early years of practice. It led to an attitude that as a GP I felt that I was not using all the training and knowledge that I had, for the benefit of my patients. I felt frustrated. I was not giving them the best of my abilities. I practiced little proactive medicine, merely performing crisis management of their problems. I felt just like a clerk at times, flogging sick notes.

But, things have improved, I have to admit, in the last two decades the NHS systematically has begun to rapidly change.

To me it was the arrival of the Labour government in 1997 that the great changes of modern general practice commenced and became apparent, "at the coalface" of medicine, the consultation with the patient. It was not just the greatest ever increase in NHS expenditure that caused this, but it was attitude and direction of general practice that changed, instigated mainly by the political masters, sadly not the medical profession! We began to practice "medicine by results". We started to in-house manage many complex and chronic diseases such as diabetes, heart disease, asthma and such, and we became proactive with the widely expanded investigative and screening techniques becoming available to us GPs.

In Wolverhampton and Dudley, we all took on our own practice nurses and attached health visitors, and in some practices specialist nurse practitioners, even physician's assistants, all to widen the service to our patients and give them more care in the community. The profession started to take notice of the fact that we humans are a group animal. We began to realize the need to communicate better, pleasingly to be more open with our patients, seeing them as the person, rather than the problem[87]. I know from my hospital appointment in Birmingham, where we had medical students that we began to stress all this into medical student and young practitioner training.

In his series of articles and lectures on "Hubris Syndrome" Dr (Lord) David Owen[88], himself unusually being both a qualified physician as well as a politician, describes Mr Tony Blair as being swept up by the intoxication of power, of being unable to listen to or accept logic or reason. Well, all I can say is that the setting up of NHS changes that commenced about his time in office was a breath of fresh air, and the government of that day must be congratulated on the inception and improvement of modern medical practice. We still have problems today, but pleasingly continuing governments of all political parties now have continued the changes and attitudes that commenced around this time.

Despite the daily continuing publicity in the media of doom and gloom and of "NHS catastrophes and mistakes" it cannot be ignored that looking at the bigger picture as well as my practice, there has been a marked improvement in the general health of the population of the country as a whole, all from around this time. This has become apparent now with a decrease in overall disease morbidity and an increase in life expectancy, in the new millennium.

I am pleased to have taken part in all these new developments of the National Health Service.

I am content with all my reflections.

References and Author's comment:

84. Home Deliveries. Interim Life tables. UK Statistics Authority. 1 Drummond Gate. London SW1V 2QQ. www.statisticsauthority.gov.uk/:

Birmingham and the Black Country Reducing Perinatal Mortality Project. T. Martin, J. Gardosi. 2007. West Midlands Perinatal Institute:

NICE Intrapartum care. www.nice.org.uk/cg190 CG190:

Infant Mortality. N. Watson. 05/12/2008. The BBC Politics Show:

The incidence of UK home births is illustrated by the figures of the Office for National Statistics (ONS) that show the great reduction in the numbers of home deliveries in the UK in the latter half of the 20th century.

This trend continues up to date.

In...

1958   36.0% of all births were by home delivery.
1970   12.0% of all births were by home delivery.
2010   2.30% of all births were by home delivery.

More recently in December 2014 the National Institute for Health Care Excellence,

NICE, revised their previous recommendations (CG190)

for the delivery of women with low risk of complications. It was stated that such cases should have their baby in an environment where they feel most comfortable, preferably a midwife-run unit not connected to a hospital, or at home. This was psychologically much better for the mother.

However, as recently as 2007-8 the West Midlands Perinatal Institute and a survey commissioned by the BBC found that the West Midlands, including Birmingham and the Black Country, still had the highest rate of infant mortality than anywhere else in the UK! The complex causes of this included poverty and deprivation, poor general health and pregnancy health awareness, as well as smoking and poor diet.

As a GP working for many years in the Black Country, I was always depressed and alarmed by the statistical analysis of these local infant mortality figures. The reasons for these results were certainly not evident in my practice areas, which had little or no infant death rate at all over many years, although this I suspect was due to the excellent midwifery and health visitor cover available to me and my patients, not my particular personal care or expertise.

Also up to retirement I was one of the few doctors still working who had wide experience of home deliveries. There is no doubt that a home delivery in a low risk patient is psychologically better for the mother. However, you have got to be faced with doing a forceps delivery for a late turned breech delivery presentation baby, on a wet bed, under a sloping tenement roof illuminated by a 40 watt bulb, to know what I am talking about. Before making such sweeping generalizations, I bet none of the clever NICE professors have done this. Well I have. Even today with a home delivery, if faced with unexpected dire complications such as foetal distress or respiratory distress syndromes, which although rare, can still occur in low-risk patients, in my opinion this markedly puts not the psyche, but the child's life at risk.

It is debatable on whose care we should focus upon.

Note, the cost of an obstetric unit hospital birth in (NICE 2012 figures) was estimated to be approximately £1,631. A midwife-led unit birth cost was £200 cheaper. A home delivery was £600 cheaper still.

But cost was never involved in the recent edict!

85. Ether. Exploring the History of Medicine. The Science Museum. Exhibition Rd. London SW7 2DD. www.sciencemuseum.org. uk/:

(Diethyl) Ether is colourless liquid, first used as a surgical anaesthetic agent in 1846. Its use has now been superseded by modern anaesthetic agents due to the marked side effects exhibited when used, and because it is highly volatile and a highly inflammable substance.

Ether usage is, however, not confined to antiquity or medicine. Its volatility confers on it other uses, such as being a constituent of starter fluid for combustion engines, and usage as a laboratory solvent.

I saw it used in both hospital practice as an anaesthetic agent, especially on children, up to the 1970s, and even in my early GP practice, when my partner carried it in the surgery emergency bag, and when it was used as a skin cleansing agent on swabs prior to giving injections.

Ether has been used up to recently for recreational and addiction purposes, and incredibly, drinking the neat liquid or mixed with milk and/or juice was common at one time in places such as Scotland, France, and the Scandinavian countries!

86. The Rt. Hon. Kenneth Clarke QC MP. www.gov.uk/ government/poeple/:

Kenneth Clarke. Wikipedia. The free encyclopedia:

Kenneth Harry Clarke (02/07/1940-) is a British Conservative politician. Educated at Nottingham High (Grammar) School and Cambridge University, he is MP for Rushcliffe in Nottinghamshire, and was first elected to parliament in 1970. He has held a multiplicity of ministerial posts, and he has contested the leadership of the Conservative party (unsuccessfully, poor chap) on three occasions. He is a leading pro-European, and his long and distinguished political *curriculum vitae* is well documented outside of this book. In particular, despite being at one time an ardent pro-tobacco advocate, he was appointed Secretary of State for Health (July 1988-November 1990) when he introduced the somewhat controversial concept of the "Internal Market" i.e. competition between NHS providers, still a very debatable subject. Whilst Mrs Thatcher and others professed him to be a great communicator this is not always correct, in my opinion.

He does have certain other less well-known attributes ("detributes"?) which includes a love of Hush Puppy shoes, smoking cigars, jazz music and soccer. A keen Nottingham Forest football fan, he would like to be remembered as being instrumental in helping England win the World Cup in 1966!

His explanation for this is that whilst in attendance at the match at Wembley, in direct line behind the "Russian linesman", Tofiq Bahramov, who was actually an Azerbaijani, he purports to have shouted to the linesman to award a goal in extra time when the ball crossed the line after striking the West German crossbar. A "great communicator"? How this cry could have been heard by the linesman who was several yards away at the time, whilst being almost deafened by the roar of 100,000 spectators, and how he and the Swiss referee, all with no common language understood all this, he has never explained. Like many of his political claims or speeches say his critics, it matters not. In the last minute of extra time Geoff Hurst scored a fourth and quite definite winning goal for England to settle the controversy!

87. Developing Presence as a Doctor. K. Oxtoby. 02/02/2013. The British Medical Journal. Polestar Ltd:
    The Language Instinct. S. Pinker. 1994. Harper Collins:
    Evolutionary Psychology. D.J. Buller. Vol.22. Winter Edition 2013. Scientific American:
    In her article Katie Oxtoby, not a doctor, but a freelance journalist, outlines what is required of a doctor to communicate and indicate a presence to a patient, to develop a proper

appearance, use body language and to take time to listen and not to be afraid to say "I don't know". Talk. Take time. Be honest with the patient.

This all concurs with the eloquent argument of Pinker, a leading language expert, who in his book wrote extensively that language, is indeed an adaptation for verbal communication of infinite combinational complexity between all the parties concerned. Buller, writing about human evolution in his article, further expanded on all this, and explained how communication and language is all a part of our human evolutionary psychology, whatever we are talking about or whoever we are talking to.

When I first read these widely differently sourced and very involved references, I was somewhat at a loss to comprehend the concepts involved due to both the complexity of the subject and the expressions used within them. However, on rereading them all, eventually I began to realize that they both complemented and agreed with each other, hence my huge precis above for the reader.

Essentially they disclose to the medical profession that we should learn to listen and communicate openly to all, not only with the patients primarily, but also our overseers, in actual practice our political masters, as well.

88. *In Sickness and in Power*. David Owen. 2008. Methuen:
David Owen. Hubris. Wikipedia. The free encyclopedia:
Lord (Baron) David Anthony Llewellyn Owen (02/07/1938-) is both a Member of Parliament and a qualified doctor of medicine. After schooling in Tavistock and Berkshire he qualified in medicine at Cambridge in 1962. He entered Parliament in 1966 and was elevated to the peerage in 1992 after serving as both a Labour and then a Social Democrat member. His political career is well documented elsewhere. Specializing in Parkinsonian disease and neurophysiology he has written and lectured widely on the interaction between illness and politics. In 2002 he gave his first lecture on "The effect of serious illness on heads of State or Government" and since that time he has expanded on

this theme on many occasions. In 2008 he wrote his definitive book on "Hubris Syndrome", that he postulates is an acquired personality disorder affecting those at the pinnacle of power. He describes how an exuberant overconfidence takes hold which leads to an intoxication of power turning many leaders into tyrants who are no longer willing or able to listen to rational or respected argument. He has examined many leaders, British and foreign, as far back to Ancient Greece, and includes Anthony Eden, Margaret Thatcher and Tony Blair especially in his articles, but oddly not others such as Winston Churchill or John Major. He highlights 14 markers for the syndrome which at present is not treatable, and he suggests that it requires recognition as a true medical disorder.

He further suggests that the Cabinet of the day, or the equivalent in the USA or elsewhere, is the only restraining influence on the condition at any particular time.

Dr (Lord) Owen certainly fulfils the required language and communication skills between professions as discussed in reference. no. 87 above. Could it be then that he himself has a degree of hubris syndrome to make these assertions?

Whether his complete postulate is correct is somewhat questionable, and intense medical and political debate on the issue continues.

24. Tomorrow

I see that with better health we all prosper and live longer.

The grey days and times of the Black Country have gone.

The skies are brighter, the folk are happier. Colour has returned.

Even clothes now are of a *melange*. The anaemic amorphous dress of my childhood has resolved.

You can now buy a car of any manufacture, of any type, and of any colour.

You can holiday at home or abroad with profligate impunity.

I am happy with all my memories and I look to the future with anticipation.

Unfortunately *Anno Domini* rules. I am slowing down physically and mentally. As Benjamin Frankin[89] once said, I can "retire to the joys of senility".

Who did you say, said that?

No, not our coalman this time. It was some old bloke from America!

Reference and Author's comment:

89. *The First American*. H.W. Brands. 2010. Knopf Publishing: The Benjamin Franklin House. 36 Craven St. London WC2N 5NF.

www.benjaminfranklinhouse.org/:

Benjamin Franklin (17/01/1706-17/04/1790) American

politician, writer, theorist and diplomat, was also a scholar of the arts, music and science.

He was one of the Founding Fathers of the United States, often being known as the "First American" for his work in campaigning for colonial unity. He was signature to both the United States' Declaration of Independence and of the Constitution, when despite being disabled by an acute attack of gout he was still able to alter the original draft of Thomas Jefferson.

He spent much of his early life abroad in Britain and elsewhere, and he was the first American ambassador to France.

Whilst mainly remembered for his political career and writings, he is not so well renowned for his many inventions and ideas that include the lightning rod, identifying the positive and negative poles of electricity and such medical innovations as bifocal spectacles and the flexible urinary catheter, which I imagine was less painful than the rigid tubes employed at that time!

Postscript

1. Dialectic expression (Black Country-speak) is included in the book, as spoken to the author. Full translations are not included, although some difficult words are explained (in brackets), and readers requiring comprehensive interpretation are advised to refer to the multiple articles of Prof. Carl Chinn or Mr Ed Conduit (references no. 1 and 2 respectively).

2. Handwritten quotes (Lucida Handwriting font):

Page	Quote	Derivation	Translation
15.	Grand seigneur	French	A dignified or aristocratic man.
32.	En famille	French	With one's family, casual and informal.
33.	Fait accompli	French	Something already done and decided that seems unalterable.
59.	Flagrante delicto	Latin	Caught in the act of committing an offence, (Legal). In the midst of sexual activity, (euphemism).
62.	Ad hoc	Latin	To this, for a specific purpose.

99.	Gemütlichkeit	German	Comfortable ambience, friendliness, snug and cosy
152.	Ad nauseam	Latin	To a disgusting extent, the point of nausea.
181.	Hoi polloi	Greek	The many, the majority. Derogatory English The commoners.
185.	Virgo intacta	Latin	A female who has never had intercourse, whose hymen remains unbroken.
229.	Joie de vivre	French	Enjoyment of life or living.
230.	Compos mentis	Latin	Of sound mind, sane.
257.	Cri de Cœur	French	A cry from the heart, a sincere appeal.
275.	Curriculum vitae	Latin	Course of life.
278.	Melange	French	A mixture.
278.	Anno Domini	Latin	In the year of our Lord.

3. Names written as colours (ColorHexa colour encyclopaedia classification) in chronological order as they appear in the book:

White. Olive. Green. Cherry. Magnolia. Rose. Magenta. Brown. Amber. Coral. Cerise. Taupe. Sepia. Jasper. Pearl. Gold. Black. Carmine. Fuchsia. Myrtle. Ginger. Ruby. Buff. Scarlet. Fawn. Veronica. Gray. Iris. Champagne. Lavender. Laurel. Rackley. Violet.

4. Mentors, counsellors and trusted advisors to the author:

William Edward (Bill) Cooke (30/12/11/1914-08/02/2002):
My father, who left school at the age of 16 years to start

work, running 10 miles per day delivering hot meals to men in the local foundries. He passed the entrance exams for grammar school, but in 1930 it was impossible for my grandparents to pay for his education on a coal miner's wage. Nevertheless, he always believed in the value of furthering one's education and knowledge and although he subsequently went into the foundry himself as a moulder, an extremely heavy manual occupation, he went on to self-educate himself in all methods of manufacture of metal and design technology, to eventually retire as the founder and managing director of...

Trucastite Foundry Ltd. Upper Gornal, Dudley.

Olive May Cooke (04/05/1920-19/09/2005:

My mother, who did not see the necessity for higher education. She was the first female licensee to be granted a licence to run a public house, the Blue Gates pub, in Dudley in 1950, albeit "limited to the sale of beer and wines only" selling Edwin Holden's beer and ales. Even when she moved to the Park Inn, in Woodsetton, despite an exemplary record, it was not until 1957 was she granted a "full licence to sell wines and spirits". Later despite moving on to work at Springvale Social Club at the steelworks in Bilston, and being a member of the Licensed Victuallers Association, she still managed to bring up six children in the meantime.

Edwin Holden (13/11/1907-1981):

Chairman was a founder member of Edwin Holden's Brewery and Bottling Company, one of the largest independent Black Country breweries, still run by the family, was a governor in my time at Dudley Grammar School. In his youth he passed the entrance examination for Birmingham Medical School, but because of wartime pressures he had to transfer his occupation into the family brewery trade, and always had secret aspirations to do medicine.

A friend of my father, he urged me to enter such a career, whilst his son, Edwin Holden junior (deceased 2002), a dear schoolboy chum, went on to succeed him as a director and expand the brewery and bottling company into business as it is today, with over 20 Black Country pubs and producing in excess of 75,000 pints of ale per week.

The company site still rests in part on land purchased in the 1920s, after extensive coal mining by my grandfather.

Dennis Turner (26/081942-25/02/2014):

Born into a working-class family background, Dennis Turner was a staunch trade unionist, an ex-market trader and worked for many years at the steelworks in Bilston. Both a Wolverhampton and county councillor, he went on to be elected the Member of Parliament for Wolverhampton South East in 1987, and a Labour parliamentary whip, and in 2005 eventually became a life peer, Baron Bilston in the upper house of Parliament.

I, the author, first met him as a choirboy in my teens when he advised me on how to obtain a higher fee, i.e. 2 shillings and 6 pence, for choirboys at weddings… "Refuse to attend, go on strike Edwurd" was his advice. Lambasted in the national press for the delay in making his introductory speech to Parliament, he was adored in the Black Country by his constituents and was famous for introducing a private member's bill to legislate the correct amount of froth on the top of a pint of beer!

He became a great drinking and social friend of my father at Springvale Social Club in Bilston, and he advised me later in life on the awful conditions that the steelworkers had to endure and on the "night workers" in Bilston at one of Mr Holden's pubs.

The same age as myself, we joked on us sharing the same age in years as Paul McCartney, Billy Connolly and Colonel Gaddafi! A true Black Country man, sadly he died in the course of my writing this book.

13727415R00161

13727415R00161

13727415R00161

13727415R00161

13727415R00161

13727415R00161

13727415R00161

13727415R00161

13727415R00161

13727415R00161

13727415R00161

13727415R00161

13727415R00161

13727415R00161

13727415R00161

13727415R00161

13727415R00161

13727415R00161

13727415R00161

13727415R00161

13727415R00161

13727415R00161

13727415R00161

13727415R00161

13727415R00161

13727415R00161

13727415R00161

13727415R00161

13727415R00161

Printed in Great Britain
by Amazon.co.uk, Ltd.,
Marston Gate.